SMOKESTACKS IN THE HILLS

THE WORKING CLASS
IN AMERICAN HISTORY

Editorial Advisors
James R. Barrett, Julie Greene, William P. Jones,
Alice Kessler-Harris, and Nelson Lichtenstein

*A list of books in the series appears
at the end of this book.*

SMOKESTACKS IN THE HILLS

Rural-Industrial Workers in West Virginia

LOU MARTIN

UNIVERSITY OF ILLINOIS PRESS
Urbana, Chicago, and Springfield

© 2015 by the Board of Trustees
of the University of Illinois
All rights reserved

1 2 3 4 5 C P 5 4 3 2 1
♾ This book is printed on acid-free paper.

Library of Congress Control Number: 2015948316
ISBN 978-0-252-03945-4 (hardcover)
ISBN 978-0-252-08102-6 (paperback)
ISBN 978-0-252-09756-0 (e-book)

CONTENTS

List of Illustrations — vii
Acknowledgments — ix
Introduction — 1
CHAPTER 1. A Rural Place and a Rural People — 13
CHAPTER 2. Building Factories in the Country — 29
CHAPTER 3. Rise of the Rural-Industrial Workers — 63
CHAPTER 4. Prosperous, Independent Rural-Industrial Workers — 92
CHAPTER 5. Work and Identity in the Factory and at Home — 125
CHAPTER 6. Movements for Equality in a Time of Industrial Restructuring — 155
Conclusion: Country People and Capital Mobility — 179
Notes — 187
Index — 233

ILLUSTRATIONS

MAPS

1. Hancock County and the region — 14
2. The towns of Hancock County — 49

FIGURES

1. Lyman Stedman farm and residence, 1877 — 17
2. A jiggerman, Homer Laughlin China, ca. 1950s — 35
3. Decal girls, Homer Laughlin China, early 1900s — 40
4. W. E. Wells — 50
5. Homer Laughlin China Company — 52
6. Ernest T. Weir, ca. 1923 — 53
7. Early postcard of the Weirton mill — 56
8. Tunnel kilns, Homer Laughlin China — 59
9. Julia Ellis feeding her poultry, ca. 1930s — 64
10. Weirton's North End, ca. 1920s — 69
11. A finisher, Homer Laughlin China, ca. 1950s — 111
12. Arch A. Moore — 120
13. Three-legged race on Fourth of July at Washington Park — 162
14. The Weirton Steel can in front of the Millsop Community Center — 173

TABLES

1. Population of Hancock County by
   Civil Divisions, 1900–1930 — 66
2. Workforce of Newell, 1930 — 67
3. Workforce of Downtown Weirton
   (North), 1930 — 71
4. Hancock County Church Membership, 1952 — 73
5. East Liverpool–Chester–Newell District
   Locals by Gender, 1953, 1959 — 131–32
6. Male and Female Labor Force Participation
   by County, 1950 — 145

ACKNOWLEDGMENTS

I began working on this book in the summer of 2001 when Joe Shemenski spent four hours telling me about his experiences working for Wheeling Steel in the 1920s and 1930s. When I think about this book, I first think of the many people who shared their stories with me over the past eight years. Even though the project changed over time and some of their stories did not make it into the final draft, they all played an important role in helping me understand the experience of living and working in the upper Ohio Valley in the twentieth century. I will always be grateful to John Alatis, Cecelia Arnett, Francis Asfour, Paul Barkhurst, Carlos Beagle, Al Boniti, Gizella Brown, Henry "Tex" Burns, Richard Cameron, Walter Danna, Linda Dickey, Alex Fiedorczyk, Michael Garan, Frank Gregory, Chester Grossi, Karen Williams Harris, Fay Haught, Margaret Heaton, Boots Hines, Mike Jacob, Mary Jacob, Cheryl Mader, Frank Maslowski, Mario Patrizio, Bill Pomeroy, Tom Rector, Lula "Pug" Rigdon, Bob Rossell, Joe Shemenski, Hugh and Garnet Snider, Walter and Helen Szczepanski, and Alex Zucosky.

Several people helped me find people to interview, including Bill Barrett, Sean Adkins, Brad Barkhurst, Mark Glyptis and the Independent Steelworkers Union, Linda Dickey, Fay Stump, Bud Rector, Mindy Lamp, and Chris Mader. I also want to thank Paul Zuros for accompanying me to some interviews. Sean Adkins and Dennis Jones provided helpful information along the way.

A lot of folks I went to grad school with gave me support and feedback over the years, including Mark Myers, John Hardesty, Elizabeth Lee, Jen Egolf, Connie Rice, Carletta Bush, Jay Smith, Allison Fredette, Krista McCart, and Hal Gorby. I owe a special thanks to Becky Bailey, John Hennen, Diane Barnes, and Paul Rakes, who were always willing to help a junior grad student. Shera Moxley, Lisa Johnson, and Peter Gilmore read and commented on chapters I was working on. Their support and insightful readings really helped me when the task seemed so large and my research seemed so inadequate.

Thanks to Elizabeth Fones-Wolf, Michal McMahon, Steven Zdatny, and Lisa Fine for offering helpful criticism. Lisa Fine and Daniel Walkowitz gave me vital feedback at the North American Labor History Conference in 2006. Conversations early on with Joe Trotter and Ron Lewis helped me conceptualize this project, and both have been important role models for me as I have grappled with how to be a scholar who is still engaged in the real world. I want to thank Jim Green for his support and friendship from the time we drove up Cabin Creek together. I also need to thank Jessie Ramey and Mike Finewood for giving me valuable feedback on chapters.

Thanks to the staff at the West Virginia and Regional History Collection for all their patience and assistance, including Harold Forbes, Christy Venham, Mike Thobois, Michael Ridderbush, Viktoria Ironpride, Judy Sirk, Kevin Fredette, Catherine Rakowksi, and especially Frank Tovar. I also appreciate the efforts of archivists of the special collections at Kent State, Penn State, and the West Virginia State Archives. Thanks to the History Department at West Virginia University, the Eberly College of Arts and Sciences, Janice Bagby, the Labor and Working-Class History Association, and Chatham University for funding my research trips and conferences.

One night in 2003 when I was ready to give up on academia, I read Jack Metzgar's *Striking Steel: Solidarity Remembered*. Jack's book reminded me that you could write history with passion and purpose about regular people, for regular people. Ironically, after reading his book I began searching for the Johnny Metzgar of Hancock County. When I could not find him, I realized that I would need to write a different book. I feel fortunate to have found *Striking Steel* and gotten to meet Jack, and I am grateful for his camaraderie and the interest that he has since taken in my work.

I thank Chris Michelmore for reading my manuscript and giving me thoughtful and invaluable feedback on the writing and the argument. I also thank her for encouraging me to finish this book and for being a wonderful leader, mentor, and friend. I am glad she is enjoying her retirement, but after two years I still look at her office door and wish that she were there.

I am also grateful to the staff at the University of Illinois Press for their hard work and to the peer reviewers whose comments made this a better book. I am particularly indebted to Laurie Matheson for all her words of encouragement and advice and the interest she took in this project nearly seven years ago.

I want to thank Ken Fones-Wolf for everything. Years before we began working together, he was already encouraging me, telling me that the history that I wanted to write was an important one. He has put in countless hours to help me become a better researcher, writer, and teacher. He has guided me through the biggest and the smallest challenges of academia. He read the earliest drafts of these chapters, the later drafts, and even the nearly finished manuscript. I cannot thank him enough for his guidance and his friendship.

I have been blessed with a loving and supportive family. My sister, Nancy Basile; my aunt, Liz Brown; and my uncle, Allan Brown, have all shared my enthusiasm for history and have cheered me on. My parents, Jeanne and William Barrett and Lou Martin, have always believed in me and supported me when I needed it the most. I am also very grateful for the support of my father-in-law, Al Stiller, and my late mother-in-law, Pat Stiller. Lastly, I want to thank Mary Ann Henderson for her support and help through some tough times. Without all of them, I would not have been able to pursue my career in history.

Krista, the love of my life, has always been there to support me, encourage me, and reassure me. I cannot thank her enough.

Nearly two decades ago, I sat at a carrel in Wise Library at West Virginia University in a part of the library that has been renovated out of existence. I was reading a book on American labor history. I can't remember which one, but I came across the list of books in the Working Class in American History series. I did not know anything about publishers or book series, but I realized that most of my favorite labor history books were on that list. Being part of this series is an honor and a dream come true, and I will be forever indebted to the people that I have listed above and many more for helping me make that happen.

LOU MARTIN
Daisytown, Pennsylvania
2015

SMOKESTACKS IN THE HILLS

INTRODUCTION

Louis Truax grew up on a farm in Hancock County, West Virginia, in the early 1900s. His family raised some forty-two different varieties of apples in addition to peaches, corn, grain, and hogs. Truax's early memories were of following his father around their orchards, harvesting corn, hunting local game, and sitting with the family in front of the fireplace while his father read the *Farm Journal*. In the last days of the summer of 1919, he helped pick the corn, butcher hogs, and make the "best sausage anyone ever ate," but rather than return to school, the seventeen-year-old Truax went down to the mill gate and got a job as a catcher's helper. His first day "seemed so strange," he recalled. All the noises from motors, shears, rolling mills, and cranes running overhead frightened him "half to death," but he decided that if boys even younger than him could do it, so could he. Truax said that around his home town of Weirton, by 1925, nearly "all of the younger men on the farms went to work in the mills."[1]

This is the story of the forces that brought factories to the countryside in the twentieth century and the emergence of a rural and small-town working class in northern West Virginia. Steel and pottery companies relocated their production facilities to Hancock County in the early 1900s and hired local farm kids as well as rural migrants from far away. As rural people joined the industrial workforce, they adapted to the dictates of industrial capitalism—as millions of others did—but with access to land in and around these steel and pottery towns, they were able to preserve far more of their rural habits than rural migrants who moved to the city. The resulting rural working-class culture privileged place and local community over class, and they were never fully integrated into the national labor movement. While many urban-industrial workers preached the gospel of unionism, the rural-industrial workers of Hancock County worked to place limits on the power of unions and credited companies and self-help activities for their improved standard of living.

Important differences in the local histories and community structures of small towns and rural settings like those found in Hancock County—or Spartanburg, South Carolina; Bogalusa, Louisiana; Ottumwa, Iowa; or Anaconda, Montana—influenced the identity and culture of the industrial workers who lived in those places.[2] Locality shaped class identities and produced a myriad of working-class cultures across the country, even in an era of mass culture.[3] Our understanding of twentieth-century labor history is largely based on the experiences of the urban working class, but studying the distinctive experiences of small-town and rural workers reveals a greater diversity of identity, culture, and behavior than labor historians have acknowledged.

This study contributes to a growing literature on the shifts in national politics in the years after World War II. For decades, historians have been investigating the rapid growth of industrial unions in the 1930s and 1940s and their subsequent failure to reform American society in more fundamental ways. As industrial unions became powerful institutions, labor liberals imagined that the working class would make progress on long-held visions of social democracy. Instead, in the late 1940s and 1950s, Congress enacted legislation to restrict the power and influence of unions, and once-progressive union leaders abandoned broad social programs to focus narrowly on wages and benefits at the same time that working-class whites defected from the New Deal coalition.[4] Labor activists initially viewed the postwar shift to the right as an order imposed on working people by their foes in business and in the government.[5] In the 1970s and 1980s, historians saw top union officials as conservative, undermining their own unions' influence in society by restraining rank-and-file militancy to achieve narrow goals.[6] More recently, scholars have argued that the political conservatism of working-class whites arose out of their racism, status as new homeowners, and precarious grasp on a middle-class lifestyle.[7]

Race has been central to recent histories of the postwar working class, and while race was certainly central to the identities of workers in Hancock County, it was not the driving force in local politics that it was in places like Detroit and Los Angeles. Rural working-class culture likely worked in concert with racism by underscoring differences between small towns and big cities, especially as racial strife rocked northern cities in the 1960s. But in Hancock County, there were no race riots, battles over public housing, or major challenges to white privilege that would have made racism the most instrumental force in shaping local politics. Instead, aspects of their rural working-class culture, especially their localism and their ethic of self-sufficiency, conditioned the entry of Hancock County's factory workers into the national labor movement and tempered their support for New Deal initiatives.

Workers in rural places and small towns have not captured the attention of historians for several reasons. Histories of the countryside in the period of industrialization have tended to focus on the mechanization of agriculture and the effects of commercialization on the family farm.[8] At the same time, historical narratives of the late nineteenth and early twentieth centuries have strongly linked industrialization and urban growth, largely disregarding or glossing over the industrialization of rural places.[9] Certainly industrialization fueled the growth of major cities, and manufacturing jobs were highly concentrated in urban areas between 1880 and 1920. In 1889, 57.8 percent of the nation's manufacturing jobs were located in thirty-four industrial areas, and despite the incredible growth of manufacturing in the United States over the next thirty years, those areas retained 56.2 percent of all manufacturing jobs by 1920. Industrialists concentrated production in those areas mostly because of several economies of agglomeration including large labor pools and the concentration of transportation, communication, and other support services.[10] This concentration of industry helped to create the "manufacturing belt" that stretched in a great arc from Boston and New York down through Pittsburgh, Cleveland, and Cincinnati, and up into Detroit and Chicago.

In addition to fueling the growth of major cities, industrialization also transformed many dusty crossroads and mountain valleys. Processors of agricultural products and manufacturers of agricultural implements often located facilities in the hinterlands with easy access to farming areas. Extractive industries like mining and timbering required companies to build new camps and small towns in the mountains and forests. Often, such boom towns declined and vanished after the companies extracted the profitable natural resources. Some industrialists built towns in the countryside to escape the chaos of the city, envisioning greater control over their facilities, employees, and the surrounding communities. These factory owners often ascribed values such as tranquility, harmony, and individualism to rural areas and hoped these values would rub off on their workers.[11] Furthermore, by the 1920s and 1930s, the supremacy of the manufacturing belt was beginning to crumble. Diseconomies of urban agglomeration increasingly overshadowed the earlier advantages as, among other things, real estate, labor, and service costs increased while regional transportation cost disparities decreased, making it equally if not more profitable to locate in suburbs, small towns, and rural places.[12]

While rural-industrial workers lived in places without significant populations, as a whole they accounted for a sizable portion of the American working class in the early twentieth century. In 1921, 40 percent of all manufacturing wage earners, about 3.7 million, worked in rural places and towns of twenty-five thousand or less compared to the 42 percent that labored in cities with populations of one hundred thousand or more.[13] Thus, for nearly every garment worker in New York City or steelworker in Pittsburgh, there was a packinghouse worker in rural Austin, Minnesota, or a potter living on a farm outside of Newell, West Virginia.

The history of West Virginia between 1880 and 1920 does not fit well into the dominant rural-agricultural or the urban-industrial narratives. In fact, historian Ronald Lewis argues that the stereotypical images of West Virginia—that of rural "hill folk" plowing worn-out fields in "isolated hollows"—may be so persistent because of the unusual nature of the industrialization of the Mountain State. By 1920, only a quarter of the workforce still made a living by farming, but the development of mines, timbering operations, railroads, and even factories did not result in the development of big cities. Seventy-two percent of the population in 1930 lived in rural areas even though the economy was by then overwhelmingly industrial.[14]

Studies of the industrialization of rural places like Hancock County can help us better understand the nature of industrial capitalism, particularly the relationship between capital mobility and the working class. Industries periodically entered periods of crisis that required a general restructuring for companies to remain profitable, and relocations were a key component in the process. When labor gained power through solidarity and organization and resisted certain changes, capital had the geographical mobility to move beyond tight-knit worker communities. Industrialists exploited regional inequalities and local variations, such as low wages and company loyalty, and used relocations as an opportunity to reorganize production, build factories that employed the latest technologies, and adopt new organizational structures. In "undeveloped" rural areas, some manufacturers believed that they could create new environments free of discord and find a grateful and compliant pool of rural laborers—often women and other low-wage workers—to surround a core of handpicked skilled workers.[15] Thus, manufacturers' old labor problems and their high hopes for an improved workforce figured prominently in the migration of capital to rural places.

Throughout the nineteenth and twentieth centuries, industries were constantly on the move. Both capital and workers migrated from Britain, France,

Germany, and Belgium to the United States during the nineteenth century, sometimes draining Old World factory towns of their lifeblood.[16] Beginning in the late nineteenth century, textile companies and investment capital relocated from New England to the Carolina Piedmont in search of cheaper, nonunion workers.[17] In the 1930s and 1940s, garment manufacturers opened new factories in the Deep South as part of a more general migration of manufacturing to the burgeoning Sun Belt, a shift facilitated by policies of the federal government and the passage of antiunion laws at the state level.[18] In the 1950s, city centers like Detroit lost industrial jobs as corporations "decentralized," moving production facilities to suburbs, leaving many thousands behind to face a devastating unemployment crisis.[19]

Recently, historians have paid more attention to capital migrations and their effects. Jefferson Cowie's groundbreaking study followed RCA's multiple relocations from the 1930s through the 1990s as the corporation shifted production from New Jersey to Indiana to Tennessee and ultimately to Juaréz, Mexico.[20] In her book *Capital's Utopia*, Anne Mosher examined the efforts of steel magnate George McMurtry to respond to the crisis the industry experienced in the 1890s. An important part of McMurtry's response was the creation of the model town of Vandergrift, Pennsylvania, designed to be free from the labor strife that afflicted industrial cities. Mosher examines the labor relations that emerged along with changes in production technology, composition of the workforce, and managerial organization.[21] Similarly, Ken Fones-Wolf examined the glass industry leaders' responses to that industry's crisis in the 1890s, which also included changing locations, technologies, workforce composition, and labor-management relations of glass production.[22] Patterns emerge from these studies. Relocation was one of many strategies industry leaders pursued in response to a crisis in their industry, but it usually preceded other changes in technology, managerial organization, and labor. Industrialists searched for locations where they could tap into pools of low-wage, first-generation, often female workers.

Both the pottery and steel industries experienced industrial restructuring in the 1890s that led to the construction of new factories in Hancock County and transformed what had largely been a rural place. During that decade, the pottery industry in Trenton, New Jersey, and East Liverpool, Ohio, entered a period of crisis, and owners and managers responded with several strategies: new technologies, a reorganization of production, greater reliance on female labor, new marketing campaigns, vigorous pursuit of protective tariffs, and relocations, including the construction of new plants in Hancock County. The industry's adaptations led to a period of great growth and prosperity for pottery owners and workers before World War I.[23] Steel also experienced a dramatic transformation in the 1890s, particularly the segment of the industry that produced tinplate, a thin plate or sheet of steel coated with tin to prevent rusting. Through the 1890s, workers continued to do most of the production work by hand, unlike most of the rest of the steel industry. The biggest change during that decade was the mass migration of Welsh producers—the longtime world leaders in the industry—and investment capital to America. Newly organized American tinplate firms typically located their rolling mills in small towns in Pennsylvania, Ohio, Kentucky, Indiana, and West Virginia (including Hancock County) and built the mills with new technologies, new groups of workers, and eventually a new business organization.[24]

Initially, the construction of new potteries and tinplate mills in Hancock County attracted a class of skilled craftsmen who had little interest in country living. The skilled rollers of the mills and the jiggermen of the clay shops maintained an urban lifestyle, often riding new streetcar lines from nearby cities across the Ohio River. Many of these craftsmen did not develop an attachment to place, remained mobile, and moved freely from one factory town to another all around the northeastern United States. Their effort to control production and negotiate high wages continued to frustrate industrialists who had hoped to start over in rural Hancock County. This led them to reorganize production around new technologies and to hire more first-generation factory workers who had no experience with unions or even with working-class traditions.

Rural migrants and young people from local farms brought their own ideas, goals, and culture—distinct from those of the skilled craftsmen—and came to constitute a truly rural-industrial workforce. Whether they were peasants from Southern or Eastern Europe, African Americans from the South, or the sons and daughters of local farmers, these workers hailed from rural places, and in this setting, more of their rural ways persisted than among migrants who ended up in major cities. With greater access to cheap land and few restrictions on land use, many of these rural-industrial workers' country habits took root in and around the factory towns of Hancock County. Communities that had been overwhelmingly native-born, white, and Protestant experienced a series of transformations in social relations and social structures. Oftentimes, the local industries hired low-cost female labor to fill jobs formerly labeled "men's work," and the new rural-industrial workers were less resistant to such changes than their skilled predecessors had been.[25] In the small towns and rolling hills of Hancock County, where industrialists' schemes met rural-industrial workers' values, a rural working-class culture emerged.

Yet little is known about the cultures of the rural working class. The "development of a rural-industrial culture within a rural rather than an urban context," as historian Ronald Lewis observed in 1993, "represents still another subtlety in the industrial transformation which has been ignored by scholars."[26] Most labor historians have focused on workers in big cities, and with good reason. Many of the most dramatic clashes in the history of the labor movement occurred in cities like New York, Chicago, Pittsburgh, and Detroit, and historical sources for these major cities on the whole are richer. Those who have studied rural-industrial workers such as miners and lumberjacks have been interested in their class consciousness, racial identities, and contributions to the national labor movement more than in the distinctiveness of rural working-class cultures.[27]

Another reason for the paucity of studies of rural-working class cultures may be the decreasing attention paid to twentieth-century workers' cultures and communities overall. When labor historians have turned their attention to the twentieth century, their focus has mostly shifted from communities to the role of the state and national organizations. One explanation for the shift is that historians found in nineteenth-century workers' culture a source of activism, whereas twentieth-century workers' culture was frequently used to explain workers' "passivity" within narratives of the "taming" of the working class. Compared to the power of the state and markets, local cultures and communities had limited utility in opposing global forces and instead became obstacles to broader solidarity. Labor historians have understandably turned their attention to the economic and political structures that shaped the experiences of the working class in the twentieth century. This led to an impression that local culture disappeared in the face of modernizing forces and that what local culture remained was irrelevant to studies of power and control in American society.[28]

The history of workers in Hancock County demonstrates that labor historians may be mistaken about the passivity of twentieth-century workers and their homogeneity. Local communities and cultures may be ill-suited to oppose global forces, but it is debatable whether economics, the state, and large institutions are the homogenizing forces they are often made out to be. As historian Lizabeth Cohen observed in her study of industrial workers in Chicago during the 1920s and 1930s, the rise of mass culture did not obliterate ethnic and working-class identities or cultures but instead interacted with them to create something new but not homogeneous.[29] The same could be said for rural people and their cultures. On the one hand, twentieth-century American popular culture often exaggerated the cultural differences between urban and rural life, portraying country people as lagging behind modern times in their style of dress, consumer goods, and even cultural traits.[30] On the other hand, some historians have overstated the degree to which modernizing forces such as the federal policy, corporations, and mass culture homogenized rural and urban people, noting that country people began to talk, dress, and shop like city people.[31]

While there is no doubt the gap between the two narrowed when it came to modern amenities, merely analyzing superficial characteristics like statistics about electricity, refrigerators, running water, and radios ignores deeper social structures that help us comprehend cultural transformation and reproduction among country people. In the 1970s and 1980s, anthropologist Susan Carol Rogers observed that the men and women in the tiny village of Ste Foy, France, participated "in the wider world" but did so "largely on their own terms," still retaining some "ties to an old identity."[32] She writes that "however universal the process glossed as 'modernization' may be, its effects are far from universal," and it produces no more homogeneity than existed when the world was "peopled largely by subsistence agriculturalists."[33] The rural-industrial culture of workers in Hancock County is further evidence for Cohen's and Rogers's arguments about modernization and heterogeneity. Rural-industrial workers in Hancock County certainly experienced cultural change in the twentieth century as they participated in a national mass culture, worked in modern factories, and increasingly lived within a web of federal regulations, but they did so—to quote Rogers again—"largely on their own terms."

This study argues that in the emergence of a rural-industrial culture in Hancock County in the early twentieth century, we see country people adapting to the dictates of industrial capitalism in a setting that allowed important parts of their rural culture to persist. One aspect of these workers' rural culture that persisted into the industrial era is localism, a strong attachment to place and community and a desire to maintain local control over the government and the economy. While a homogeneous rural culture has never existed, localism—often appearing as "self-reliant independence"—appears to be a common characteristic of American rural cultures according to recent studies.[34] Localism was sometimes a reaction to the shift in power from local governments to urban centers.[35]

In mid-twentieth-century Hancock County, the localism that was part of rural-industrial workers' local culture shaped their response to national events. The most profound transformation in twentieth-century American labor history was the creation of a national union movement between the 1930s and the 1950s out of what had been fragmented and isolated communities of workers, but these rural-industrial workers remained isolated to a surprising degree from that national movement. It is in the contrasting responses of rural-industrial workers and urban-industrial workers to those national organizations and national actions that we can best see the deeper logic of local cultures at work.

The success of union organizing in mass-production industries required workers to identify their interests with the interests of workers in distant places and to be able to cooperate with them. Urban workers' entry into the national labor movement was precipitated by the collapse of their local institutions. Industrial workers in Chicago, for example, relied heavily on mutual benefit societies and neighborhood churches, but when the Great Depression devastated those institutions, working families found themselves at the mercy of corporations, landlords, and soup kitchens. As old survival strategies failed, those workers eagerly turned to national politics through the Democratic Party and national unions through the Congress of Industrial Organizations (CIO) to empower them. Lizabeth Cohen argues, "State and union, workers hoped, would provide the security formerly found through ethnic, religious, and employer affiliation as well as ensure a more just society."[36]

Such a reorientation laid the groundwork for the "disciplined collective action" that was evident by 1946 when 800,000 steelworkers nationwide went out on strike together and returned to work together.[37] The national strikes of the late 1940s and the 1950s were the culmination of more than a decade of historical experiences that unified workers in far-flung factories into a single, well-disciplined body. During those years, shop stewards preached not only the gospel of unionism but also a culture of unity. During mass strikes, as workers became aware of their common sacrifice for one another, solidarity crystallized. The "end product of this process," according to historian Jeremy Brecher, "is the sense of being part of a class."[38] And if all that did not convince workers of the importance of national unions and well coordinated actions, the tangible rewards of those strikes probably did. For example, between 1945 and 1956, steelworkers saw their hourly rates double as a result of a series of well-executed national strikes, and they won several new benefits including vacation pay, pensions, and health insurance.[39]

That reorientation to national labor unions and participation in national strikes never happened in Hancock County. Instead, the rural-industrial workers of Hancock County remained part of a local system of grievance and contract negotiations. The roughly 13,000 steelworkers who worked in Hancock County were among the very few in the industry who did not participate in the 1946 walkout of 800,000 workers.[40] This kind of localism has cropped up in the work of those labor historians who have studied rural workers in the twentieth century. The "fiercely independent" packinghouse workers in outlying areas in the Midwest believed in direct action to reform labor relations but failed to see a need for any fundamental reform of the society as a whole.[41] The "local orientation" of autoworkers in and around Lansing, Michigan, was "rooted, in part, in their rural origins."[42] Textile workers living in the small mill towns of New England and the Carolina Piedmont identified strongly with their individual textile mill villages rather than with other mill hands living in the hundreds of other villages. Not surprisingly, their responses to strike calls varied wildly.[43] Many rural Iowans deeply opposed all unions, fearing that radicals would take over their small towns.[44] Thus, place could be more important than class in the formation of these workers' identities.[45]

Many of Hancock County's steel and pottery workers voiced suspicions of national unions and powerful union officials, and they often valued employers' commitment to place and the accessibility of owners and management. They preferred face-to-face communication—even when it was confrontational—to distant, impersonal bureaucracies. While they invoked the power of the state and federal agencies when it served their needs, the rural-industrial workers did not wholeheartedly embrace the Democratic Party platform in the same way that urban-industrial workers did.

In addition to localism, another important aspect of the culture of the rural-industrial workers of Hancock County was "making do," which meant meeting a lot of the family's needs through domestic production and buying fewer consumer goods.[46] The steel and pottery workers in northern West Virginia who still had close ties to the land drew on rural skills to build their own homes, grow and preserve food, raise livestock, and hunt local game. We might view household food production simply as a reaction to low wages were it not for the fact that workers continued to can vegetables, raise chickens, and hunt local game through the 1960s, when their wages and benefits helped them achieve a comfortable lifestyle. Furthermore, they often celebrated these activities. Unlike the working families of Chicago and other major cities who scrambled to find new survival strategies when their mutual benefit societies collapsed in the 1930s, the people of Hancock County found their old strategies still useful. In the 1940s and 1950s, these survival strategies tended to strengthen their localism and weaken their commitment to New Deal coalition goals such as a more robust welfare state and union protections.

Access to land and pre-existing rural values like localism shaped rural-industrial culture as did workers' historical experiences, especially with their employers. When Chicago workers were standing in breadlines, most Hancock County workers remained on the job as local mills and potteries weathered the Depression fairly well. Stable employment, rural skills, and access to land served the needs of working families and strengthened their faith in self-help and local institutions.

Some labor historians may question whether the rural-industrial workers of Hancock County never embraced the national labor movement because employers prevented them from doing so. In the 1930s, for example, Weirton Steel managers effectively thwarted unionization campaigns with a combination of coercion and legal maneuvering. Yet in 1950, in a very different political climate, Weirton steelworkers opted for a local company-dominated union over the national United Steel Workers of America. It would be a mistake to conclude that employers alone prevented these workers from joining the national labor movement. By the 1950s, Weirton steelworkers had achieved what Gerald Zahavi calls a "negotiated loyalty," using formal and informal methods to win concessions from Weirton Steel.[47] Furthermore, the pottery workers in the northern end of the county acted in ways very similar to the steelworkers even though pottery workers had unionized in the 1890s. Though courted by the CIO in the late 1930s and early 1940s, potters opted for what was essentially a local and fairly conservative union.

There are examples of rural-industrial workers in twentieth-century America who adopted radical critiques of American capitalism and American politics, including coal miners and timber workers in the early 1900s. There are also examples of rural-industrial workers becoming loyal members of the CIO after thorough and energetic organizing campaigns. But to ascribe Hancock County's rural-industrial culture to either successful company campaigns or failed union organizing campaigns denies these workers agency and views culture as merely reactive. They lived within a world of constraints, but they also made choices, maintained traditions, and held certain values dear. In the decades after World War II, not only did they not support the Democratic Party's efforts to strengthen unions and the welfare state, they actually worked to place limits on union power and the growth of welfare state, efforts that were consistent with their localism.

As a result of their localism and distinctive historical experiences, these rural working-class voters helped create a less hospitable political environment for unions and helped halt the expansion of the welfare state. While the industrial workers who gathered in union halls in Chicago in the 1930s helped forge a New Deal for labor, the steel and pottery workers of Hancock County fought in the 1950s and 1960s for their vision of independence, a vision rooted in rural-industrial values. The distinctive features of working-class life in and around the steel and pottery towns of northern West Virginia are a reminder not only of the diversity of American working-class culture in the twentieth century but also of the significance of local cultures in shaping workers' politics and, beyond that, national politics.

Capital relocation to undeveloped places is an ongoing process. The capital mobility and industrial restructuring that brought new opportunities to Hancock County in the early twentieth century presaged the sometimes wrenching restructuring of postwar America. Industries that once arrived in Hancock County and other rural areas in America moved on to yet newer frontiers in Latin America and Asia. As weeds grow around many American factories, working families have been left behind, often unemployed and robbed of pensions and health insurance.[48] Meanwhile, in places like Chengdu, China, a new generation of factory workers is emerging and developing a new rural-industrial culture, retaining aspects of their rural backgrounds while adapting to their new settings and the dictates of industrial capitalism.[49]

CHAPTER I

A RURAL PLACE AND A RURAL PEOPLE

In the 1880s, Lyman Stedman spent most of his days doing chores on his farm on Brown's Island, a sliver of land in the Ohio River within the boundaries of Hancock County, West Virginia. Like many in the northern panhandle of the Mountain State, Stedman was a Republican who favored modernization, and he had served as a delegate in the West Virginia state legislature in the 1870s. Now in his fifties, he spent his time planting corn, hauling manure out to the fields, and mowing hay. On Sundays, the family attended the Methodist Episcopal Church, but the rest of the week, Lyman and his twenty-six-year-old son, Audubon, attended to the numerous tasks their farm required of them. In his diary, the patriarch of the Stedman family seldom mentioned his wife, Emily, his daughters, Blanche and Mabel, or his younger sons, Sedgwick or Chester, evidence that in many ways they lived separate lives.[1] As a family, the Stedmans organized the tasks of agricultural production by gender, produced most of the food they ate, and sold surpluses at local markets and to merchants.

Before the rapid industrialization of Hancock County, farming dominated the economy and defined the lives of residents of these rolling hills along the Ohio River. Most of the local yeoman farmers like Stedman raised sheep, grew grain for their livestock, and tended apple orchards. In the late nineteenth century, the rural culture of farming families privileged local institutions over distant bureaucracies such as state agencies and large corporations. The habits and values of this rural existence shaped their survival strategies and notions

CHAPTER I

MAP 1. Hancock County and the region
Source: Jessica Brewer

of work, community, and politics in ways that long outlived the county's reliance on agriculture. Therefore, an examination of the rural culture of this place prior to industrialization helps us understand local rural-industrial workers in the twentieth century.

Hancock County sits in a bend in the Ohio River about forty miles west of Pittsburgh, Pennsylvania, where the waterway forms the border between Ohio and West Virginia. This land of green rolling hills, small creeks, and large stands of oak, maple, and pine trees held great potential for the farming people that migrated westward in the 1750s.[2] Early settlers to this region traveled across the Allegheny Mountains from eastern Pennsylvania, eastern Virginia, and Maryland. Many of them originated in the British Isles and used techniques passed down through the generations to carve farms out of frontier forests.[3] In the early 1770s, at the age of four, Joseph Doddridge migrated to the area with his family. He later remembered how difficult it was to make "new establishments in a remote wilderness," especially because they had to violently displace the Delaware, Mingo, and Shawnee Indian nations, who lived and hunted there. Fighting a war and eking out an existence from the fields and forests pushed these pioneers to the limits of their endurance.[4] Doddridge and his generation transformed the land during their lifetimes, clearing timber, planting crops, raising livestock, and laying the foundation for an economy that rested on commercial agriculture. So much had changed by 1824, Doddridge wrote, that the countryside's former appearance was "like a dream." As the pioneer looked around, he found that his father's little cabin no longer existed and the "little field and truck patch, which gave him a scanty supply of coarse bread and vegetables," had been "swallowed up in the extended meadow, orchard, or grain field." The old pioneer was now "surrounded by the busy hum of men, and the splendor, arts, refinements and comforts of civilized life."[5]

Farmers in the panhandle secured their food supply first but also participated in market exchanges. In the early 1800s, they grew potatoes, beans, and corn to eat and wheat to sell to local flour mills. By 1830, the northern panhandle of what was then western Virginia was an important center of flour milling, and merchants shipped between thirty and forty thousand barrels of flour down the river to New Orleans every year.[6] Growing wheat for external markets, however, pushed the soil of northern panhandle farms to its limit, and soil exhaustion and erosion—not to mention declining grain prices—forced farmers to reconsider the crop.[7] They shifted their efforts from growing wheat to planting apple trees and raising sheep. Raising sheep had several advantages. Sheep naturally fertilized the soil and prepared pastures for plowing, and the price of wool was on the rise.[8] Also, many area farmers had either raised sheep in the British Isles before migrating over the Allegheny Mountain or came from families who had a tradition of raising sheep in Ireland and America. These farmers observed that the climate, soil, and topography of this region were ideally suited to sheep.[9] While the average farm in the northern United States in the mid-nineteenth century only had 11 to 12 sheep, a survey of the farms in Hancock and neighboring counties revealed that these farms averaged 157.[10] Hancock farmers sold their wool to the woolen mills downriver in Wellsburg, West Virginia, and Steubenville, Ohio.[11] During the 1860s and 1870s, New England mills bought the greatest percentage of wool from West Virginia's northern panhandle.[12]

Apples were another important crop for the nineteenth-century commercial farmers of Hancock County. One early settler, Jacob Nessly, planted fifty acres of apple and pear trees and made fruit brandies with the produce. His farm was situated at a convenient landing on the Ohio River, and his distilling business netted him and his heirs a small fortune. By the time of his death, he owned some five thousand acres of land along a five-mile stretch of the river.[13] His profitable example undoubtedly encouraged others, as did amenable conditions like cool breezes off the river and rich soils. By the 1880s, it was common for Hancock County farmers to tend two or three hundred apple trees on their land, but more ambitious entrepreneurs had orchards of as many as eighteen thousand trees. They also experimented with developing new varieties of apples. One farmer in neighboring Brooke County became renowned for his "Golden Grimes" apple, while Hancock apple growers became known for their "Willow Twig." The 1896 harvest in Hancock yielded 300,000 bushels of apples, attesting to the decades of labor needed to grow and maintain the orchards.[14]

While most sold their farm products to merchants connected to national markets, local farmers spent considerable time producing for their own subsistence as well. The diversity of crops and animals they raised was part of a "subsistence-surplus" strategy.[15] In 1880, Lyman Stedman and his family farmed one hundred acres of improved land. They had a six-acre apple orchard of two hundred trees that produced 450 bushels of apples, and their 35 sheep produced 200 pounds of fleece. That year, they also harvested 800 bushels of Indian corn, 300 bushels of wheat, 150 dozen eggs, and 25 bushels of Irish potatoes; they kept five horses, five milk cows, and about 75 chickens and made 300 pounds of butter and 40 gallons of molasses.[16] Similarly, Jane Adair Truax owned a farm in nearby Hollidays Cove. She and her family tilled 97 acres of ground and had a seven-acre orchard. In 1880, they harvested 300 bushels of Indian corn, 200 bushels of wheat, 15 dozen eggs, and 30 bushels of Irish potatoes. Unlike the Stedmans, who had no hired hands, Truax paid $25 that year for help on the farm. It is likely that she hired someone to help her churn the incredible 900 pounds of butter that her farm produced, which would have netted her a considerable amount of cash. Sometimes twelve- to fourteen-year-old girls would come to stay with a family and help out with domestic manufacture. The Truax family also kept 43 sheep whose wool they could take to market as well.[17]

James Dietz grew up in the early 1900s in central West Virginia on a farm that was probably very similar to the farms of Hancock County at that time. His childhood memories suggests that many farming families still practiced a blend of subsistence and market activities and that they still tried to limit purchases by making products themselves or doing without. He recalled, "Both Dad and Mother were hard workers and scrupulous about the way they spent their money. They bought only bare necessities."[18] Farmers called this "making do," and it became a central tenet of farming culture that lasted well into the twentieth century.[19] In fact, the habits and values of making do would remain important to rural-industrial workers in the mill and pottery towns of Hancock County in the mid-twentieth century.

Commercial farming in Hancock County reached its pinnacle in the last quarter of the nineteenth century. In 1879, one observer remarked that a hus-

FIGURE 1. Lyman Stedman farm and residence, 1877
Source: West Virginia and Regional History Center, WVU Libraries

bandman in Hancock County could rejoice at the productiveness of his acres and "smile at the long waving green that covers his pasture fields. His cattle are sleek and fat, sheep in good order, with promising abundance of wool of the finest quality yearly."[20] The county's towns and villages were gathering places for farmers. The villages of New Manchester and Hollidays Cove contained post offices, hardware stores, and blacksmiths that catered to farmers. In 1868, Hollidays Cove had 250 inhabitants, two wagon makers, two shoe shops, a drug store, and three churches.[21] The only manufacturing of significance occurred in New Cumberland, also known as "Brickyard Bend." New Cumberland started as a convenient riverfront landing and developed into a center for brick manufacturing in the late 1830s and the 1840s. A particularly rich vein of Kittanning Fire Clay lay underneath Hancock County and adjacent areas. Manufacturers began clay mining operations in the county's hills and along the river. They shipped bricks down the Ohio and the Mississippi and sold them in towns all along the way. While the burgeoning western markets stimulated the mining and shipping business, the brickyard crews remained small, four or five men. Even in the late 1800s, brick manufacturing only employed several dozen and drew few farmers away from their land.[22]

Farming Families, Work, and Independence

Many of the family dynamics of Hancock County farmers rested on centuries of tradition as well as adaptations to their setting in northern West Virginia.

They organized their work, planned their estates, and participated in the market economy, all designed to achieve a particular sense of independence.

Men and women largely worked in separate spheres, spending most of their day on different parts of the farm and at tasks assigned by gender. Within the family hierarchy, the father stood at the head and in many ways controlled the lives of the other members of the household. His dependents by law and by custom included not only his children but also his wife, and the father held title to the family's property and was entitled to the fruits of the labor of his family and any servants. Parents socialized their children from an early age to respect the gender boundaries of their society, instructing them on what it meant to be manly and womanly.[23]

In northern states in the nineteenth century, yeoman farmers such as Lyman were much celebrated for their independence. Many believed that farmers made good citizens because, unlike manufacturers, they were not dependent on the whims of the market. Americans also equated family farming with egalitarianism. In 1815, a minister in neighboring Brooke County waxed about this aspect of life in his community:

> I cannot speak too highly of the advantages that the people in this country enjoy in being delivered from a proud and lordly aristocracy.... I have had my horse shod by a legislator, my horse saddled, my boots cleaned, my stirrup held by a senator. Here is no nobility but virtue; here there is no ascendance save that of genius, virtue and knowledge. The farmer here is lord of the soil, and the most independent man on earth.[24]

Having emigrated from County Antrim, Ireland, this minister knew from experience what it was like to live under a "lordly aristocracy." The yeomanry of western Virginia also contrasted with the wealthy planters of the Tidewater, particularly in that yeomen owned relatively modest tracts of land and relied on family labor rather than slave labor. But the livelihood and the celebrated independence of the yeoman farmer rested on his ability to control the labor of his "dependent" family members and to reap the fruits of that labor. Therefore, the patriarchal system, which perpetuated inequality within the family, formed the foundation of the "egalitarian" yeoman's independence.[25]

The men and women of nineteenth-century Hancock County were socialized into gendered roles on the family farm. Hancock County farmers treated their sons like apprentices, training them from an early age. In 1907, the editor of the *New Cumberland Independent* estimated that it took twenty years to learn to be a farmer; some never learned.[26] Farmers also intended for their sons to eventually inherit the family farm and continue to plow the same fields. One writer noted that E. Langfitt "grasped the plow left in the furrow by his progenitor, and continued tilling and breaking up the fallow-ground" and that Jonathan Allison "settled upon the old home farm, remaining there engaged in tilling the ground until his death."[27]

Men and boys would spend most of their time in the fields, pastures, orchards, and woods where sons would learn how to raise livestock like cattle and, in Hancock County, sheep. The seasons dictated many of their duties. Raising sheep had seasonal rhythms. In the spring and summer, the men herded sheep onto the hills and knolls for grazing. They gave them grain before lambing in the spring and salt in the summer. The warm months were also a good time to wash the sheep in nearby creeks and shear them. In winter months, farmers finally had time to build sheep barns and sheep sheds that helped them supervise breeding and provide shelter when the animals were sick or giving birth. Some of the larger "wool growers" also sowed their pastures with timothy, red clover, and rye.[28] All were skills sons would learn by watching and helping.

Lyman Stedman's diary of his widely varied daily chores provides a glimpse of how subsistence and market strategies intersected with daily life. In the fall of 1880, harvest time, Lyman and his sixteen-year-old son, Sedgwick, were busy harvesting corn, picking apples, plowing fields, mowing grass, sowing wheat and timothy, and threshing wheat, several dozen bushels of which they took to the mill. They also butchered a calf, dug potatoes, built a corncrib, sold some of their livestock, and spent weeks husking corn.[29] In the winter of 1880–1881, with no planting or harvesting to be done, Sedgwick went to school while Lyman and Audubon, his oldest son, butchered hogs, made sausage, hauled coal up to the house, fed the cattle, and made skiff oars out of red elm planks. They also sold produce, poultry, and lumber in Ohio. With temperatures in April still below freezing, Lyman sowed clover and tapped his maple trees, "closing up the business" of drawing syrup on April 12.[30] As the weather got warmer, Lyman and Sedgwick spaded up the garden, spread manure on the potato patch, rebuilt some of their fences, plowed fields, and planted beets, peas, lettuce, radishes, tomatoes, peppers, potatoes, cabbage, cucumbers, and beans. In May, they sorted apples in the cellar, packed fifty-two barrels of them, and spent two days downriver selling them.[31] During the summer months, they hoed the corn fields and the potato patch, washed the sheep, sheared the wool, split locust logs for fence posts, and then watched helplessly as floodwaters washed away some of their wheat, corn, and new fence. The Stedman men repaired the fence, plowed and replanted corn and wheat, hauled hay, took a dozen bushels of wheat to the mill, and paid a bill with a local merchant.[32] And when the leaves fell to the ground, it was time for the Stedmans to start the cycle over again.

Men in Hancock County also hunted during every month that contained an "r," meaning September through April. Hunting provided settlers like Joseph Doddridge and his generation with the "greater amount of their subsistence," since deer, bear, squirrels, beavers, and turkeys were plentiful. Local game was not only an important source of food, but hunters could also sell pelts and hides at trading posts for cash or trade them for store goods.[33] While pioneers successfully transitioned to commercial farming in Hancock County by the 1820s, hunting and trapping retained pragmatic as well as cultural importance into the late nineteenth and early twentieth centuries. Many descendants continued to hunt as a pastime, for solitude, and sometimes for food and cash. Louis Truax recalled that as a boy he made money by taking care of his brother's team of horses and by trapping muskrats and raccoons. He sold about $85 worth of pelts that winter, which he said was enough for "a young man to spend."[34]

The image of men hunting in the forests and plowing fields inherited from their fathers obscures the crucial role that wives and children played in the success of any yeoman farm.[35] Farm women's work fell into three categories: child rearing, food production, and domestic manufacture. First, the children they bore were fundamental to the success or failure of the farm. While a patriarch's fortune may have been defined by the size of his land holdings, his prosperity had less to do with his own industriousness than with the number of his working-age children.[36] Having sons was also critical to the intergenerational succession of his family's farm ownership. Thus, farm women's reproductive labor—both their childbearing and child rearing—was the single most important factor determining the future of the family farm. Giving birth, raising the children, and maintaining the household were laborious duties for women on nineteenth-century farmsteads. For Emily Stedman and her daughters, Blanche and Mabel, the workday began before sunup. Hauling water, milking cows, starting cooking fires, and preparing meals—all before dawn—required strength, stamina, and considerable know-how. The women of the farm butchered and plucked the poultry to prepare meals, baked breads on a daily basis, made jellies and jams, and scrubbed clothes clean in steaming hot water. Mothers also monitored children's health and provided care when they fell ill. Having several children required that they spend many years pregnant without a rest from their other work responsibilities, except for one or two weeks after giving birth.[37]

Emily and her daughters also produced a good portion of the family's food supply. When the labor of the whole family was needed, women helped with fieldwork, such as when the time came to harvest corn and wheat. Because women typically worked in and around the house, they weeded and cultivated the garden patch behind the kitchen, fed the hogs and chickens, collected eggs, tended small flocks of geese, milked cows early in the morning, processed milk into cheese and butter, and sold eggs, cheese, and butter surpluses, which were an important source of income when wheat and corn crops fell short of family needs. In good times, women traditionally got to keep their "egg money."[38] In 1880, the Stedmans produced three hundred pounds of butter and the Truax family produced nine hundred pounds.

Finally, farm women manufactured a great many household items that often meant the difference between a bare existence and a comfortable one. They rendered animal fat to make lard, candles, and soap and spent nights beside the fireplace making thread, cloth, and clothing. They made other items out of fabric including curtains, bedsheets, pillows, pillowcases, and mattresses, which they filled with the down they plucked from geese the family had eaten that winter.[39] Philip Doddridge, Joseph's brother, observed, "Our clothing was all of domestic manufacture. . . . Almost every house contained a loom, and almost every woman was a weaver."[40] When the men came in from plowing, not only would there be a hot meal waiting but also a soft mattress awaiting their tired bodies. Self-sufficient farmers must have been keenly aware that their independence was largely thanks to the women of their household, because women grew, preserved, and prepared nearly everything they ate and spun and sewed nearly everything they wore.[41]

James Dietz recalled how his parents' work roles complemented one another on their Nicholas County, West Virginia, farm in the early 1900s: "Dad's portion of the responsibilities of making and maintaining a home were no less than those of Mother. We would not dare to say which of the two had the greater task and to try to defend our choice. It was a blend of efforts and a combination of responsibilities."[42] These farm families organized work in ways that dated back centuries and, like their ancestors, performed numerous and varied tasks to coax a living out of the earth and achieve a measure of self-sufficiency.

Community Solidarity

Farm families like those of northern West Virginia identified strongly with their local communities, an identity reinforced by collective activities, kinship, ties to the land, community events, and a sense of belonging. Farming often required that neighboring families pool their resources. This was especially true for harvesting, building barns and houses, and helping families struck by illness. Not only did families sometimes need help cutting wheat or picking corn, but they also helped one another thresh the wheat and husk the corn. Harvest time brought neighbors together out of necessity, but it also gave them the opportunity to socialize. John Walker Dinsmore, a farmer from across the state line in western Pennsylvania, recalled of this time: "It was very common for people 'to neighbor' as they called it; that is, if a barn was to be raised, or a job of threshing was to be done, or anything requiring a number of men, all the men in the neighborhood would be invited to attend and help." During barn raisings and collective harvests, farmers might repay their neighbors with a portion of the harvest or a feast. During such collective workdays, men headed out into the fields early in the morning while the women gathered in the kitchen to prepare the feast, which took the whole morning. Dinsmore wrote, "Along with these gatherings of men there would often be a similar gathering of women in the afternoon, for a quilting or some such work, and then after a big supper, the evening would be spent in rustic jollity."[43] Another activity that required cooperation was raising hogs. Many farmers allowed their hogs to roam free in the forests neighboring their properties or on their property. Neighbors supported this system by allowing each other to set their hogs loose on what might be part of the other's property, by recognizing the markings of someone else's hog, and by only gathering one's own hogs.[44]

Like the interdependency of the men and women of a single household, no farming family could survive without the cooperation and help of other families, and the need for collective activities instilled the value of reciprocity in these communities. When one family had the good fortune of a strong crop, they were expected to share some of that year's seed with other families so that they too could have a stronger crop the following year.[45] Such reciprocity became so commonplace that newcomers who expected to be thanked profusely for offering assistance in times of need might be disappointed.[46] And when somebody violated this social norm, it did not go unnoticed. For example, when a landowner served his helpers the harvest feast out in the field, neighbors viewed this as a selfish act because it seemed that he was trying to get the maximum amount of work out of his helpers. They repaid him by taking all the food before the host could get any.[47]

Kinship also tied together farming communities. Because sons often took up residence on the old homestead or purchased nearby land, the neighbors who came to help with harvests and barn raisings were frequently related by blood or by marriage. Families formed dense networks based on their close proximity and mutual assistance. As sons married daughters of nearby families, the web of familial connections grew until somebody would joke that they were related to half the county. To move far away from the old homeplace would also mean leaving behind a broad network of support. As the children of farmers grew up, there was an undeniable sense of belonging as even distant neighbors could ask "whose girl" you were and locate you on an imagined geographical and familial map of the community.[48]

As farming communities stabilized and prospered, residents became increasingly rooted in their place, especially as they became familiar with the peculiarities of their soil, local climate, and favorite hunting grounds. People who grew up on farms in the nineteenth century expressed a love for the natural beauty of their place, the sweet sounds of the birds, and fragrances of the honeysuckle or lilac that surrounded their homes.[49] One New York farm woman in the 1920s wrote of her relationship with the land on her family's farm, noting that there was a "comfort, a real comfort, in plain living." "In walking over the fields in the spring to see how the 'new-seeded' are coming, in watching the different birds come back from the south each spring. In tending the little lambs, and chickens and calves, in watching things grow, in making your own delicious butter, in picking the raspberries from your own patch, and in getting the first peas and sweet corn, and in the fall in gathering the apples from the trees that your own grandfather planted on the farm years ago." She continued: "They are simple things, all of them, but there are the simple virtues back of them that make life worth living."[50]

By the late 1800s, the farming families of Hancock County were firmly rooted in place. Kinship, collective activities, and interdependence knitted the local community into a dense support network that individuals both relied on and were part of. Not only were they rooted in place by their role in the community, they also formed sentimental attachments to the land and local flora and fauna. This attachment to place fostered a localism that also influenced their politics.

Localism in Politics

In the late nineteenth century, life among farming families in the North continued to be informed by values of independence and localism, leading them to resist the efforts of reformers to wrest away from local leaders various governmental functions such as maintenance of public roads and administration of public education.[51] Available evidence suggests that Hancock County was no different. On the eve of the county's industrialization, local government gave residents control over a surprising number of aspects of life. As late as 1881, Hancock County residents still administered social welfare locally by holding an annual auction wherein the county would pay the lowest bidder to take care of a pauper for the year.[52] The County Book Board met once a year to adopt textbooks for the year. In 1907, the *New Cumberland Independent* reported that "realizing that frequent changes of text books" was expensive, the board "acted with their usual conservatism."[53] And county commissioners still administered road maintenance, construction, and finance.

In the second half of the nineteenth century, the Republican Party came to dominate Hancock County politics. In the years leading up to the Civil War, the Republican Party attracted farmers, who supported higher tariffs, as well as the owners of the small brickyards in New Cumberland, who favored government-funded improvement projects. Streets in the county seat of New Cumberland bear the names of Lincoln and Grant. When they petitioned the federal government, it was often to request higher tariffs against wool and manufactured goods. Initially, local boosters hoped such policies would strengthen their local economy.[54] At the time, both Republicans and Democrats at the state level embraced the "development faith," promoting the construction of railroads and the industrialization of the state. In the late 1800s, struggling farmers were among the few dissenting voices in the rush to industrialize, and a chapter in the history of the Populist movement played out in the Mountain State. Many foresaw a tremendous increase in their property taxes with the coming of railroads as well as increased competition from larger commercial farms in the Midwest, both of which would hurt them financially. In addition to the disadvantages they faced after the arrival of railroads, they also protested the higher rates that smaller shippers paid and the lower taxes that railroad companies paid. West Virginia farmers initially used the Grange movement to organize their opposition to railroads and later reformed as the Farmers Alliance.[55]

Little is known about where the farmers of Hancock County stood in relation to the railroads and the Populist movement, but an examination of the only Democratic gubernatorial candidate, Cornelius C. Watts, to receive a majority of the county's votes in three decades is instructive. Watts ran for governor in 1896 on the Democratic ticket and lost.[56] No friend of railroad corporations, as attorney general for West Virginia he argued the pivotal 1885 case *Miller, Auditor vs. The Chesapeake and Ohio Railway Company* before the U.S. Supreme Court and won, forcing the C&O and all other railroad companies to forever pay taxes to West Virginia on their properties.[57] Watts lost the 1896 gubernatorial election to Republican candidate George Atkinson, who had a very different attitude toward corporations. In his inaugural address in 1897, Atkinson noted that West Virginia's resources were "perhaps superior to those of any other State in Union." "It behooves us, therefore, as good citizens," he said, "to do everything in our power to forward her interests, and to encourage her development." Atkinson went on to say that the Democrats had made much of the presence of corporations in the state during the election, but he saw no reason to create prejudice against men who form a corporation for "proper business purposes." He concluded, "Instead of fewer corporations in West Virginia, we need more of them. Instead of crushing out those we already have, it is our duty to invite others to come among us to aid us in the development of our almost inexhaustible natural resources."[58]

The majority of Hancock County voters who gave their votes to Watts instead of Atkinson may have done so out of their concerns about powerful outside agents that would erode their local control. In fact, Atkinson's invitation to corporations (and their distant investors) to take control of the state's resources would have made the advocates of home rule and independence shudder. After his election, Atkinson continued to encourage corporate development of the state and embarked on a program to modernize school administration and road construction.

Local road administration, Hal Barron writes, "embodied the principles of home rule and self-reliant independence that epitomized rural republican ideology."[59] Good roads were an issue in the 1909 election in Hancock County when a seemingly unknown group of men got a road bond added to the ballot. In a letter to the editor, a "Taxpayer" declared that a bond should instead have "its birth among the realty holders," adding, "We do not wish to go on record as being against the improvement of our highways—we need a better system for their improvement and need it badly—but we are opposed to the idea of voting in a large amount of money into the hands of a few, to use as they please, and perhaps, build a sort of a 'Kings highway' in some remote part of the county."[60] The following week, the county commissioners tried to allay Taxpayer's fear that decisions about roads would be made by anyone other than the commissioners who would work with committees from each district in the county.[61] Not satisfied with that response, "Square Deal" wrote to praise Taxpayer for being "very conservative, gentlemanly and very proper to caution the tax payers of Hancock County" about the bond, which he argued contrasted with the county court's "extreme heat, over anxiousness and bossism."[62] When road construction did get underway that spring, a strike foreshadowed conflicts to come. Fourteen "Americans" laid down their tools and demanded that the ten Italians be discharged from the road crew and replaced with "citizens and taxpayers of said district."[63] Interestingly, 1909 was the year that the state legislature established a state road fund and appointed a state commissioner of public roads and county road engineers, drawing away some of the county's prized local control.[64]

CHAPTER I

Decline of Farming in Hancock County

The late 1800s proved to be the golden age of commercial farming and local control in Hancock County. Raising sheep and growing apples proved to be economically unsustainable for local farmers, and both ventures reached their zenith in the last two decades of the nineteenth century and faded from prominence by 1920. Apple growers experienced a gradual decline in the late nineteenth century. Farmers had shipped many of their apples downriver to southern states, but after the Civil War, these markets bought fewer and fewer Hancock County apples.[65] Furthermore, farmers in Hancock County and throughout the state suffered from some of the increased competition that accompanied economic development. The construction of railroads in West Virginia and across the Midwest undermined the favorable conditions that had led to the expansion of commercial farming in Hancock County and in the hills and dales of many northern states. As the costs of transportation decreased, competition from large-scale midwestern farms made life increasingly difficult for older farmers back east, just as they had feared, and nearby railroads increased property values and taxes along with them. Farmers like Lyman Stedman and his family were forced to produce more just to pay their taxes and maintain their lifestyles. Farmers with smaller holdings whose products brought in less and less cash faced the choice of reverting to a more basic subsistence strategy, finding "public" work to supplement their farm income, or abandoning the farm altogether.[66] Apple farmers, like farmers in many other places experiencing industrialization, also suffered from another by-product of economic development: pollution. The smokestacks of brickyards and newly constructed potteries produced gas and smoke that killed nearby vegetation, leaving steep barren hills all around them.[67] Some of the largest apple producers in the county were located on the riverbank near the factories, and the new pollution undoubtedly affected their orchards' yields. Those that survived tended to be commercial orchards located in the hills far from the mills and potteries.

According to one 1915 study, the "sheep industry" in West Virginia reached its peak around 1890 when the census recorded that there were 785,000 sheep in the state. Twenty years later that number had fallen to 567,000. While sheep farming was still a profitable business, many complained about recent increases in the number of stray dogs and dog attacks on their livestock. In fact, 71 percent of the survey's respondents cited dog attacks as the main reason why the state's farmers were abandoning sheep herding for a living.[68] The sheep farmers also suffered from new competition from western states as well as from Australia and Argentina, which led to declining prices.[69] The number of sheep in Hancock County peaked in 1880 at roughly 25,000 and declined to a little less than 6,000 by 1910.[70]

The county's commercial farmers enjoyed a prosperous century during the 1800s, but now they faced new circumstances and new choices. Many of them chose to abandon farming or farm only part time. The number of farms and the amount of land being farmed dropped sharply. In 1890, there were 407 farms in Hancock County that averaged 117 acres. By 1920, there were 357 farms averaging 106 acres. The total farm acreage in the county decreased from nearly 48,000 to less than 38,000.[71]

Some Hancock County farmers embraced economic development, likely hoping to buoy their commercial farms. Some of the most ambitious farmers profited handsomely from the new opportunities, facilitating new ventures and courting outside capital. Cyrus Ferguson, described in some accounts as an "old settler," bridged the county's old farming economy and the new manufacturing one.[72] He spent most of his life working on farms in Hancock County until 1883, when he opened a meat market in nearby Wellsburg. Over the next decade, he became increasingly entrepreneurial, investing in businesses across the state line in McDonald, Pennsylvania, including another meat market and a brick factory as well as local oil wells. In 1902, recognizing the value of a broad flat cove that did not flood, Ferguson bought ten farms near Hollidays Cove totaling 1,700 acres.[73] He then subdivided the land into town lots, donating some of them for schools and businesses. In April 1909, he sold 105 acres to Ernest Weir, who eventually purchased about 1,200 acres from Ferguson on which the company's new tinplate mill and an accompanying town would be built.[74] After that, Ferguson retired to a nearby farm where hired hands did most of his farm work.[75]

Some older farmers continued to work the land, change their farming strategies, and chase declining profits, but their children, like Louis Truax, who left his family's farm in 1919, went down to the factory gates seeking wage work to avoid a slow economic death on the farm. Yet as a new stage of economic development swept across the county, much of the rural culture remained unchanged, as we will see in the coming chapters.

Conclusion

The culture of the farmers of Hancock County was shaped in several ways by their rural lifestyles. First, work assignments were divided among family members by gender, with women performing the bulk of household production and raising small livestock while the men tilled fields, hunted for local game, herded sheep, and harvested apples. To fit into the factory systems, these rural people would have to adapt to a new set of gender roles of the rising industries of the early twentieth century. Second, successful farming required a wide spectrum of skills that enabled farmers to coax a living out of their fields and forests. These skills would prove useful in making ends meet even after they started to draw paychecks from local factories. Finally, the farmers exhibited a preference for local autonomy, self-government, and independence from distant powers. Their ideals of self-reliance and independence in turn shaped their politics. While boosters called for better roads and schools, farming communities jealously guarded their control over local institutions. These social structures and the values of the rural farming culture would continue to exert influence over the rural-industrial workers of a later period and to shape their response to industrialism.

CHAPTER 2

BUILDING FACTORIES IN THE COUNTRY

In 1909, Ernest Weir, his brother, and two other managers of his tinplate company headquartered in Clarksburg, West Virginia, began looking for a new location. The operation would need to be close to steel mills that would supply them with the steel bars they would roll into thin metal sheets to be coated with tin, and it would need to be close to the highly skilled tinplate workers they needed to operate their mills. The executives visited many sites, primarily around the city of Pittsburgh, but did not find the space they envisioned until they came to Cyrus Ferguson's farm in Hancock County on the banks of the Ohio River. Weir recalled that, standing in the grassy field, the four men envisioned the locations for all the various structures of a "completely integrated steel plant and the community necessary to support it."[1]

Weir was similar to scores of other factory owners who experienced cutthroat competition during the 1890s, a decade of declining prices, slashed wages, labor strife, and bankruptcy. Both the steel and pottery industries emerged from those years of crisis transformed. As many owners searched for solutions, they reorganized their business structures, formed employers' associations, bought out competitors and suppliers, supported higher tariffs, adopted new technologies, and tapped into new pools of labor. When workers resisted these changes, industrialists used capital's mobility to their advantage, building new factories in other communities, sometimes pitting one locale against another. Many factory owners saw rural places as a blank canvas that offered them more control over their operations, their workers, and their businesses. They had tended to locate their factories near raw materials and markets, but now they looked for wide, flat farms where they could start over with new facilities, the latest technologies, and more harmonious labor relations. The industrialists who relocated to Hancock County intentionally created a rural-industrial place that would influence the lives of workers for the next century.

Industrialists, Pottery, and Tinplate

In the late nineteenth century, industrialists like Ernest Weir saw themselves as pioneers, bringing progress to undeveloped lands and improving the American way of life through technological innovation. At the same time, they felt trapped in a world of labor strife and chaotic business conditions. Many were self-made men who entered the business world as clerks and errand boys and capitalized on their network of contacts as well as opportunities that presented themselves during a period of tremendous economic growth. Some of them were craftsmen who banded together with their coworkers to invest in idle factories. Others were trained by their fathers, heirs to industrial empires. Whatever their background, they all struggled to remain solvent during the economic depressions and "panics" of the late nineteenth century that bankrupted many successful businessmen and taught the rest the importance of keeping costs low and adjusting to an ever-changing business environment. Out of these lean years emerged a stern and uncompromising managerial class that had no patience for inefficiencies.[2]

During the 1820s and 1830s, as Americans moved westward, industrialists flocked to the banks of the Ohio River, and the region experienced decades of steady industrialization. Centers of commerce like Pittsburgh, Pennsylvania; Steubenville and East Liverpool, Ohio; and Wheeling, West Virginia, grew into centers of manufacturing. Local entrepreneurs took advantage of the area's coal, iron ore, limestone, and clay and built a myriad of factories along the Ohio River, the region's main artery. By the end of the Civil War, manufacturers were exporting millions of dollars worth of coal, firebrick, pottery, glassware, woolen goods, pig iron, and cut nails down the Ohio River to points west.[3] During the late nineteenth century, the construction of railroads, creation of vertically integrated steel mills, and tapping of natural gas reserves fueled the continued growth of manufacturing up and down the river.[4]

Pottery manufacturers enjoyed great success in the Ohio Valley, especially in East Liverpool, which sat atop rich veins of clay. English immigrant James Bennett established the first pottery in East Liverpool in 1840, and by the end of the decade five other potteries located in the town, earning it the nickname "Crockery City." A steady stream of pottery workers emigrated from England to East Liverpool. By the end of the decade, English immigrants accounted for a third of the city's population, and they continued to have a large presence in the city for decades to come.[5] In England in the early 1840s, an economic depression led union leader William Evans to propose a radical solution: emigration to America, where potters could become farmers. One hundred potters migrated to Pottersville, Wisconsin, where their lack of agricultural skills proved too great an obstacle, and many migrated back eastward to East Liverpool.[6]

East Liverpool continued to attract capital for new potteries in the 1870s and 1880s and soon rivaled Trenton, New Jersey, as a leading center of American pottery production. In the 1870s, the city council gave Homer and Shakespeare Laughlin, two brothers from Suffolk, England, free land and a bonus of $5,000 in exchange for building a whiteware pottery. They broke ground in the fall of 1873 on a two-kiln pottery and steadily increased capacity thereafter. The firm took the name of owner Homer Laughlin, and he and his bookkeeper, W. Edwin Wells, incorporated in 1896. Homer Laughlin gradually sold his interest in the firm to Pittsburgh entrepreneurs Louis Aaron and his son Marcus, but the Homer Laughlin name remained with the company.[7] Toward the end of the century, while Trenton potteries specialized in sanitary ware (meaning bathtubs and water closets), Homer Laughlin and the East Liverpool potteries focused increasingly on manufacturing tableware.

The terminology for the pottery industry can sometimes be confusing. Ceramics is a broad class of clay products that includes bricks, tiles, sanitary ware like sinks and toilets, and tableware, which includes china. China was often used as a general term for household dishes as well as a more specific term for white, porcelain dishware. Potteries might produce sanitary ware or tableware, but rarely both. Most of the potteries of Hancock County focused on tableware.

Tariffs became a near obsession of American pottery owners. In an industry where labor made up some 50 percent of the total production costs, American potteries were vulnerable to imports from countries like England, where wages were much lower. In 1875, owners from forty-one pottery firms convened in Trenton and formed the United States Potters' Association (USPA). They vowed to share scientific and practical information with one another but decided not to fix prices because some argued that it would weaken the USPA. Instead of setting prices, the organization focused most of its energies on lobbying for tariffs, which owners considered to be critical to their industry.[8] The workers also favored high tariffs. Initially, John O'Neill, who became a potter in 1869, never "missed an opportunity to cuss the protective tariff" because tariffs "compelled the consumer to accept an inferior class of goods." But experience taught him that there was a great difference in wages and costs of production between Europe and America—"from the cellar to the garret"—and only tariffs would protect their wages and their industry.[9]

After Congress reduced the ceramics tariff in 1894, pottery owners and workers alike felt the ill effects and enthusiastically supported Republican presidential candidate William McKinley, who ran in 1896 on a platform of increased tariff protections. When news of his election reached East Liverpool, a raucous celebration ensued. Congress enacted higher tariffs on ceramics in 1897, and the twenty-two potteries operating in the city were booming. East Liverpool's population grew from 10,956 in 1890 to 16,485 in 1900.[10] By 1900, nearly 3,500 people worked in East Liverpool's potteries and produced $4.1 million worth of ceramics, slightly less than Trenton's $4.8 million. Together, Trenton and East Liverpool produced 49.7 percent of all pottery products made in the United States.[11]

The terms used in the iron and steel industry—of which tinplate is but one product—can also be confusing. First, there are different kinds of iron. Pig iron contains high amounts of carbon and is only one step removed from iron ore. Wrought iron contains very little carbon and is very hard, but it is brittle. Steel has more carbon than does wrought iron and is more malleable, making it more suitable for use in railroads and skyscrapers, which partly explains its importance in the American economy in the nineteenth century. As mentioned, tinplate refers to a thin sheet of steel coated in tin that by the late 1800s manufacturers used for canned food and boxes for cigarettes and candy, among other things. A mill referred to an individual set of metal rolls that pressed the steel thin and flat, and they sometimes talked about a fifteen-mill plant, meaning that the facility had fifteen stands of rolling mills. In the 1920s, it became common for tinplate production to be part of an integrated steel plant rather than a stand-alone finishing company, and by the mid-twentieth century, Weirton steelworkers often talked about the "tin mill," which was now but one department of the sprawling steel "mill."

Before 1890, the tinplate industry struggled to take root in the Ohio Valley. Tinplate was the most difficult of all the finished steel products to manufacture. Wales led the world in the manufacture of tinplate, and one son of a Welsh tinplate worker recalled that his people "thought that nobody but a Welshman could make tinplate."[12] Welsh tinplate rollers and heaters saw their skills as the family's most valuable asset. An industry expert observed, "Whole families worked in the mills. Boys entered the trade when still young and grew up in it, while wives and sisters followed the work open to them."

He also noted, "Zealously did the Welsh oppose all changes that tended to upset the trade's organization."[13]

The flood of imported Welsh tinplate made it difficult for fledgling American companies to compete, especially without the skilled workers needed to run the mills. In 1873, one American investor located a tin mill in Wellsville, Ohio, but it soon went bankrupt.[14] Mill owners credited the 1890 McKinley tariff (sponsored by William McKinley, then a Republican U.S. senator) for providing the protection they needed to start their businesses and compete with imported Welsh tinplate. Like pottery workers, tinplate workers in America were also strong supporters of tariffs. Even recent Welsh immigrants supported the high tariff though they knew it devastated the mills back in their home country.[15] American industrialists built dozens of new tinplate plants, and unlike the mammoth basic steel plants, these finishing mills did not require much capital to get started. With some $50,000 of investment capital, a group of skilled workers or steel company executives could finance the construction of new tinplate plants in small and mid-sized towns in Pennsylvania, Ohio, and West Virginia.[16] Being close to steel centers like Pittsburgh ensured the companies a steady, cost-effective supply of steel bars.

Ernest Weir was one of the rising stars of the tinplate industry. He was born in Pittsburgh on August 1, 1875, the son of Scottish immigrants. At the age of fifteen, when his father died, he started working as an office boy at the Braddock Wire Company. He then got a job as a clerk at the Oliver Wire Company. His employer, iron and steel magnate Henry W. Oliver, saw promise in the young Weir and made him his lieutenant in his new business venture, the Monongahela Tin Plate Company, which Oliver soon sold to the American Tin Plate Company. Weir then worked for the American Tin Plate Company and was promoted to superintendent of the Monessen mill.[17]

Industrialists' Dependence on Craftsmen

In both the tinplate and pottery industries, owners and managers found their dealings with the craftsmen most vexing. In fact, more than a decade of turmoil and labor-management conflict in both industries preceded the relocation of tin mills and potteries to Hancock County. Skilled potters and tinplate workers belonged to tight-knit communities defined by their trades and their shared values. They considered themselves the "aristocrats of labor." Jiggermen and kilnmen in the potteries as well as rollers and heaters in the mills had great authority on the shop floor; they hired and fired, supervised and paid their crew members. Much of their authority rested on their unique knowledge of the production processes that they performed and supervised. Manufacturers depended on the craftsmen and had to tolerate craft traditions that were at odds with the drive for productivity and profit. The skilled workers were steeped in a craft culture that privileged taking a "manly" posture toward bosses and fellow craftsmen. Well-established customs guided them through their workday, influencing how much they produced, the price they demanded for their labor, and under what conditions they were willing to work. These craftsmen collectively and informally enforced work rules by shaming fellow workers who violated them. By the end of the nineteenth century, they codified work rules into union bylaws and contract clauses.[18]

Because workers refused to change, the American pottery industry up through the 1880s still employed Staffordshire methods and English craft traditions in most production departments. The first department in the production process was the clay prep shop, where workers forced clay through sieves to clean it. Operators then sent the clay through a pugmill to squeeze out any air bubbles before setting it aside to "age." To make slip—a liquid clay used in the casting shop—clay prep makers used secret recipes, mixing ground flint, quartz, feldspar, and clay, sometimes crunching it between their teeth to gauge the mixture.[19]

In the clay shop, jiggering crews then formed the clay into ware. Each jiggerman employed a batter-out and one or two mold runners. The batter-out cut off the needed amount of clay and forced it down onto a mold. In crews that made cups, the batter-out was called a cup-baller. Next, the jiggerman used a water tool (also called a pulldown or a jolly) that he equipped with different profile jigs, which greatly simplified turning shallow, flat, circular ware such as plates and saucers by forcing the clay onto a spinning mold. The mold runner took the now filled mold to the stove room for drying and returned with an empty mold to give to the jiggerman. Dishmakers were part of a separate craft altogether and only made large dishes like oval platters by hand. Similarly, casters in the casting shop made complicated items like creamers, sugars bowls, and pitchers by pouring slip into molds. Casters also made lids and handles separately. A finisher, who was often the wife of the jiggerman, took the "green" ware as it was known before the first firing and removed any flashing and smoothed its rough edges with a sponge or a knife.

Cup handlers performed delicate work that required much practice. They had to slice off handles from a "handle tree" in such a way so that their cut matched the profile of the side of the cup. They then sponged the clay and applied handles to the cups manually. If the handler made a good cut, the handle would adhere well to the side of the cup. If not, the handler had to apply some liquid clay or "stickin' up slip," as they called it; the handle and cup might still be ruined.[20]

FIGURE 2. A jiggerman, Homer Laughlin China, ca. 1950s
Source: Homer Laughlin China Company

Formed ware waited in the green room until kiln placers set the pieces in saggars, ceramic boxes that protected the ware while it was in the kiln (pronounced "kill" by the potters). To prevent breakage, the kiln placers carefully "pinned" ware into the saggars with wooden dowels. They then stacked and placed the saggars, depending on the shapes and sizes of the ware, in different parts of the bottle kilns, so called because the large, circular brick ovens were topped with bottleneck-shaped smokestacks. The kiln fireman slowly built a fire and monitored the temperature in the bottle kiln through test holes. The first firing in the "bisque kiln" typically reached three thousand degrees Fahrenheit and transformed the green or soft clay into hard but porous clay that could be more easily handled. Kiln drawers removed or "drew" the saggars from the bottle kiln once it cooled down enough and carefully removed the ware from the saggars. It might be only then that mistakes in clay prep or kiln firing would be discovered, as some of the ware would not survive the firing in one piece.

Laborers then transported bisque ware, as it was called at this point in the process, to the warehouse, where various groups of warehouse women worked.

The bisque warehouse "girls" brushed the dust off the ware before the dippers lowered it by hand into a tub of liquid glaze. The dippers' helper then sponged off any excess glaze, and another crew of kiln placers, kiln firemen, and kiln drawers fired the glazed ware in the glost kiln (pronounced "gloss kill"), which fused on the glassy coating.

From the glost kilns, laborers took the ware to the decorating shop. In the nineteenth century, skilled male printers would hand stencil patterns onto the ware, and less skilled female paintresses filled in the patterns. Another group of decorators, known as the gilders, hand painted gold lines or rings on ware.[21] Kilnmen put the decorated ware in muffle kilns at low temperatures to fuse the decoration to the dish. Finally, warehouse men and women hand selected ware to fill various orders and carefully packed it in barrels, filling in straw around the ware to keep it from breaking.

The skilled workers of the potteries learned their craft through apprenticeships lasting seven years in England and five years in America. Even the profile jigs that cut the same pattern into the clay, time after time, required "a deft hand," according to potter John W. Morgan. Morgan apprenticed in England for five years before he decided he was "big enough and knew enough about the business to skip out . . . and come to America." He preferred working in American potteries because even though they worked at "a killing pace," American potters made more money.[22] Once a potter became a journeyman, his skills became a family asset to be passed on to sons, sons-in-law, and nephews, whom the journeyman employed as helpers. Journeymen were autonomous craftsmen who hired, supervised, disciplined, and paid their workforce.[23] The patriarchal aristocrats of the American potteries held their heads high and assumed leadership roles in their communities, and potters regularly expressed pride in their work. As John O'Neill put it, "I, like every good fellow in the business, felt proud I was a potter."[24]

As in the potteries, iron manufacturing was a handcraft industry until the 1870s. Crews of skilled puddlers, heaters, and rollers enjoyed nearly complete control of the manufacturing processes and strongly identified with their fellow tradesmen. The puddlers, for example, prided themselves on their knowledge as well as having the strength and stamina to stand in front of a blazing hot furnace stirring molten iron with a puddling rod. These "sons of Vulcan" demanded high wages and produced only what they deemed to be a fair day's work. In the 1870s, companies invested fortunes in research, new equipment, and new production lines to wrest control away from the fiercely independent and expensive artisan workers. When they installed new Bessemer and open-hearth furnaces, they eliminated the need for the iron puddlers and greatly reduced production costs. Furthermore, instead of wrought iron, the new furnaces produced steel, a much more uniform material, which made it possible to create continuous rolling mills. This in turn eliminated the need for highly skilled rollers and heaters. In the new steel industry, workers only needed to monitor and maintain the machinery, making adjustments here and there. Accordingly, owners hired farm boys and European immigrants to operate many departments in the mills.[25]

The only segment of the steel industry that resisted automation was tinplate. In the 1890s, as the market for canned food exploded, so too did the demand for the tinplate to make the cans, and manufacturers searched for efficiencies in the tinplate mills. The continuous rolling mills used to make bar steel proved to be too crude to roll bars to the thin gauge they needed. Thus, long after skilled workers had been banished from basic steel production, manufacturers still needed skilled rollers and heaters in the tinplate mills, and these craftsmen exerted great control over production, dictating both the pace of production and quality of the product, negotiating tonnage rates with mill owners and hiring and paying their helpers as they saw fit.[26]

The process for making tinplate was convoluted. Skilled heaters placed steel bars in furnaces until they glowed red and then passed them along to the rougher, whose crew sent the bars through a stand of rolls called the roughing mill, which flattened the steel like rolling pins flattening bread dough. Heaters reheated the sheets before rolling crews sent them through their individual stands of rolls by hand. The catcher, who was sometimes a young helper, grabbed the sheets as they came through the rolls and then passed them back over the top to the roller. The roller would carefully adjust the roll height so that the metal sheets came out the proper thickness. The doubler folded the sheets in half using a "crocodile squeezer" to flatten the edge of the sheet. Because the squeezer was connected to the main driveshaft in the mill, the doubler would have to time his movement to the closing of the crocodile's mouth, so to speak. After the sheets were folded in half, the roller sent them back through the mill and they came out the other side half as thick. After several passes, a heater would put the stacks of plate in the furnace for a second heating and send them on for a finishing rolling. They would be doubled again and rerolled. After a third and final reheating in the finishing furnace, the packs were passed through the finishing rolls again.[27]

After the skilled rollers and heaters had produced the thin squares of steel, laborers then took the black plates, as they were called at this point, from the hot mill to the tin house, where, typically in the United States, eastern European immigrants, men and women, would finish the plates. The jobs in the tin house required stamina instead of skill, as workers performed monotonous tasks in unpleasant conditions. The first operation of the tin house was shearing. When the packs of sheets had cooled, a worker put them into "crocodile shears," which opened and closed continuously, to cut them to 20-by-42-inch squares, the standard final product. The rolling and reheating process would slightly weld the sheets together, and women known as openers would pry them apart. This was physically demanding work. One Progressive Era investigator, Elizabeth Beardsley Butler, watched as five to eight sheets arrived welded together and the openers had to tear them apart while they were still hot and flexible. Wearing heavy gloves, the women would grab a stack of welded plates and "beat it on the ground" and stick a piece of lead in between the plates to make an opening. Next, they tore the plates apart, "holding part of the sheet down with one knee while tearing the metal with the other. "The violence of this work," Butler wrote, "takes all the strength of even the earth-toughened peasant women who have followed their husbands from Poland to the mill country in America."[28]

The black plates at this point were hard, brittle, and covered in iron oxide. Workers in the pickling mill sent the sheets through a bath of sulfuric acid followed by a bath of water to strip off the iron oxide, and seven or eight furnacemen would pack them in cast-iron pots and send the plates into the annealing furnace, subjecting them to intense heat for ten to twelve hours to make them stronger and more malleable. Tin house workers then sent the plates through a series of vats to finish them. The first contained boiling palm oil, or flux, that cleaned the plates and made them more absorbent, and the other two or three pots contained molten tin that formed a base coat and then finishing coats. After a washman removed excess tin, young girls would polish the finished plates with sheepskins, and female assorters would inspect and stack them based on their quality. Butler watched this work, too, and found the women in a cleaner environment assorting tinplates, an occupation that she described as "less violent." Still, she noted, the repeated lifting and handling of the plates required considerable exertion.[29] Finally, warehousemen packaged stacks of tinplate into boxes of one hundred plates to be shipped out on railcars.

The Family Wage and New Technologies

During the late nineteenth century, skilled potters and tinplate workers in America attempted to earn a "family wage," largely by banishing women from the work crews and leaving them to do unpaid household labor at the same time that men's wages were increasing.[30] In the eighteenth century in the Staffordshire pottery industry, the journeyman's wife often worked as his finisher, and some women even headed up their own cup and saucer jiggering crews. Females made up one-third of the workforce. When English potters migrated to Trenton, New Jersey, in the mid-nineteenth century, women were restricted to working as finishers, decorators, and warehouse workers and prohibited from running their own crews, and by 1860 they accounted for less than one-tenth of the Trenton workforce.[31] Male journeyman had direct control over the gender of their helpers. In 1901, one potter remarked, "I engage a woman myself and pay her. Every jiggerman employs what he wants. So far as I can remember, and I have worked on a jigger for thirty-eight years, there were always women engaged to do the finishing work—to make the finishing touches."[32] By 1890, women accounted for only 5 percent of the workforce in the East Liverpool district.[33] Thus the skilled male potters had succeeded in banishing most women from the potteries up to that time.

The gender roles of the tinplate industry were also undergoing change. Men controlled the production processes as well as the hiring of their crews, which strengthened the patriarchal culture of these artisans. Male tinplate workers believed that the presence of women in the mills was a drag on wages and saw the shift in location from Wales to America as an opportunity to reshape the workforce to their advantage. In Wales in 1890, as much as 25 percent of the workforce was female, but when Welsh workers crossed the Atlantic to work in American mills, they attempted to create an all-male workplace that paid a family wage to the male breadwinners, and they were largely successful.[34]

During the 1890s, manufacturers in both the pottery and tin plate industries responded to increased competition and declining profits by adopting new procedures and technologies, which sometimes also meant changing the gender composition of the workforce. American potteries adopted the new process of decalcomania, which enabled pottery owners to replace most of the highly paid male printers with working-class women known as "decal girls" to work in separate decorating shops.[35] Bill Pomeroy, a twentieth-century pottery executive, described what was still a "pretty labor intensive" process: "They used round cylinders that had been engraved with a pattern, and they would run those on a lathe. And they would use tissue paper to print the pattern from the cylinder onto the tissue paper. Then they would rub that down to transfer the ink off the paper onto the ware. And it was pretty damn slow." Once the decorator transferred the ink from the decal to the ware, they submerged it in a trough of water for a half hour to forty-five minutes. Eventually the paper would float off and leave the ink transfer on the ware. The ink could easily be smeared when the decorator applied the decal, and some colors, like cobalt blue, were

CHAPTER 2

FIGURE 3. Decal girls, Homer Laughlin China, ca. early 1900s
Source: Homer Laughlin China Company

more difficult than others. So decorators and "decal girls" had to apply decals with precision and care, and they had to get it right the first time lest the ware be ruined.[36]

The advent of decalcomania in the 1890s coincided with East Liverpool potteries' shift to the production of schemeware, inexpensive dishes often used as premiums, marketing gimmicks to help sell oatmeal and other mass-marketed products like cereal and soap. The low standard of quality for schemeware enabled potters in East Liverpool to produce it rapidly, make excellent wages on piece rates, and conceal defects with decoration.[37] In the late nineteenth and early twentieth centuries, the East Liverpool district gained a reputation for paying little respect to output restrictions and producing far more ware than the Trenton or Staffordshire pottery districts. East Liverpool operatives increased their daily production from about 125 dozen in 1896 to 175 dozen by 1904. That was at a time when English potters only produced 75 dozen and Trenton potters approximately 100 dozen (although in those districts they made ware of much higher quality).[38] Homer Laughlin and other major potteries in the East Liverpool district relied more and more on nationwide chain stores, premium distributors, mail-order businesses, and department stores to buy and market their schemeware. By 1900, the American Cereal Company was demanding forty-eight thousand decorated bowls per week from Homer Laughlin for a Quaker Oats cereal promotion. By the end of the first fourteen months of their partnership, Quaker Oats premiums accounted for nearly one-fifth of all of Homer Laughlin's sales.[39]

With a new focus on schemeware, potteries in the East Liverpool district hired more women. Between 1890 and 1900, the number of women in the potteries of Ohio and West Virginia increased from 616 to 2,417, and their proportion of the total workforce increased from 5 percent to 13 percent.[40] Such monikers as decal "girls" or bisque warehouse "girls" were misleading. When one Ohio labor arbitrator spoke about the bisque warehouse "girls" to the U.S. Industrial Commission, confused commissioners thought he was referring to children, but the arbitrator clarified that the bisque warehouse "girls" ranged from eighteen to forty years old, with some of them "turning a little gray."[41] Unlike many industries at the time, potteries hired married women. Interestingly, Bill Pomeroy recalled that they still hired family units as jiggering crews as late as the 1950s. He recalled "in lots of cases it was a family: the husband was the jiggerman, the wife was the finisher, and a son or son-in-law was mold runner and/or the batter-out."[42]

American tinplate manufacturers faced greater resistance when they tried to employ more women. In 1895, Henry W. Oliver—president of the Monongahela Tin Plate Company and Ernest Weir's first mentor—hired a young Welsh woman named Hattie Williams to train other young women, but his male employees protested mightily. Although tinplate workers had succeeded in banishing women from many mills in America, companies like Monongahela started hiring women to work primarily as openers, prying apart hot plates, and as assorters, polishing and inspecting plates for defects. Despite the fears of male workers, the hiring of Williams did not signal the beginning of the widespread employment of Welsh women, nor did women get employment outside of opening and assorting. Instead, employers filled those two departments (and only those two departments) with young eastern European women, especially Poles, who they believed were stronger and would work for less.[43] Most of the work of the tinplate mills was still considered "men's work." For example, in 1926, women made up only 2 percent of the workforce of the tinplate mill in Chester and 1 percent in Weirton.[44]

Instead of employing low-wage female workers, tinplate manufacturers took advantage of their relocation from Wales to America to adopt new procedures and technologies. Many of the same Welsh workers who opposed changes back home now belonged to the Amalgamated Association of Iron, Steel, and Tin

Workers, which had a different attitude toward technological improvement. "The Association never objects to improvement," president William Weihe said in 1894. If changes "do away with certain jobs they make no objection. They believe in the American idea that the genius of the country should not be retarded."[45] American tinplate manufacturers adopted larger rolls that increased capacity and reduced the number of times the plates needed to be rolled. The larger equipment usually required a seven-man crew instead of the traditional four-man crew used in Wales, but companies still saved money by increasing output. By 1910, most companies had built narrow-gauge railroad tracks through the mills and used trains to transport slabs and stacks of plate from one department to the next. They also used electric cranes to unload slabs from the trains and swing them over to the furnaces. The trains and cranes eliminated the need for several crews of transport laborers. These changes increased productivity from 1.15 tons per man per day in 1895 to 5.96 tons in 1910.[46] Unlike other sectors of the steel industry, however, the changes in tinplate production did not reduce the need for skilled workers.[47]

Because tinplate production proved so difficult to automate, there was no substitute for the close supervision of an experienced worker. One 1913 report noted that to be a heater required "long experience and considerable practical knowledge of the heat treatment of metals." Furnace temperatures, for example, were largely judged "by the heater's eye" as he watched for a certain shade of cherry. A single error meant the "loss of a valuable steel slab."[48] The report also explained that the roller's job remained unaffected by the technological changes around him: "This is a very responsible and highly skilled occupation, which requires a special knowledge of the working of iron and steel that can be gained only by long experience. It is impossible to convey in a description the kind and degree of knowledge required to produce uniform plates of the proper width and thickness on which the loss shall be as little as possible."[49] Rollers not only had to carefully measure the distance between the rolls but also had to closely monitor the shape and temperature of the rolls. Periods without metal passing between them could allow the rolls to cool and change shape. One company executive argued that if a worker was "real clever he can learn the business in 3 years from the time he starts in," and he was probably underestimating.[50] One Weirton Steel executive explained that while the roller was a worker, he was "generally regarded as the 'boss' of his mill." With a pair of tongs, he carefully made the final passes to bring the plate to the proper thickness and quality, and the higher the quality the more valuable the sheet, which was a matter of "great importance" to his crew and the company because they both made more money.[51]

Craft Unions in the Potteries and the Mills

While industrialists in the steel and pottery industries in the 1890s pursued similar strategies such as adopting new technologies and attempting to employ more female labor, they diverged sharply in their attitudes toward unions. While tinplate executives detested unions, pottery owners supported the unionization of their industry. In December 1890, delegates from potteries in and around East Liverpool voted to form the National Brotherhood of Operative Potters (NBOP), an affiliate of the American Federation of Labor.[52] The NBOP modeled its bylaws on those of the American Flint Glass Workers Union (AFGWU), strictly a union of skilled workers. The NBOP used strikes, albeit judiciously, to achieve better wages and working conditions and required all locals to adhere to a uniform working price list, something owners found very attractive.[53] In the 1890s, several of the pottery owners who were facing ruin encouraged this movement in the hopes of bringing uniform wages to a chaotic industry. They reasoned that "regulatory unionism" might bring the kind of stability to potteries that the AFGWU brought to the glass companies in the 1880s.[54] Yet in 1894, four years after its formation, the NBOP had only four locals, garnered little support among the pottery workers in the East Liverpool district, and lacked the clout to enforce any industry-wide standardization.

That changed when the Wilson Tariff of 1894 reduced the duties on ceramics, and pottery owners responded by cutting wages by up to 20 percent. Albert Hughes, the new NBOP president, saw an opportunity to strengthen the union. Elected president in 1892, he had already made several important changes to the union's structure, including securing an annual salary for the union president so he could act as a full-time organizer. Hughes argued that the union needed a man who did not have to "depend on his earnings at the bench."[55] When the local potteries announced the wage reductions, Homer Laughlin employees unanimously rejected the new rates, and employees from the other local potteries followed. At a mass meeting two days later, speakers noted that the new rates would bring American wages below those paid in England, which they found unthinkable.[56] They voted to strike, but as one union official later recalled, there were "a large number of potters who, while willing to resist the reduction offered, would have nothing to do with the Brotherhood." So Hughes created an independent advisory board to act as the voice of the strikers, and they chose him, the NBOP president, to chair the board.[57] Ultimately, the pottery owners in the East Liverpool district offered a compromise that the clay shop workers voted unanimously to accept, but Hughes had to lobby each craft of pottery workers to convince them to sign the agreement as well.[58] This was the beginning of a truly industry-wide union among the tableware potteries.

For nearly a decade after the strike, Hughes served as the NBOP president and worked to strengthen the union's solidarity and the industry's stability. He oversaw the creation of craft locals, established a solvent strike defense fund, and, on March 10, 1900, brokered the first industry-wide agreement between the NBOP and United States Potters' Association (USPA), which now became the bargaining agent for several companies.[59] The union also played an important role in bringing order to shopfloor relations, acting as a mediator between the skilled crew leaders and the companies. Ever-changing pottery fashions required constant changes in the production process, which in turn created multiple conflicts over the many minute changes that resulted. Union and company officials created the standing committee to handle grievances as they arose. Made up of three national union officers and three company representatives, the standing committee set piece rates for new lines of ware and changed work rules in the months between annual contract negotiations.[60]

The NBOP remained true to its conservative craft traditions. It was exclusive, and only the skilled journeymen were well-represented in the union's national offices and at negotiating conferences. Each trade in each district formed a separate local union, just as they did in the American Flint Glass Workers Union, after which the NBOP founders had modeled their union. As one government report on the union explained, "The jigger men have their own local union; the kiln men theirs; the saggar men, pressers, packers, painters, decorators, and so on through all the minute trade divisions."[61] Furthermore, the jiggermen belonged to a local union but their batter-outs, mold runners, and finishers did not; they were employees of the jiggermen.[62] Finally, the potters rarely went on strike. As one NBOP delegate said, "Be sure the money is in the business before you ask an advance, and be sure of your ability to fight before you take off your coat."[63] The NBOP—with the support of pottery owners—brought uniform wages and acted as a regulatory force in an unstable industry.

Labor relations in the tinplate mills took a very different path than in the pottery industry. The rise of the tinplate industry occurred at the same time that steel magnates like Andrew Carnegie were driving the steelworkers' union, the Amalgamated Association of Iron, Steel, and Tin Workers, from their basic steel mills. The Amalgamated Association was so named because it was an amalgamation of the craft unions that had once represented iron puddlers, rollers, and heaters separately, just like the AFGWU and the NBOP. Withholding skilled labor was the key to any success they enjoyed. When the Amalgamated Association lost the infamous 1892 Homestead Strike, it signaled the end of the union era in modern, mass-production steel mills, and union leaders looked to the new tinplate mills—the last refuge of the skilled steelworker—to be the foundation of their membership, which helped to offset losses in automated mills.[64]

After its rapid growth in the early 1890s, the tinplate companies were soon fiercely competing with one another, and they reduced their prices by from more than five dollars per box in 1893 to less than three dollars in 1898.[65] In these years of razor-thin profit margins, tinplate mill owners came to despise union work rules, particularly union limits on production. At its 1894 convention, the Amalgamated Association of Iron, Steel, and Tin Workers placed a limit of five thousand pounds of standard plates on the daily production of each crew. At the time, the limit was greater than the average output, and union officers believed it would prevent manufacturers from demanding more and more and lowering wages accordingly. They also believed that the limit would spread work around to more crews and force manufacturers to put more mills into production.[66]

Managers complained that when machinery broke, they could not make up for lost time the next day because of the limit on daily production. They also complained that when they made improvements over the old Welsh machinery by making bigger and heavier rolls with greater capacity, they had to wait until the next negotiation to establish a new output limit. Furthermore, some orders, because of the size of the sheet or the quality specified, were easier to produce than others, which should have resulted in greater output. According to one executive, the majority of workers were still "bound by the union fear of unrestricted output," afraid that if limits were abolished energetic workers would set new records, the rest would struggle to keep up, and wages would decline. This executive believed that wages would actually increase if output restriction were abolished.[67]

Because they were locked in a "condition of excessive competition," according to one tinplate executive, struggling companies scrambled for solutions.[68] In fact, few tinplate manufacturers went bankrupt despite the falling prices, but because none were able to gain a competitive advantage, they turned to business mergers to bring order to the industry.[69] Daniel Reid, president of an Indiana firm, teamed up with a small group of influential owners and executives and began offering stock options to the other tinplate companies from Indiana to Maryland. The new American Tin Plate Company, organized on December 15, 1898, with $46 million issued in capital stock, brought together nearly forty different companies that, in all, owned more than 275 mills and employed between twenty and twenty-five thousand workers. In another round of mergers in 1901, the American Tin Plate Company, along with several other steel concerns including the mammoth Carnegie Steel Company, became part of the first billion-dollar corporation, the United States Steel Corporation. Controlling more than 50 percent of the nation's steel production capacity, executives at U.S. Steel shut down some plants, modernized others, and illegally fixed the whole industry's prices and wages.[70]

Initially when the American Tin Plate Company incorporated, the Amalgamated Association signed contracts for all of their mills but one: the Monessen plant that Ernest Weir managed. The company insisted the union make an exception for that mill because they were experimenting with rolling the sheets continuously, which would not work with union rules.[71] Then the formation of U.S. Steel gave management a tremendous advantage over the union. Previously, the key to breaking the union in many segments of the steel industry had been technological improvements that reduced the need for skill, but unlike its predecessors, U.S. Steel did not have to fight to maintain a tenuous hold over a small share of the market for its basic steel or its finished products like tinplate. It had excess sheet and tinplate capacity as well as other product divisions to help keep it profitable in the event union workers shut down the tin mills. Even though they had not developed the technology to eliminate skilled tinplate workers, managers could now starve the union out of the mills.[72] This was consistent with the psychology of steel industrialists, who had little sympathy for the workers. As one U.S. Steel executive said, he had a simple rule: "If a workman sticks up his head, hit it."[73]

In 1901, an imbroglio in the sheet mill division turned into a national strike. When Amalgamated Association president T. J. Shaffer could not get contracts for all the sheet mills, he called on all union members employed by U.S. Steel to strike, gambling the future of the union on its ability to force the corporation back to the bargaining table. The only union workers left to answer his strike call were employed in the finishing mills, which included sheet, tinplate, and hoop mills. Less than two weeks into the strike, U.S. Steel's board of directors, deeply concerned about the public's opinion of the first billion-dollar corporation, offered to sign an agreement that included six more mills than the union had before the strike, but union officers had already decided that they needed a contract that covered all the mills of the tin, sheet, and hoop subsidiaries, and they rejected U.S. Steel's offer.[74] Shaffer confidently told a crowd of strikers in Wheeling: "The trust can't run the mills without you. There is not enough skilled labor left to make more millions for these men who have centralized capital."[75] Yet when the union finally signed an agreement after two and half months, it had lost fifteen mills where the men had given up and gone back to work, and the treasury had been depleted.[76]

The two managers at the Monessen works, Ernest Weir and J. R. Phillips, were hard at work trying to perfect what was called the two-roll or two-mill system for making tinplate. It involved using one set of rolls for roughing and another set for finishing. They lined up the two rolls to imitate continuous rolling even though men were still passing the sheets through by hand. After the strike, other nonunion mills started to adopt this system, and workers complained bitterly because they claimed the process reduced their wages, reduced the number of skilled rollers by half, increased the number of helpers, and increased the tonnage.[77] In 1904, the Monessen mill became the first to use open-hearth steel on the two-roll system, and Weir complimented his workers by saying that "the fact that the men employed at the Monessen mill have successfully worked the open-hearth steel on the two mill system goes to show that they are as skilled in the rolling of tin-plate as any workmen in the world."[78] While he praised his workers, Weir undoubtedly knew that tinplate rollers strongly disliked the two-roll system.

Between 1901 and 1909, U.S. Steel often ran nonunion mills to full capacity and idled union mills until the workers signed contracts that disavowed any connection with any labor organizations. One worker complained, "Ostensibly we are idle through want of orders, but as a matter of fact we are locked out because we will not work at a lower rate of wages, as do the men of Monessen."[79] Union officials were powerless as more and more of the plants fell to this method, which they dubbed "starvation and petition."[80] One official described the union's policy in this era as "giving way to every request that was made by the company when they insisted upon it," as in 1904 when they insisted the union remove all production restrictions from the wage scale agreement.[81] In 1909, U.S. Steel announced that neither it nor its subsidiaries would bargain collectively with the union anymore. The announcement threatened the union's very existence, and officials called a strike that lasted up to twelve months at a handful of mills. The corporation barely noticed, and after the workers drifted back, the union existed only at "independent" steel companies that were not owned by U.S. Steel.[82] This period of intense conflict coincided with Ernest Weir's early career and began his lifelong hatred of unions.

Expanding to the Farmland of Hancock County

The transformations that took place in the pottery and tinplate industries in the 1890s ultimately led factory owners on a search for new locations, which brought them to the cheap, flat land of Hancock County. There was little manufacturing in the county save a few brickyards in the riverfront town of New Cumberland, which began exploiting veins of clay and coal in the 1830s. As farming declined toward the end of the nineteenth century, some residents hoped manufacturing would buoy the county's economy, and in 1884, anticipating the importance of the riverfront to the manufacturing economy, voters decided to move the county seat to New Cumberland. One local entrepreneur, Captain John Porter, led New Cumberland's industrial development during the 1880s. A riverboat captain who operated a line of barges, Porter invested in a handful of brickyards and a sewer pipe manufacturing company. In 1887, he brokered a deal to bring a branch line of the Pennsylvania Railroad to the county and started the Chelsea China Company, the county's first pottery, in New Cumberland.[83] By 1890, the county had thirty manufacturing establishments that employed a scant 250 people, five of whom were women and nine children. Frequent floods and fires in New Cumberland seemed to discourage further industrial development, and the town remained small, with a population of 2,300.[84]

In the early 1900s, rural places like Hancock County began to figure into industrialists' schemes. J. Russell Smith, a professor of industry at the University of Pennsylvania's Wharton School of Business, included two chapters on the importance of factory location in his textbook on the best practices of industrial management, and he pointed out that rural and suburban locations had some advantages that city locations did not. Cities were far better than the country when it came to supplies, services, and fire protection, but land cost more, which often led to "cramped and crowded" spaces that inhibited expansion and forced employees to work in dark, "unwholesome" places. Furthermore, cities had to closely regulate construction, fire hazards, noises, and smells, which might make production more costly.[85] The country location, on the other hand, had the great advantage of cheap land, plenty of space for "economies of structure," and new railroad connections, which meant not having to truck goods through city streets. The cost of living in the country was usually lower, which meant that wages could be lower as well. Smith also noted that disadvantages of the countryside included the lack of housing, leading to greater construction costs, and the paucity of skilled laborers. Finally, the suburban location had many of the advantages of both the country and city, namely cheap land within close proximity to city services and skilled labor. Smith worried, though, that the "suburb of to-day becomes the city of to-morrow and we tear down and tear down and tear down—a frightful waste for which there is no return."[86]

Pottery owners in East Liverpool took advantage of the cheap farmland in Hancock County to expand their operations. Tired of the cramped conditions,

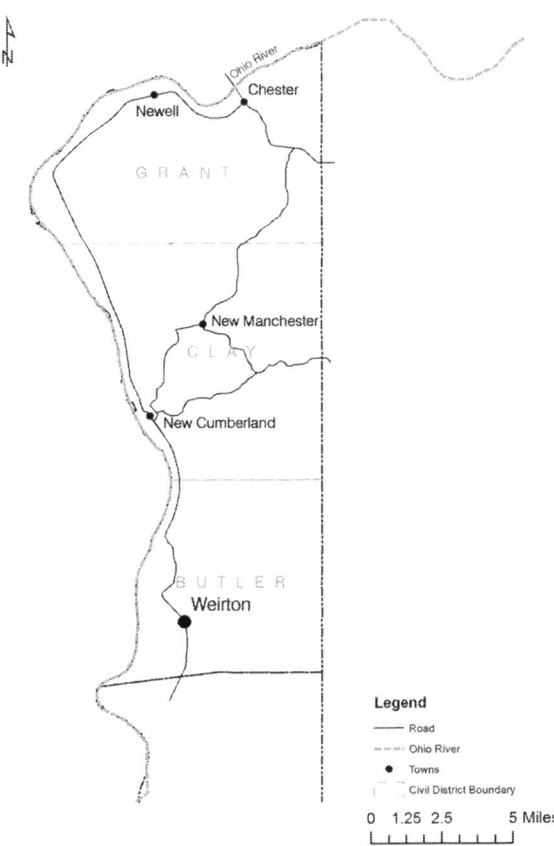

MAP 2. The towns of Hancock County
Source: Jessica Brewer

they longed for the room to create large new facilities with easy access to rail transport. W. E. Wells explained to East Liverpool boosters that if the city had adequate railroad facilities his company could gain 25 percent more business. Pottery companies banded together to create two new towns—Chester and Newell—on Hancock County farmland. Since there were no bridges to the West Virginia side, pottery manufacturers formed companies to build them. Because the new towns were but a bridge away from East Liverpool, J. Russell Smith might have classified them as "suburban" locations. Excavations on the Chester Bridge began in March 1896 and, on New Year's Day 1897, some 2,500 people paid a nickel each to walk across it.[87]

Local businessmen advertised the new town's advantages to potential factory owners. Charles A. Smith, who purchased the Chester Bridge in 1901,

FIGURE 4. W. E. Wells
Source: Hancock County
Museum in West Virginia

published a promotional pamphlet titled "Chester on the Ohio" that extolled the new town's virtues to prospective investors. Its level ground was "ideal for factories," the pamphlet read, and the scenery was such that from "almost any position in the town a noble prospect unfolds itself."[88] Equally important was its proximity to East Liverpool, the center of the pottery industry, with twenty-five thousand "busy inhabitants" and thirty factories. Smith stressed the combination of rural elements like the "dark green high hills," the "quiet stream," and "picturesque landscape" and the industrial elements like the riverboat hauling freight and the stern-wheeler with "its acres of coal."[89] He also listed the many improvements on which city fathers were working, including a sewer system, water works, paved streets, electric light and power plant, streetcars, a hotel, and Rock Springs Park, an amusement park of rides, a dance pavilion, and a lake. Finally, the "Pennsylvania lines" were also completing an extension of the railroad through Chester. Smith concluded with an appeal directly to manufacturers in Pittsburgh, explaining that within twenty miles of Pittsburgh there were few sites for factories and those that were available were prohibitively expensive. He concluded that the "future land of promise for manufactures therefore lies down and along the Ohio River valley."[90]

Cheap land and good infrastructure did help to lure capital investment to the town. In 1899, the company became Taylor, Smith, and Taylor—or TS&T—and began construction of a pottery that went into operation the following year. By 1913, TS&T had seventeen kilns in operation and employed about four hundred people. In 1900, the Edwin M. Knowles China Company built Chester's second pottery. It began as a five-kiln operation, added two more kilns by 1907, and employed more than five hundred. In 1900, steel industrialist William Banfield invested in a new tinplate mill there named the Chester Rolling Mill, but it soon joined the massive American Sheet and Tin Plate Company merger. Employment at the rolling mill hovered around five hundred.[91]

The success of the town of Chester led the pottery owners to create the town of Newell a few miles downriver. On the Fourth of July 1905, pottery owners W. E. Wells and Edwin Knowles drove an automobile across the newly constructed Newell Bridge with one thousand people following behind them on foot. Along with Louis and Marcus Aaron, they financed the construction of the bridge and the Newell Street Car line to shuttle people between East Liverpool and Newell. By the end of 1906, the Homer Laughlin China Company constructed its Plant No. 4 in Newell. At the time, it was hailed as the single largest pottery facility in the world, a million-dollar structure that housed thirteen bisque kilns, seventeen glost kilns, and twenty-four decorating kilns and that employed 1,200 workers.[92] Homer Laughlin—now operating four factories employing 1,800 people—was the largest pottery company in the United States, producing one-tenth of the nation's ceramic products in 1912.[93] In shifting its operations to Newell, company executives saw an opportunity to escape the costs and overcrowding of East Liverpool and create a more modern, spacious, and better-organized facility.

In short order, the construction of Homer Laughlin's Plant No. 4 transformed a patch of level land along the Ohio River into the town of Newell. The company had to build houses for its workers, but most of them still chose to live in East Liverpool because in the early days there were houses but "no town."[94] Only a few houses dotted the dirt streets during construction of the pottery, but by December 1907, after Plant No. 4 began operations, Newell had 130 homes and a population of about seven hundred. The company gradually

FIGURE 5. Homer Laughlin China Company
Source: Author's collection

shut down its East Liverpool facilities and continued to expand its Newell site, adding Plant No. 5 in 1914, No. 6 in 1924, No. 7 in 1927, and No. 8 in 1931. A handful of other smaller ceramics companies, such as the Edwin M. Knowles Pottery, Globe Brick, Metsch Refractories, and the Kenilworth Tile Company located in Newell, but none of them equaled Homer Laughlin's impact. Homer Laughlin not only built the town and accounted for a majority of its jobs, but also took over ownership of the bridge and the town's water and sewage systems through subsidiaries.[95] With roughly 1,800 inhabitants, the town remained small and unincorporated.[96]

After considering all his options, Ernest Weir located his tinplate plant in Hancock County. In 1905, he and the district operations manager, J. R. Phillips, left Monessen to buy their own tinplate mill in Clarksburg, West Virginia. Phillips died a month later, but Weir went on to win a contract with the National Biscuit Company. The Phillips Sheet and Tin Plate Company soon could not keep up with orders and built four more mills or individual stands of rolls.[97]

As Weir began to expand his operations, new Belgian, French, German, and English glassworkers brought socialist ideas to Clarksburg. They saw worker-

FIGURE 6. Ernest T. Weir, ca. 1923
Source: West Virginia and Regional History Center, West Virginia University Libraries

owned cooperatives as the solution to increasingly acrimonious labor relations and declining wages, but Weir worried about the creeping influence of radicalism, viewing such ideas as a threat to private ownership.[98] Weir, along with other mill owners, looked to the countryside to escape radicalism. In 1909, *Iron Age*, the leading steel industry journal, printed an article titled "Labor Conditions in Country Towns," which reported that some mill owners believed that "farm bred labor is good to get." Though inexperienced, the boys were "intelligent and adaptable to their new conditions."[99] Mill owners believed that farm boys were patriotic, hard-working, and loyal—and devoid of the radicalism that was pervasive among the urban working class. The same year *Iron Age* published its article on country towns, Weir decided to build his new tinplate mill on 1,200 acres of farmland near Hollidays Cove in Hancock County.[100]

Weir told a newspaper reporter that he chose this location because of its access via the Ohio River to cheap raw materials and because it was only about forty miles from Pittsburgh's steelworkers. He explained, "We get the better class of workmen here because the best labor will not leave the Pittsburgh district. They have been here for generations and refuse to change. For this reason we elected Weirton for the new plant which will start with eight hot mills and a tin house."[101] Weir also believed that cities, "if not breeders, were certainly magnifiers of discontent among workers." In cities, he argued, managers and workers lived too far apart. Plus, when different industries were located in close proximity to one another, unrest became "contagious," spreading from one industry to another. In the rural setting in Hancock County with no established working-class neighborhoods, he hoped to attract a workforce free from radicalism and discontent.[102] In short, Weir set out to create a rural-industrial place.

Weir's vision undoubtedly owed much to another steel magnate, George McMurtry. In the 1890s, after a bitter strike at his steel mill in Apollo, Pennsylvania, McMurtry decided to build a modern mill and a more stable town. He hired the firm of Frederick Law Olmsted of Brookline, Massachusetts, to help him design the new town of Vandergrift, which would attract good workers with American values. McMurtry believed that a sanitary town with no taverns or alcohol, with well-functioning sewers and water lines, and with streets bearing the names of American statesmen and commanders would make for healthy, happy, and patriotic workers. The Olmsted firm added curvilinear streets, single-family detached houses, and plenty of trees and shrubs to help create a stable, peaceful environment. Finally, McMurtry insisted there should be low-cost housing and low-interest loans to encourage high levels of home ownership, thereby tying workers to the town and the company. He combined the new town plan with the standard union-busting tactics of the time, such as blacklisting and brutalizing organizers, and was tremendously successful at preventing unionization.[103] When Weir managed the Monessen works during the 1901 strike, McMurtry managed one of U.S. Steel's largest sheet and tinplate plants, one of its only nonunion mills, and the only sheet and tinplate plant to not be idled, thanks in part to his paternalistic company town. What a powerful example for young Ernest Weir.

Construction of Weir's new tinplate plant began in May 1909 in what was then northern Hollidays Cove, which the steel magnates declared would now be known as Weirton.[104] The mill began production in December 1909 as a nonunion plant.[105] Among the first to arrive in Weirton were the skilled tinplate workers who were attracted by the opportunity for advancement and who were willing to work without a union contract. In the early days of the Phillips Sheet and Tin Plate Company, Weir was just as likely to hire helpers rather than master craftsmen. He later remembered that in Weirton many heaters' helpers became heaters and roughers became rollers, getting their first chance to lead their own crews.[106] At that time, skilled tinplate workers were almost nomadic, traveling between towns like New Castle, Pennsylvania; Wheeling,

West Virginia; Newport, Kentucky; and Elwood, Indiana; searching for work, better pay, and better working conditions. One tinplate worker boasted that he held forty-one different jobs in 1915 alone, some for only two or three days before he moved to another town.[107]

Weir initially brought a lot of workers—including a cadre of Finnish tinplate rollers—from the company's Clarksburg location to work at the new facility in Weirton, but he said that "tin mill men came to Weirton from all parts of the country."[108] Louis Truax, who grew up on a nearby farm, estimated that the twenty mills in Weirton in 1912 would have required nine men each to operate. With three shifts of crews, they would have totaled 540 men. If you included the millwrights, maintenance men, shearmen and their helpers, openers, cold rollers, tinners, picklers, cranemen, roll turners, and barshear workers, the mill employed a thousand men, he figured. Truax recalled that "things sure were buzzing around there" as men came from mill towns all around the region. A "great many" came from the American Tin Plate Company mill in Chester, including his future father-in-law, Emery Tingler, a skilled roller who brought his whole crew with him.[109]

William Reardon was a typical roller who came to Weirton in search of work. Born in Fort Wayne, Indiana, in 1887, Reardon attended high school in Elwood, Indiana, the original home of the American Tin Plate Company. He arrived in Weirton in 1913 and became a founding member of the Weirton Boosters Club, an officer in the Odd Fellows, and a member of the Kiwanis Club, and in the 1920s he helped organize the Weir-Cove Fire Department. A civic leader and business booster, Reardon certainly fit the image of an aristocrat of labor.[110]

Workers flocked to the new mill in Weirton in such numbers that housing construction could not keep up. Four years after operations began, some workers were still living in tents or shacks.[111] Because there were not enough houses in Weirton, many of Weirton's skilled steelworkers settled across the river in Steubenville, Ohio.[112] The skilled craftsmen who came to Hancock County—potters and tinplate rollers alike—were urban people accustomed to refined living. Tinplate rollers were said to live as well as rich men with pianos, lace curtains, and horses and buggies.[113] With little experience farming or living in the country, few of the recently arrived rollers and heaters were interested in living in a rustic, country town and preferred to commute from nearby Steubenville.

Local farm boys like Louis Truax also got an opportunity to join a skilled work crew. Truax's first job was spelling the catcher on the No. 10 mill. That meant the catcher would give him a part of his wages to step in and do his work for fifteen minutes here and there. Truax remembered that it was "not a hard job," but there was "a great amount of heat on your face, as you shoved the packs

CHAPTER 2

FIGURE 7. Early postcard of the Weirton mill
Source: Dennis Jones

over the rolls to the rougher or roller."[114] He married the daughter of a skilled tinplate roller and at the wedding reception was offered a job as a pair heater on the No. 2 mill, starting the next day. Fifty years later he could still list the names of all of the rollers who headed crews, a testament to their importance in the mill and the community.[115]

Weir's employment of helpers and farm boys was consistent with his antiunionism, a sentiment that became even more apparent in 1913, when Phillips Sheet and Tin acquired a new mill in Steubenville where workers belonged to the union. Weir refused to negotiate with the Amalgamated Association and locked the workers out. The American Federation of Labor sent John L. Lewis, then a young labor organizer, to Weirton, and he reported back that the company had imported between three and four hundred strikebreakers, half of them acting as armed guards on company property. Lewis also noted that Weirton was a small town that was "practically owned by the steel companies" and that fellow organizers were forced to leave town "by the agents of the steel corporation."[116] Weir ultimately broke the union when company guards and strikebreakers fired rifles in the direction of mill workers' homes and gunmen shot at several strike leaders from a moving automobile.[117] The clash in Steubenville was the first but not nearly the last act of violence and intimidation in Weir's growing empire.

Fall of the Aristocracy of Labor

In 1930, pottery owner Edwin Knowles, owner of the Edwin M. Knowles China Company, told a reporter, "The most interesting thing about the pottery industry is the employees. They are the aristocrats of labor."[118] Yet at that very moment, local factory owners in both the pottery and tinplate industries were pursuing new technologies to reduce the power of those "aristocrats" to control the pace of production and the quality of the products. During and after World War I, pottery owners became increasingly concerned with wages and work quality. NBOP negotiators won multiple rate increases for pottery workers, but inflation outstripped their wage gains. The USPA, which negotiated labor contracts on behalf of several member companies, contended that shoddy workmanship and price hikes were costing them customers and that additional wages increases would make it impossible to lower prices to win back those customers.

Between 1920 and 1922, the USPA and the NBOP argued repeatedly about wages and quality. In 1920, W. Edwin Wells, president of Homer Laughlin and chair of the Labor Committee for the USPA, agreed to an additional 10 percent wage increase to offset inflation but insisted on new standards and work rules designed to reduce waste and improve quality. When these rules limited hourly production—thereby cutting wages—the jiggermen and kilnmen walked off the job and only returned after union officials agreed to resolve the matter at the next wage conference.[119] In 1921, USPA owners complained that they had sat through "many long and tedious conferences" to discuss matters that might benefit the employees, but now that the owners had proposals to improve quality and cut down on waste, the union did not have the authority to call a special conference.[120] When business conditions worsened, NBOP negotiators agreed to a 10 percent wage cut in August and a 7 percent reduction in November, but they were determined to recoup the lost wages the following year. At the 1922 conference, however, Wells reiterated the USPA's complaints about quality, noting that the speed of production had increased by 80 percent over the previous eight years but the quality of the ware had deteriorated, hurting business. The USPA proposed that wages stay the same, and both NBOP officials and the membership at large rejected the offer and went on what would be a pivotal strike in the industry.[121]

The nationwide 1922 strike involved ten thousand potters. Trenton district strikers failed to win concessions from producers of sanitary ware and returned as nonunion workers. After two months, the East Liverpool district owners agreed to a four-and-a-half cent raise and workers returned to work, but the union's defense fund was empty and morale was low. After 1922, poor business conditions and high unemployment in the pottery industry weakened the union's bargaining position, leading union officials to accept wage cuts that further frustrated rank-and-file potters. Membership fell from the prestrike high of 9,360 members to just over 6,000 eight years later.[122]

Immediately after the 1922 strike—the largest in the history of the tableware industry—Homer Laughlin pursued new technologies that automated much of the handwork in the clay shop and the kilns and that reduced dependence on skilled workers. New contracts with W. W. Woolworth and Company required such great volumes of tableware from Homer Laughlin that the company had to expand its production capacity, a good opportunity to construct new potteries with new technologies at its Newell location. The union, with empty coffers and fewer members, was in no position to oppose changes to the organization of production.

In 1923, the company constructed Plant No. 6, which industry experts heralded as "the world's most modern pottery."[123] Instead of the old bottle kilns, Plant No. 6 was equipped with the industry's latest innovation, tunnel kilns, which no longer required highly skilled kilnmen who knew where to place the ware and how to monitor and manage the kiln temperature. Tunnel kilns were different from bottle kilns in that the ware passed through them on a train of iron cars with firebrick decks, entering at the cold end, passing by the hot furnace at the center, and cooling off as it exited at the other end. In other words, the ware no longer had to be fired in batches that required heating the furnace up and waiting for the whole furnace to cool off. They were more reliable, increased throughput, saved the company money, increased quality, and lowered wholesale prices, allowing Homer Laughlin to remain profitable during the age of chain stores. Over the next decade, the company replaced all their bottle kilns with tunnel kilns, and kilnmen found themselves at a disadvantage when negotiating with the company.[124]

The NBOP had less and less power to make demands on behalf of the kilnmen, who had no choice but to adjust to the new tunnel kilns. Because the tunnel kilns had to be run continuously, the kilnmen of Local Union 9 demanded double time on Sundays. At a 1925 conference to discuss the matter, an exasperated W. E. Wells offered time and a half and stated, "No. 9 needs a good spanking. If the kilnmen do not want to accept this, they can quit. You can close

FIGURE 8. Tunnel kilns, Homer Laughlin China
Source: Homer Laughlin China Company

No. 5 down if you want to. I don't care that much [snapping his fingers]."[125] By 1932, manufacturers were refusing to pay even time and a half, saying that the pottery industry needed to adopt "modern equipment and conditions" like other industries and "where continuous operation is necessary it should be done on regular time."[126]

In 1934, Homer Laughlin hired Walter Emerson, a graduate of the Massachusetts Institute of Technology, to run the newly created mechanical engineering department. Emerson supervised a number of projects that continued to decrease the company's dependence on skilled labor. First he eliminated the unskilled labor involved in moving materials and ware around the plant by installing a system of overhead trolleys, conveyor belts, elevators, and trucks.[127] He explained that he wanted "to keep the product at all stages of the process either moving or mobile."[128] Next he introduced the "Iron Horse," a mechanized trolley that moved workers and stacks of saggars toward the kilns. The kiln placers, who had to place ware on the Iron Horse while it was moving, complained about the stress that caused them, and the NBOP president declared that the new working conditions were inhuman.[129] The union ultimately negotiated a slower speed of movement, an increased wage rate, and shorter working hours for those who were assigned to the Iron Horse, but the company refused to discontinue use of the new machinery.[130]

In the late 1930s, skilled jiggering crews still performed their work much as they had for several decades, and their wages accounted for 40 percent of the company's labor costs. In 1940, Emerson unveiled "King Kong," an automatic jigger that mechanically pressed clay into molds and could make 9,600 plates in eight hours compared to the jiggering crew's 2,400. In the mid-1940s, Homer Laughlin installed Emerson's improved version, called "Big Flat," which could make a greater variety of shapes as long as they were flat or shallow forms, a limitation of King Kong as well. The Big Flat could produce twenty-four plates per minute to King Kong's twenty.[131]

By the mid-1950s, skilled workmen, reflecting on their fall from grace, observed that the new technologies were their undoing. At a meeting of the kilnmen, the recording secretary asked, "What has happened to our trade?"[132] He concluded that the current "deplorable" conditions could be traced back to the introduction of the Iron Horse in the 1930s.[133] Similarly, the kiln firemen of Local Union 130 recalled that when tunnel kilns were first installed in 1924, the company put them and their helpers on an hourly rate that declined gradually over the years. In 1955, a member of Local Union 130 asked, "Who ever heard of a kiln fireman getting a merit increase?"[134] Clearly they were no longer in the position to demand one. Not only did the new machines eliminate skilled labor, the jiggermen's helpers—the mold runners, batter-outs, and finishers—were no longer members of his crew. Now they reported directly to the company.[135]

Eliminating Skill in the Mill

When Ernest Weir began production in December 1909, there was no way to circumvent the skilled heaters and rollers. Increasing production meant adding more mills, and the company did so by acquiring the Pope Sheet & Tin Plate Company plant and by expanding its existing facilities in Weirton and Clarksburg. By 1915, it operated twelve mills in Clarksburg, twelve in Steubenville, and twenty-six in Weirton. Weirton Steel then took steps to become a fully integrated steel plant. He recalled, "As it was then, we had to buy raw material—sheet bars—from large steel companies which also sold tinplate, so our very life depended then on our competitors."[136] In 1918, the company changed its name from Phillips Sheet and Tin Plate to Weirton Steel, and it incorporated with a capitalization of $30 million. The following year, it constructed a six-hundred-ton blast furnace. In 1920, Weirton Steel erected seven 100-ton open hearth furnaces, a blooming mill, and two continuous rolling mills. In 1923, the company also put thirty-seven of the most modern, efficient by-product coke ovens in the country into production.[137] Those facilities made Weirton Steel an integrated steel plant, able to convert coal into the coke that fueled its blast furnaces, convert iron ore into pig iron, covert pig iron into steel slabs with the open hearth furnaces, and roll the slabs into bars in the blooming mill, all using automated processes. But when the bars arrived in the rolling mill to be made into tinplate, the highly paid rollers and heaters finished them by hand.

It was not until 1927 that Weirton Steel finally automated the rolling process. That year, engineers developed a continuous process for rolling sheet steel thin enough to be made into tinplate. In May and June, the industry publication *Iron Age* reported that the Columbia Steel Company of Butler, Pennsylvania, and the American Rolling Mill Company of Ashland, Kentucky, successfully rolled steel from the roughing mill through the finishing mill.[138] The new production line was called a "stripsheet mill" because instead of making small square sheets, it produced long strips of steel. At the end of the process the strips were rolled into mammoth coils. Millworkers remarked that they no longer made tinplate by the box; now they made it "by the mile."[139] *Iron Age* dubbed it the "sheet mill of tomorrow" because it did "in a large part mechanically what is now done by hand."[140] Its success depended on a number of technological innovations including roller bearings, furnaces between each roll, and adjustable-speed motors at each set of rolls.[141] Operators had to carefully monitor and fine-tune the roll speed, the temperature of the rolls, and temperature of the material passing through them. Engineers also realized that slightly convex rolls kept the steel centered and that the convexity could be reduced as the product neared the end of the line to make the strip flat. Close inspection of old Welsh rolls revealed that they were not always perfectly cylindrical. Thus, it was not until the late 1920s that managers would finally discover all the secrets of the skilled tinplate rollers.[142]

Weir's company quickly adopted these innovations, investing $5 million in a new hot strip mill, which was more than the company's profits for the year. Weir announced, "Very thorough and careful consideration has been given to the planning of this mill, and we are all very confident that, when complete, it will be one of our great and permanent assets."[143] In December 1927, six months after the successful trials at American Rolling Mill, Weir paid for a license to use all that company's patents and processes, enabling him to install the same equipment.[144] Steel managers had finally brought automation to tinplate production and ended their reliance on skilled rollers. The Weirton hot mill, where the skilled rollers were still using hand methods, discontinued production in 1938.[145] Just as in the potteries, the era of the craftsmen of the tinplate mills had come to an end.

Conclusion

Industrialists saw in Hancock County an undeveloped countryside where they could create factories and factory towns that would give their businesses a fresh start. Relocating allowed them to adopt new organizations and new technologies, to reshape their workforces and labor relations, and to have greater control over their businesses. The erection of the steel mills and potteries on grassy fields along the Ohio River also transformed the local economy. In 1890, the majority of the county's 6,500 residents lived and worked on 408 farms, and only 250 worked in manufacturing. By 1910, the population had grown to 10,000, and tin mills and potteries now stood on the bank of the Ohio River, surrounded by small factory towns on what had once been farmland.[146] In the decades that followed, the county's population would triple, but as we shall see, much of the rural nature of the place and rural habits of the people remained intact. So too did the contentious nature of labor relations in the two industries, leading to another round of industrial restructuring and the rise of a truly rural-industrial workforce.

CHAPTER 3

RISE OF THE RURAL-INDUSTRIAL WORKERS

In 1901, Paul and Julia Illes left Hungary and came to the United States. They changed their name to "Ellis" and settled in Mingo Junction, Ohio. As soon as Julia had gotten rid of the cockroaches and bedbugs in one house, Paul would decide to move again. So Julia saved her money and found a Hungarian contractor to build them a home on Sixth Street in Weirton, West Virginia. That way, she figured, Paul would have to "stay put." In the north end of downtown Weirton in the 1920s and 1930s, Julia raised much of the family's own food. A hard worker, she always planted a big garden. In the spring, she would have hot beds with tomato and pepper plants that she sold to neighbors, who then started their own gardens. The family had a cow, and every day Julia's son led it over the ridge to Kings Creek to let it graze. Her daughter delivered some of the milk to neighbors, and Julia would use some to make butter and cottage cheese. She also kept chickens in the backyard so that the family always had eggs. Living in the shadows of the smokestacks, Julia Ellis adapted many of the folkways of Hungarian peasants to the steel town of Weirton where—with no zoning laws and ample access to land—they could take root.[1]

The Ellis family was typical of many families of unskilled and semiskilled rural-industrial workers who came to Hancock County in increasing numbers in the 1920s and 1930s to work in local factories. In the early 1900s, industrialists had believed that building new potteries and tinplate mills in rural Hancock County would result in more disciplined and loyal workforces, but they soon

CHAPTER 3

FIGURE 9. Julia Ellis feeding her poultry, ca. 1930s
Source: The property/estate of Margaret Heaton

discovered that many of the conflicts they had had with craftsmen in urban centers followed them to the countryside. In the 1920s, owners in both industries began another round of technological innovation that reduced the power of skilled craftsmen and allowed managers to hire more unskilled laborers and semiskilled operatives, mostly from a large pool of rural migrants. Between 1910 and 1930, Hancock County's population increased from ten thousand to thirty thousand.[2] Rural migrants came from the peasant villages of southern and eastern Europe, the sharecroppers' patches of South Carolina and Georgia, and the failing farms of central West Virginia. In contrast to the skilled jiggermen and rollers, few of these rural migrants had any factory experience, but local employers were grateful for a steady stream of new workers that would accept low wages and harsh working conditions. Employers hired and quickly trained these men and women to do simple, repetitive tasks.

Because these recruits came from rural places in the United States and Europe, they brought with them rural habits like the household production of food. Once hired on at the factory, they had very different experiences than the skilled craftsmen. Rather than working in their own crews, they fell under the direct supervision of the company, and the increasing numbers of semiskilled operatives and common laborers rocked labor relations in both industries. In the potteries, the National Brotherhood of Operative Potters (NBOP) struggled to apply the old logic of the craftsmen's organization to new situations, while in Weirton the creation of the "foreman's empire" bred discontent and led to tumult in the 1930s. The influx of a wave of rural migrants also led to a political realignment in the county. Thus the fall of the skilled craftsmen coincided with the rise of a new workforce that lived on the land, labored among the new machines of the potteries and tin mills, worked under close supervision, and altered the county's politics.

Rural People in Factory Towns

Unlike the craftsmen, who preferred urban amenities and rode streetcars to work, these new arrivals were truly rural-industrial workers, forming communities in and around the factories and often adapting rural lifestyles to their new circumstances. They arrived during the decades of Hancock County's greatest growth. The construction of new potteries in the first decade of the twentieth century spurred the county's population from less than 7,000 to more than 10,000. Between 1910 and 1920, with the construction of Weirton Steel and the expansion of the potteries, the population doubled to nearly 20,000. Another wave of 8,000 arrivals brought the population to 28,511 by 1930.

In Europe and America, rural ways of life underwent a radical transformation in the late nineteenth and early twentieth centuries that loosened many peoples' ties to the land and set them on a quest for wage work, typically in industrializing cities. This was certainly the case in Appalachia, where farm output per capita was already in decline by 1860 because of population growth and the limits on available land. The penetration of railroads into mountainous parts of West Virginia in the 1870s brought new competition and rising property taxes, creating new challenges for farming families.[3] The farm economy of the state did not collapse all at once, but in the first decades of the twentieth century, thousands were leaving annually to search for work in logging, mining, and manufacturing. In the 1920s alone, nine West Virginia counties on or near the Ohio River lost more than two thousand, or more than 16 percent, of their farms, and two of those counties lost one-third of their farms. Between 1900 and 1930, seven of those nine counties combined lost a total of twenty-six thousand people—22 percent of their population—while the population of the remaining two counties, buoyed by the city of Huntington's thriving manufacturing economy, increased by 50 percent.[4]

Hancock County's burgeoning industries attracted thousands of rural migrants in the first decades of the twentieth century. Between 1900 and 1910, the

TABLE 1. Population of Hancock County by Civil Divisions, 1900–1930

	1900[b]	1910[b]	1920[a]	1930[a]
Grant District (Chester & Newell)	1,758	5,666	6,268	7,835
Clay District (New Cumberland)*	3,855	3,387	2,316	3,513
Butler District (Weirton)	1,080	1,412	10,739	17,163
Hancock County	6,693	10,465	19,975	28,511

Sources: [a] U.S. Bureau of the Census, *Fifteenth Census of the United States: 1930, Population, Volume I*, p. 1167. [b] *Thirteenth Census of the United States: 1910*, Bulletin, "Population: United States, Number of Inhabitants, by Counties and Minor Civil Division" (Washington, D.C., 1913), 559.

Note: * Includes the Poe District's population, which was annexed by Clay District in 1922.

population of the Grant District, home to the new pottery towns of Chester and Newell, increased from 1,758 to 5,666 before leveling off to 7,835 by 1930 (table 1). Many of the district's potters traced their origins back to those central West Virginia counties that had declining farm populations: Pleasants, Ritchie, Wirt, Wood, Jackson, and Wayne.[5] Pottery companies focused a lot of their recruiting efforts on native-born, rural, white migrants to fill unskilled jobs, especially in the warehouses. This included packing tableware into wide, squat barrels along with straw to prevent the dishes from breaking, as well as building the barrels and hammering the barrel hoops into place. Because of this, locals derisively called migrants from south of the Mason-Dixon Line "hoopies." According to one local joke, migrants who left southern and central West Virginia kept moving north until they reached the potteries at the north end of the state. When they saw the letters "HLC" emblazoned on one of the stacks at the Homer Laughlin China Company, they thought it stood for "Hoopies' Last Chance," meaning it was their last chance for employment before they left West Virginia.[6]

The influx of migrants breathed life into the fledgling pottery towns. By the 1920s, the town of Newell boasted 1,800 residents and included a post office, automobile service station, drug store, hardware store, butcher shop, lumber company, newsstand, variety store, and half a dozen or more groceries.[7] It never achieved even the modest stature of its upriver neighbor Chester, with its 3,700 inhabitants. Aneita Jean Blair grew up in Chester and Newell during the 1920s and 1930s, and according to her biographer, she was born in Chester, a "factory town, tiny and blinkered and perched precariously on the banks of the Ohio River." The Blair family lived "just on the cusp of the good neighborhood, where the people didn't have to stretch sugar or send their kids to the government depot for cans." The differences between Chester and Newell were subtle:

TABLE 2. Workforce of Newell, 1930

Industry	%	Birthplace	%	Father's Birthplace	%
Pottery	73	West Virginia	53	West Virginia	46
Store	4	Ohio	27	Ohio	28
Tile works	3	Pennsylvania	14	Pennsylvania	16
Private homes	3	Other	6	Other	10
Public works	3				
Steel mill	1				
Grocery	1				
Porcelain works	1				
Other	11				
	100		100		100

Source: U.S. Bureau of the Census, Fifteenth Census of the United States, 1930, Population Schedules. Hancock County, West Virginia, microfilm, West Virginia and Regional History Center, West Virginia University Libraries, Morgantown, West Virginia. Sample was constructed using individuals with listed occupations from every tenth household.

"Newellies still kept chickens in their yards," whereas in Chester "there were fewer chickens and more flower beds, and on occasion, in the nicer homes, wallpaper."[8]

While Chester residents worked in the rolling mill and at the amusement park in addition to the potteries, an overwhelming number of Newell residents were potters (table 2). In 1930, three-quarters of its residents worked in the pottery industry while the rest were evenly divided between public works, stores, the tile works, and housecleaning. Furthermore, 94 percent of Newell's workers were born in West Virginia, Ohio, or Pennsylvania, and some 90 percent of their fathers were born there.

Recruiting white rural migrants preserved the ethnic and racial homogeneity of the pottery towns' populations through the 1930s. In 1936, *West Virginia Review* noted that "practically all of the workmen" at Homer Laughlin were "of American or English ancestry" and that there were "none from Southern Europe."[9] This pattern of hiring owed as much to the workers as it did management. Native workers walked off the job more than once when companies attempted to hire European immigrants, and during the 1920s the Ku Klux Klan was active in the pottery towns.[10] The Klan held a number of ceremonies in these years, such as a July 1924 initiation ceremony at Rock Springs Park in Chester, where they burned several crosses. At the end of the 1920s, the Klan faded from the local scene, suffering from poor leadership and waning popularity, but it remained a force that operated in secret to enforce certain vague notions of racial purity.[11] In 1930, only seven African Americans lived in Newell, all of whom were domestic servants. Leona Hopkins and Caroline Lumkin, for example, were live-in maids at the Joseph M. Wells house.[12] Arthur Wells remembered that the longtime British dominance in the potteries finally came to end during World War II, and the first wave of new workers was a "great influx of West Virginians"—probably meaning central and southern West Virginia migrants—but by the war's end, workers in the potteries had come "from many different ethnic backgrounds."[13] But neither eastern and southern European immigrants nor their children were ever hired in large numbers, and African Americans continued to be almost completely excluded from pottery work for decades after that.

The Butler District, home to Weirton Steel, experienced the most dramatic growth in this period, as its population increased from roughly a thousand in 1900 to seventeen thousand in 1930. In stark contrast to the pottery towns, Weirton became home to a diverse population: European immigrants as well as black and white migrants from Appalachia and the American South. Managers welcomed diversity in the steel industry, as many believed that certain ethnic and racial groups were well-suited to work in particular departments. Some companies actively sought recruits from different backgrounds to keep the workforce divided and undermine solidarity among the workers.[14]

Weirton Steel labor agents recruited heavily among recent European immigrants to perform unskilled labor in many of the new departments. By 1920, there were more than six thousand immigrants in Hancock County, the overwhelming majority of whom lived in Weirton. Ten years later, there were also almost sixty-five hundred sons and daughters of immigrants.[15] During the 1930s, Weirton's population reached fifteen thousand residents and included some forty-seven different nationalities.[16] The North End, a neighborhood adjacent to the mill, was home to thousands of immigrants. Margaret Heaton, the daughter of Hungarian immigrants Paul and Julia Ellis, remembered her neighbors on Sixth Street: "There was two American families that I know of, close by. But everybody else, they either stepped off the boat from Poland or were Russians, Slavish, you know, and all those different nationalities . . . Italians, a lot of Greek. That upper part of Weirton, those avenues and those streets . . . like I said there were two American families I knew of."[17]

Native-born residents eyed the immigrants suspiciously. One recalled that immigrant steelworkers led austere lives in "special boarding houses with six or eight rooms." She remembered, "They would get a blanket, Dago bread, fruit, and wurst. Ten to fifteen men on a floor in bare rooms. They just wanted shelter and seldom changed their clothes." She also noted that they saved "every cent of

FIGURE 10. Weirton's North End, ca. 1920s
Source: Dennis Jones

their money" and would send it back to their families in Europe via the foreign money exchange in local Weirton banks.[18] In 1936, a local schoolteacher wrote that a two-story house was "likely to contain three families, one on each floor and one in the basement." The families were large, she continued, the parents uneducated, the homes "generally poor," and the conditions "often unsanitary."[19]

Italians and Greeks were two of the largest immigrant groups in Weirton. There were 100 Italian adults living in Weirton at the start of World War I and 420 by 1920. Many of them clustered in the North End, especially on Fifth and Sixth streets and Avenues A and B.[20] By 1930, one of every five people in the North End had been born in Italy (table 3). In the town's early decades, even more Greeks than Italians settled in Weirton. The largest wave of Greek immigration to the United States occurred during the first decade of the twentieth century and coincided with the establishment of Weirton. Of the more than 160,000 Greeks who arrived in America then, an estimated 25 percent worked as laborers either in factories or on railroad construction gangs.[21] Weirton became known for its "colony of Greek steel workers," and in 1920, their population topped 1,300.[22] One wave of Greek immigrants who fled the Turkish massacres in Palea Phocaea, a part of Asia Minor, reunited in Weirton and formed a society named El Elpis, meaning "The Hope."[23] Evstratios (Charles) Koukoulis left Palea Phocaea shortly after he received a letter in 1911 from his fiancée's brother telling him that there was work in Sabraton, West Virginia, probably at the American Sheet and Tin Plate Company mill located there. Koukoulis and his future brother-in-law then moved to Weirton, where Charles's wife joined them.[24] In 1930, one of every four people living in North Weirton had been born in Greece (table 3). One extraordinary household had eleven unrelated Greek men living together.[25]

African Americans were the third largest ethnic group that made their way to Weirton. Hancock County's black population grew from a mere 46 in 1900 to 573 by 1920 before topping 1,000 by 1930, and 95 percent of them lived in the Butler District, where Weirton is located.[26] When the U.S. Congress placed restrictions on immigration in the 1920s, Weirton Steel turned to African Americans to fill unskilled positions, employing a black minister as a labor agent to travel south and hire new workers.[27] In the early 1900s, southern blacks left their homes in search of new lives in northern cities because of a complex mixture of factors, including chronic poverty, the declining price of cotton, destructive boll weevils, and a rising tide of white violence in the rural South. Although many chose to remain home and continue to struggle, a million and a half African Americans chose to permanently move to northern cities between 1915 and 1945.[28]

Steel industry jobs were a welcome opportunity for African Americans from the Cotton Belt. Unskilled work on the labor gang, around the coke ovens, and in the tin mill afforded black migrants a steady income and a higher standard of living.[29] By 1930, there were 382 gainfully employed African American men in Hancock County, more than 70 percent of whom worked for Weirton Steel.[30] Barth Jeter Sr. and Eddie Jim Jennings both came from Union, South Carolina. Jeter arrived in Weirton on August 15, 1922, and became the manager of the Harlem Club by the 1930s. Eddie Jim Jennings was hired to be a tinner in the Tin Plate Department, and in 1935 he became the employee representative of the Tin House & White Pickle workers, the second African American to hold this position.[31] Frank Gregory's ancestors were among those African Americans who came from Union County, South Carolina, and he said that a whole wave of migrants came to Weirton from there as word of opportunity in the mill spread.[32] Weirton's black community also hailed from Virginia, Alabama, and Georgia. African Americans clustered in the North End, where about 5 percent of the residents had been born in either South Carolina or Georgia (table 3).

The local industries also employed residents of the hills and valleys outside of Weirton and the pottery towns. In 1930, the people who lived on Hardins Run

TABLE 3. Workforce of Downtown Weirton (North), 1930

Industry	%	Birthplace	%	Father's Birthplace	%
Tin mill	42.7	Greece	23.9	Greece	23.9
Steel mill	20.2	Italy	16.1	Italy	17.0
Hot mill	5.5	Pennsylvania	9.2	Poland	15.1
Coke plant	5.5	Yugoslavia	8.3	Yugoslavia	10.1
Grocery	3.7	Poland	8.3	Turkey	5.0
Open hearth	2.3	West Virginia	6.9	West Virginia	4.6
Strip steel	1.4	Ohio	6.0	Ohio	3.7
Blast furnace	0.5	Turkey	5.0	Spain	2.8
Other	18.3	Spain	2.8	South Carolina	3.2
		South Carolina	3.2	Czechoslovakia	1.8
		Czechoslovakia	2.3	Georgia	1.8
		Georgia	1.8	Pennsylvania	1.8
		Other	6.4	Other	9.2
	100		100		100

Source: U.S. Bureau of the Census, Fifteenth Census of the United States, 1930, Population Schedules. Hancock County, West Virginia, microfilm, West Virginia and Regional History Center, West Virginia University Libraries, Morgantown, West Virginia. Sample was constructed using individuals with listed occupations from every tenth household. I considered North Weirton to be any households north of Pennsylvania Avenue.

Road, a sparsely populated country road nearly equidistant from Weirton to the south and Chester and Newell to the north, worked variously in the steel mill and the potteries. Richard Gillis worked as a shooter in the clay mine, and his neighbor, Harry Beattie, was a miner at the same pit. Beattie's fifteen-year-old son worked as a sponger at a pottery. Just down the road, James Wyekoff and his son worked as clay miners, as did their neighbor William Beattie. William's children worked in the potteries: Gertrude was a cup handle finisher, Florence finished bowls, and George was a bowl taker. At the Canter residence next door, George Canter also worked at the pottery, but his son Samuel had a job at the steel foundry in New Cumberland. Further down the road, Alexander Jones worked as a teamster at the clay mine, and Harry Phillips, son of English immigrants, was an electrician at the tin mill. The only farmers on Hardins Run Road were Wilbert Patterson, his wife, and their five children.[33]

The new residents in Hancock County began building churches shortly after they arrived. In Chester, the only church that predated the construction of the potteries or the American Sheet & Tin Plate Company mill was the United Presbyterian Church, built in 1895. The potters and tin mill workers who came to town tended to be Methodists, Catholics, and Episcopalians.

Starting in 1899, local Methodists held regular camp meetings in an orchard until they built the Free Methodist Church in 1904. In 1902, a group of Catholics—including a foreman from the tin mill, three potters, a housewife married to a potter, a farmer, and a man who did odd jobs, mostly of Irish and German ancestry—met at City Hall to discuss organizing a parish, and Sacred Heart Catholic Church was constructed the following year. In 1914, about seventy Episcopal employees of the tin mill, with the help of their superintendent, built St. Matthew Episcopal Church.[34]

Many of the rural migrants from northern West Virginia belonged to a denomination founded in the 1830s in nearby Brooke County. Alexander Campbell, a Scots-Irish minister, and his congregants split from the Presbyterian Church over baptism by immersion and congregational polity, and the new denomination became known as the Disciples of Christ. The Church of Christ and the Christian Church had similar nineteenth-century origins over theological differences, and they merged with the Disciples of Christ in the twentieth century. In Chester, the First Christian Church began services in 1903 with thirty members, and the Church of Christ organized in 1936 and attracted a congregation of a few hundred in the coming decades. In 1920, some thirteen newcomers established the Church of the Nazarene, a denomination associated with the Holiness, an evangelical movement of the early twentieth century.[35]

In Weirton, residents established churches that reflected their ethnic diversity. The only churches that predated the construction of the tinplate mill were the Cove Presbyterian Church and the Cove Christian Church. After the construction of the mill, residents built two Roman Catholic churches, a synagogue, an Eastern Orthodox church, two Baptist churches, a Greek Catholic church, an African Methodist Episcopal church, a Church of Christ, and a Nazarene Church.[36] By 1926, the Roman Catholic Church had the largest membership in Hancock County, with some 6,700 members, more than four times the members of the second largest, the Presbyterian Church. The Disciples of Christ had some 840, and the Church of Christ had 450. The Episcopal and Baptist churches in the county also had hundreds of members. Little changed over the next three decades. The only major change between 1926 and 1952 was the establishment of Lutheran churches and the Church of the Nazarene, both of which gained about 500 members (table 4).

The U.S. Census notoriously undercounted Holiness and Pentecostal groups, and there were undoubtedly gatherings of these faiths among the factory workers of Hancock County that census takers ignored. Yet while West Virginia and Appalachia more generally have become associated with sect-like

TABLE 4. Hancock County Church Membership, 1952

Denomination	Members	%
Roman Catholic	8,260	58.6
Presbyterian Church USA	1,928	13.7
Disciples of Christ	1,767	12.5
American Baptists	583	4.1
Nazarenes	558	4.0
American Lutherans	535	3.8
Protestant Episcopal Church	136	1.0
United Presbyterian Church	126	0.9
Free Methodist Church	102	0.7
Church of God	28	0.2
Seventh-day Adventists	26	0.2
Finnish Evangelical Lutheran	22	0.2
Wesleyan Methodist	17	0.1
Total	14,088	100.0%

Source: National Council of Churches, *Churches and Church Membership in the United States: An Enumeration and Analysis by Counties, States and Regions* (New York, 1952); accessed online at http://www.thearda.com/Archive/Files/Descriptions/CMS52CNT.asp on February 9, 2015.

religious groups, Hancock County did not have significant numbers of such groups, and their prevalence in Appalachia has often been overstated. Writers traveling through the region have been drawn to religious groups that, though smaller than other denominations, helped to characterize Appalachia as more exotic than "mainstream" America. In the 1960 presidential election, the region's presumably backwards religious beliefs took the national spotlight when political pundits wondered whether the Protestant voters of West Virginia would opt for a Catholic candidate. John Kennedy won the state's primary election, but it did little to change the nation's view that Appalachians were "backwards" and that their religious must be too. In reality, the influx of immigrants into the region during its industrial transition resulted in a great diversity of religious communities that outside observers have often ignored, such as Hancock County, where Catholics were the majority. When it came to church membership, Hancock County in the mid-twentieth century more closely resembled the urban-industrial centers of the North than it did farming communities in other parts of the Mountain State.[37]

CHAPTER 3

Rural-Industrial Folkways

Producing their own food came naturally to many first-generation industrial workers from rural places in West Virginia, the American South, and Europe. In the 1920s, many coal camps and factory towns in West Virginia were dotted with large gardens and livestock pens, tended by people who maintained a close relationship to the land.[38] Women of the coal and mill towns performed household labor and raised the next generation of workers, and working families produced much of their own food. These activities actually subsidized the industrialization of the Mountain State because they enabled employers to pay less than a living wage. Companies were then able to invest more of their budgets in capital improvements and in expansion.[39]

In dense cities, the rural ways of new immigrant factory hands could be a nuisance or even a health hazard. Progressive reformer Jane Addams noted that many of the "faults" of the city could often be traced back to the "congested housing of the immigrant population, nine-tenths of them from the country, who carried on all sorts of traditional activities in the crowded tenements." Addams disapproved of Greeks slaughtering sheep in the basement, Italian women sorting rags from the dump, and immigrant bakers making bread in "unspeakably filthy places under the pavement."[40] Immigrant steelworkers transplanted rural ways to steel towns like Pittsburgh, unaware that what was safe in the countryside was unhealthy in the city. They fetched their water from the river and refused to boil it. When they had indoor toilets, they often did not use them.[41] Because Pittsburghers used the rivers as both sewers and a source of drinking water, typhoid epidemics claimed hundreds of lives.[42]

In the small factory towns of Hancock County, rural folkways helped industrial workers cope with low wages and hard times, and because they had access to land, they could hold on to their country ways without creating health hazards. Henry Burns's parents were sharecroppers in Georgia, and when they came to Weirton in the 1920s, they brought a lot of their survival strategies with them. He recalled with fondness the gardens his family had when he was growing up in the 1940s. Because they had a large family and his father's wages were inadequate, they depended on the food those gardens produced. They had two gardens, one on a hill beside their house and another up in the hills above town. He remembered, "Everybody used to go out and fix themselves a plot someplace out in the hills. Clean it off and plant tomatoes and you name it . . . corn. Had to. Had to go out in the hills and stake your land and clean it off." Working families treated land just beyond city limits as common land. Henry said, "They didn't mind in them days. Now everybody own everything.

We used to go out there and have to throw the rocks off of it. Build scarecrows and keep the birds off of it." Before and after school, he would chase birds and rabbits away, and pick some of the tomatoes if they had turned red. "What times!" he said. "Welcome to hard times, you know?" The Burns family also raised chickens and hogs in the backyard of their company house.[43]

Because Weirton remained unincorporated until the late 1940s, there were few building codes and zoning ordinances, and working-class families could build outbuildings and fences and raise a variety of livestock. By cultivating gardens and raising small livestock such as rabbits, chickens, and goats, working-class residents fused their rural traditions and self-help values with their new life in an industrial suburb.[44] New arrivals in the pottery town did likewise.

While the skilled workers tended to aspire to the male breadwinner ideal, the families of unskilled and semiskilled workers were closer to what historians have called the "family economy." Many immigrant families acted as mediating institutions between the economy and society in both subsistence agriculture and industrial capitalism. By prioritizing family goals over individual ones and by pooling their incomes and their resources, immigrant families could better withstand the ups and downs of life in mine and factory towns and might even improve their standard of living through cooperation. The family economy could be traced back to traditions in their home countries, but it also flourished in America because of the less-than-subsistence wages paid to unskilled labor in many industries.[45]

Many of the immigrant families of Hancock County had to have most members of the household earning wages. In 1930, for example, Mary Yobbczyc, a Czechoslovakian immigrant, headed a household of six in Weirton. Her two daughters were laborers in the can factory, her son was a laborer in the blooming mill, and her two boarders, also Czechoslovakian immigrants, worked as laborers in the hot mill. Yugoslavian immigrant Matt Reven and his two sons worked as laborers in the mill. Polish immigrant Walter Kalinkewicz, two of his sons, and two boarders worked in the mill while Walter's wife Alice, daughter, daughter-in-law, and two youngest sons did not work outside the home. Among the immigrant households of Weirton's North End in 1930, if they did not have teenage sons and daughters bringing home paychecks, they more often than not had boarders to help with expenses. There was an average of two and a half wage earners per household, and often the wife or mother earned money from cooking and doing laundry for boarders.[46]

Incidentally, there were more opportunities for women to work for Weirton Steel by the end of the 1930s. In 1926, only 60 women worked at Weirton Steel out of a workforce of nearly 8,000. That figure increased to 108 in 1930 and 293 by 1940.⁴⁷ Women worked almost exclusively in the assorting department. Margaret Heaton grew up in Weirton during the 1930s and fondly remembered the "girls in the tin mill." They all wore blue uniforms, she said, and if you were Polish and knew Anne Kostur, you were "guaranteed a job down there."⁴⁸ Heaton also remembered that any woman who got married immediately lost her job.

The family economy encouraged a wide array of activities by the entire family to support the household, and in this way it dovetailed nicely with the rural ways of new factory workers. With access to land, lax regulations, and few reformers to disapprove, the rural-industrial workers of Hancock County planted gardens, raised livestock, hunted and fished, and produced a substantial portion of their own food supply. Chapter 5 explores these activities and values in greater detail.

Changing Labor Relations

Just as life around the factories was much different for semiskilled operatives and unskilled laborers than it had been for the craftsmen, so too was life inside the factories. The introduction of new technologies, the deskilling of work in both the union potteries and the nonunion steel mill, and the new labor laws of the 1930s resulted in a period of unrest and renegotiation. Working in automated factories and labor strife were certainly not unique experiences in these decades. In the 1920s, companies in Detroit, Chicago, Pittsburgh, and other major industrial centers overhauled their factories and invested in new technologies, and in the 1930s new labor laws protected the right of workers to form unions. Section 7 (a) of the National Industrial Recovery Act (NIRA) of 1933 recognized the right of workers to organize. The passage of Section 7 (a) was a watershed moment for labor law in the United States. It emboldened many unskilled and semiskilled factory workers to organize and become a powerful voice for change in American society.⁴⁹ The NIRA also granted the president the power to fix prices and wages in industries, but two years later the U.S. Supreme Court ruled that those sections of the law made it unconstitutional. Congress responded by passing the National Labor Relations Act, also known as the Wagner Act, which restated workers' right to organize, created the National Labor Relations Board (NLRB) to guarantee fair elections and collective bargaining, and outlawed several strategies companies had used to prevent unionization.

Also in 1935, John L. Lewis and several other labor leaders left the more conservative American Federation of Labor (AFL) and created the Congress of Industrial Organizations (CIO) for the purpose of organizing the mostly unorganized mass-production workers. By 1940, CIO unions like the United Steel Workers, the United Auto Workers, and the United Mine Workers were the most powerful labor organizations in the country, and Lewis, president of the CIO, was the most powerful labor leader. For many workers, unionizing under the CIO banner meant being liberated from the tyranny of foremen, low wages, and harsh working conditions. In addition to the mass unionization movement, the 1938 Fair Labor Standards Act made the eight-hour day standard, established the first minimum wage, and defined overtime pay. Industrial workers, especially unskilled laborers, experienced a dramatic change of fortune during the decade. After years of powerlessness and poverty wages, they now demanded better treatment, an end to favoritism, and a greater share of the company profits. For hundreds of thousands if not millions of industrial workers, the labor reforms of the 1930s were tremendously empowering and transformative.

But in Hancock County, the changes were not so unambiguous. In both industries, the deskilling of work resulted in a new labor system based on more direct relations between the company and workers without the mediating influence of skilled crew chiefs, but the changes affected the union shops of the potteries and the nonunion workplace of Weirton Steel quite differently.

In 1930, pottery owner Edwin Knowles said that they had never had "any labor trouble" and that "if the workmen protest about something in the factory, their complaints are referred to a standing committee.... Both employees and employers accept the decision as final."[50] The reality was that the system worked quite well when crew chiefs acted as a mediating influence between the standing committee and the crew members, but with more and more workers falling under the direct supervision of management, the committee found itself inundated with grievances.

The most common grievance involved piece rate compensation. When companies introduced a new product line, there would be a trial period during which pottery workers received a day rate while managers and foremen timed them. After the trial, managers set a quota based on the average daily production of the workers. The company paid a day rate to those who fell below the quota and paid a piece rate to those who produced above it. Workers would often drag out the production process while they were being timed to influence the new piece rate to their advantage, a practice known as "playing off."[51] They tried to get the rate set so that the average worker could earn a living as well as the speedy workers, and they resented "hoggers-in" who jeopardized the current rates. Employers vigilantly watched for evidence that a rate had been set too high and often adjusted them down.[52] If workers disagreed with the rate, they could appeal to the standing committee.

The standing committee functioned well early in the twentieth century when crew chiefs made many of the decisions related to production and pay, but after the technological revolution in the potteries was complete, the committee staggered under the weight of numerous complaints. In 1945, for example, sales manager C. L. Sebring of Knowles China Company complained to James Duffy, president of the National Brotherhood of Operative Potters, that the mold makers refused to make eight-inch plate molds for the automatic jigger even though the standing committee settled the "price for making these molds" several weeks before. They could have continued to make the molds under protest while the committee considered their second request for an increase, but they refused to do even this. At the same time, the casters refused to make the "Regent chocolate pot" after making it under protest for several weeks. Finally, because of a shortage of packages, the company—which no longer used barrels for shipping ware by this time—acquired plywood boxes in which to pack ware. The packers agreed to work with the plywood boxes at the list price under protest but would not, even under protest, pack them with the number of pieces that the company specified. Sebring believed that it was up to union officers to use their "good offices to get these men back into line."[53]

The increasing numbers of unskilled and semiskilled potters forced the union to change. In 1930, Duffy explained that the union had lost members because of the Great Depression and "the introduction of labor saving machinery," and it was only able to maintain its membership numbers by recruiting new members. He wrote, "We have, however, reached out among workers formerly looked upon as semi-skilled and taken them into the organization and this has been of great help in keeping up the membership."[54] In 1933, NBOP officials believed that the National Industrial Recovery Act, which recognized the right of workers to form unions, was "truly revolutionary" and would usher in "a new social and economic order in industry that should go a long way toward lifting the depression and giving working people, and people of the nation as a whole, a 'New Deal' in the broadest and best sense of that term." The *Potters Herald* reported on a spontaneous upsurge in membership as new workers signed up in the wake of the act.[55] With new legal protections and the union's new strategy of recruiting semiskilled workers, membership more than tripled from 5,530 in 1932 to more than 19,000 in 1941.

In the 1930s, after the old crew chief system collapsed, union officials often found themselves in the unenviable position of mediating between helpers and craftsmen as well as between workers and managers. The installation of conveyor belts was one point of contention because the new methods of moving clay and ware between departments in the potteries eliminated many mold runners and batter-outs. The NBOP had a history of accepting any new technology that would increase production. In 1920, union officials set a precedent of accepting lower wages after conveyor belts were installed at the Warwick China Company of Wheeling, West Virginia, a practice they continued in the 1930s. Union officials reasoned that jiggermen would no longer have to pay helpers. Such thinking revealed the NBOP craftsmen's disregard for helpers and unskilled workers.[56]

In the 1930s, the NBOP leadership had to convince helpers that they would receive equal representation from the union. In 1931, the mold runners and batter-outs approached Duffy about forming their own local after they felt left out of the 1931 wage conference with the United States Potters' Association, and Duffy agreed to allow them to form Local Union 131. In 1933, the USPA refused to negotiate with LU 131, insisting on only talking with their bosses, the jiggermen. In the spring of 1934, LU 131 demanded a wage increase, insisting that batter-outs receive 32 percent of the jiggermen's wages and mold runners receive 28 percent. This was a challenge to the jiggermen's autonomy and authority. When NBOP leaders could not resolve the dispute, LU 131 went out on strike and argued that their right to union representation under Section 7 (a) of the NIRA had been violated. In March 1934, after a two-month wildcat strike, the newly created National Labor Board (NLB) ordered the helpers back to work without an increase. Opposed by the USPA, the NBOP, the NLB, and the jiggermen, the helpers ended their strike. The five strike leaders of LU 131 were called before the NBOP executive board and expelled from the union. Joseph M. Wells, who had taken over the leadership of both Homer Laughlin and the USPA Labor Committee in 1928, was deeply concerned—like his father—about rank-and-file militancy. He blamed Section 7 (a) for the latest conflict between the jiggermen on one side and the batter-outs and mold runners on the other. That same year, Homer Laughlin tasked Walter Emerson with installing the conveyor belts that eliminated many of the batter-outs and mold runners.[57]

In the late 1930s and early 1940s, some helpers and laborers in the potteries were receptive to the new Congress of Industrial Organization's brand of industrial unionism, which held the promise—if not always the reality—of being inclusive, progressive, and strong enough to protect its members. CIO officials sent organizers to visit several potteries around the country, often competing with the NBOP, which belonged to the older, often more conservative American Federation of Labor.[58] Duffy warned that the CIO could present a real danger to the potters' union if they started to organize large groups.[59] Conservative trade unionists, like Duffy, contrasted the majority rule of the AFL to the "minority dictatorship" of John L. Lewis and the CIO.[60] The CIO had some successes in pottery, winning over an NBOP local in Barberton, Ohio, in 1938 and defeating the NBOP in union elections in Baltimore in 1939, Trenton in 1941, and at the Shenango China Company in New Castle, Pennsylvania, in 1943. Despite these losses, the NBOP held on to most of its locals and all its locals in the East Liverpool district.[61] Nevertheless, the few inroads the CIO did make at this moment—when craftsmen were losing control over the potteries and the union—were likely a result of resentment building among helpers and semiskilled potters. In 1937, NBOP officials attempted to placate helpers and semiskilled workers by negotiating bigger raises for them than for skilled workers. The 1937 contract granted wage increases of 9 percent for skilled workers but 12.5 percent for semiskilled and 15 percent for the unskilled.[62] Still, no truly revolutionary changes followed the passage of New Deal labor laws, and the NBOP found its membership divided just as its base of skilled workers was dwindling.

The Foreman's Empire

In Weirton, rather than a mill run by skilled crews, production now depended on machine operators, labor gangs, and foremen. In previous decades, young men turned to their fathers, fathers-in-law, and uncles to get a job on one of their crews. By the 1930s, immigrant laborers left run-down boarding houses, gathered at the factory gates, and waited for the foreman to simply point at them to indicate that they had a job on their "bull gangs" for the day.[63] Life in the "foreman's empire"—a hierarchical system of control—was far more impersonal, brutal, and open to exploitation.[64] Foremen, or "pushers," made certain that their subordinates worked at a fast pace to ensure high productivity. One immigrant steelworker at Weirton complained, "In tin mill boss pushes and kicks me."[65] Another reported, "At the Weirton Steel Mills, in West Virginia, we are not allowed to quit no matter how sick, until we fall down. The result is that in the last two days no less than 45 men have been carried out of the mill on stretchers. From the tin mill alone 25 were carried out within 15 hours."[66]

Some foremen abused their authority for personal gain. One daughter of a foreman recalled that at Christmas, immigrants would give fruit, pictures, and gifts to her father in hopes of getting extra turns.[67] Some particularly corrupt foremen openly demanded bribes from workers who were fearful of losing their jobs. One immigrant steelworker in Weirton told an investigator that when he complained to a manager because his foreman deducted money directly from his paycheck, the manager replied, "Everybody pays. You're no better." That same corrupt foreman reportedly demanded that another man pull a lever knowing it would injure a coworker atop the ladle so that there would be an opening for his son-in-law.[68] While most foremen were not so exploitive or sadistic, they all clearly wielded great authority over the operatives and laborers under their supervision.

Foremen were only one part of what Progressive-era reformer John Fitch called a "regime of exploitation" created by mill owners to control workers.[69] Steelworker-turned-labor-journalist Horace Davis documented many grievances at Weirton, which he called the "most tightly 'closed' company town of any size." All workers' organizations, he explained, were "watched for evidences of Communism or unionism," and union organizers took "their lives in their hands" when they came to Weirton.[70] Outside the mill, Ernest Weir created a community that rewarded company loyalty and punished unionism. He hoped to secure loyalty by promoting home ownership, providing amenities to townspeople, and subsidizing most of the community institutions. Between 1910 and 1940, he created an elaborate array of welfare capitalism programs that included funding ethnic churches and organizations, providing health care services, and building recreational facilities. In the spirit of community building, Weirton Steel also started a newspaper and a handful of banks and underwrote or outright owned city services and utilities. At the same time, Weir's private police force, called the "Hatchet Gang," terrorized union organizers and union supporters. This system of harsh punishments and generous rewards proved effective. One scholar concluded that those who did not run afoul of the company "came to see themselves as special and unique."[71]

In Weirton, the passage of Section 7 (a) of the NIRA brought workers' frustrations to the surface. Shortly after the NIRA became law, Weirton Steel created an employee representation plan (ERP) ostensibly to give the workers a voice in their working conditions, but like most ERPs, it was dominated by "company men," and its officials were prohibited from discussing wages and other fundamental concerns. It became clear that steel magnates designed these organizations to circumvent the spirit of Section 7 (a) by being able to claim that their employees were already represented by a labor organization.[72] On September 28, 1933, a dispute in the tinplate department exploded into a full-blown strike over the next four days involving all ten thousand employees in Weirton as well as National Steel's workers in Steubenville and Clarksburg. Skilled steelworkers Mel Moore and William Jennings Bryan Long, also known as Billy, organized Weirton workers into lodges of the Amalgamated Association of Iron, Steel, and Tin Workers. Despite the groundswell of support by previously unorganized workers, Michael Tighe, president of the Amalgamated Association, denounced the walkout as a wildcat strike, disillusioning thousands of would-be union members. Tighe and other conservative unionists feared that, left unchecked, massive rank-and-file rebellions could tear the union apart.[73]

Ernest Weir masterfully thwarted the unionization drive. Under the scrutiny of the federal government, he walked a fine line between brute force and maintaining the façade of a law-abiding businessman. The West Virginia State Police launched tear gas attacks against the striking crowds in Weirton while Weir argued that there was no need for arbitration because his employees had no grievances. The NLB convinced strike leaders to agree to arbitration, but Weir did his best to ignore the newly created board. The strike began to weaken as some 1,200 workers crossed the picket lines. On October 16, Weir finally conceded to the NLB that the company would hold representation elections. Struggling to hold the strike together, Billy Long and Mel Moore agreed to return to work with the promise of elections to come. Weir then denounced the NLB, claiming that the board sought to force the Amalgamated Association on the workers even though, in his estimation, they had already chosen the company's ERP. On December 15, Weirton Steel sponsored dances and liquor parties where employees were told to vote for the ERP. After the festivities, the company held an election for new officers of the ERP in which no "outside" unions appeared on the ballot.[74] Louis Varvakas testified that the company threw a similar party for Greek employees, and Katherine Zinaich recalled that the company held a party for the girls in the assorting room at Williams Country Club, where they were told if they wanted their "bread and butter" then they should "vote the right way."[75]

Section 7 (a) proved ineffective in protecting the new unionists. Long and Moore went to Washington to spur President Roosevelt to action, and in February 1934 Roosevelt issued Executive Order 6580, which restated the NLB's authority to conduct union elections when requested by a substantial proportion of the employees. Unfortunately, Roosevelt and the NLB had to rely on the Justice Department to enforce the NLB's "authority." The Justice Department sought an injunction against Weirton Steel in the U.S. District Court in Wilmington, Delaware, but Judge John P. Nields, who harbored corporate sympathies, doubted the constitutionality of the NIRA and ruled against an injunction. The ruling exposed that the New Deal legislation's ability to protect workers' right to organize had been more apparent than real.[76] The failed steel strikes of 1933 and 1934 heartened radicals like Horace Davis, who saw them as a sign that steelworkers were awakened to the promise that collective action held.[77] But the failure of the government to protect their rights and the failure of the Amalgamated Association to support their strike disillusioned many steelworkers in Weirton for years to come. One labor leader recalled that Mel Moore was "sorry that he ever listened to Section 7 (a)."[78]

After the strike, workers came to fear Weirton Steel's blacklist. Those who had created lives for themselves in Weirton had few alternatives for employment besides the mill, which employed about one of every three town residents. John Alatis recalled that the blacklist devastated the Greek community in Weirton. "They joined the union, and there was somebody there who was Greek. And he would tell who joined the union. And in the next couple days, they were fired. Some of them, like I said, went to Youngstown . . . all over. Baltimore, most of them. Right now, as a matter of fact, we had a reunion not too long ago. Weirton reunion in Baltimore."[79]

Paul Barkhurst's father joined the 1933 strike, which caused his entire family to be blacklisted. When Paul started to look for work a few years later, he knew he could not get a job in the mill even though he was a skilled ironworker. It was not until several years later when a foreman offered to vouch for him that he was able to get hired at Weirton Steel.[80]

Ironically, the balance of power in the steel industry tipped toward the steel unionists in the years after Judge Nields's decision in the Weirton case. In 1935, two years after the Weirton steelworkers' failed strike, Congress passed the Wagner Act, which outlawed ERPs like the one at Weirton Steel. That was also the year John L. Lewis helped create the CIO to organize the unorganized. Targeting the employees of the steel industry specifically, Lewis created the Steel Workers Organizing Committee (SWOC) in 1936, and in March 1937 Lewis signed a union contract with Myron Taylor, chairman of the board of directors of U.S. Steel, that covered all employees of Carnegie-Illinois Steel, a subsidiary of U.S. Steel. When officials at several other steel companies, including nearby Wheeling Steel, signed union agreements, it appeared that the nonunion era in the steel industry had come to an end. Many assumed that with the approval of the president of the United States, Congress, the Supreme Court, and U.S. Steel, unionization was inevitable.[81]

But not Ernest Weir. He portrayed himself as a champion of individual freedom in the face of tyrannical New Deal socialism.[82] Weir continued his strategy of positive rewards through welfare capitalism, legal foot-dragging, and intimidation of union organizers and supporters. John Alatis recalled the tactics of the Hatchet Gang: "During the Depression, if they knew that you belonged to the union, they'd come down to your house, take you out and beat you up. It happened. They took people out in the woods, tied them up to a tree, and left them there." Alatis also remembered that the members of the Hatchet Gang got the best jobs, but he explained that "you couldn't say anything."[83]

The Hatchet Gang was particularly active during SWOC's campaign to organize Weirton in 1936 and 1937. In a December 1936 letter to members of the

Weirton Steel Employee Security League (also known as the Hatchet Gang), Weir charged them to fulfill their "duties that arise from within the plant" and to "guard against dangers that arise from the outside." They alone, he wrote, stood between the "sinister threats" of the CIO and continued prosperity in Weirton, and they would have the "fullest cooperation" of Weirton Steel management.[84] Evelyn Kazienko later told the NLRB that her husband was a "special policeman" for Weirton Steel who would participate in beating SWOC organizers and would then leave home for weeks at a time. Her husband told her that company officials had "authorized them to use whatever force they deemed necessary in preventing any union organizer to engage in any activity in Weirton, West Virginia."[85]

John Kazienko, Claude Conway, William Foster, George Bush, and several other "special watchmen" for the company, as some called them, created a chilling atmosphere for those who supported unionization. On August 31, 1936, Kenneth Koch was fired for supporting the union and became a full-time SWOC organizer. The next evening someone threw a rock through his window, and a few nights later he saw Foster parked at one end of his block and Kazienko parked at the other end. Around 1 a.m., they circled his block, and an anonymous phone caller threatened to wreck Koch's car. The Hatchet Gang kept up the threatening behavior for six weeks. On October 16, Koch, his wife, and some friends were driving to a card party at the Democratic Club when three cars full of men carrying bats and bricks blocked their car. Conway, Bush, and Kazienko were among the men who dragged Koch out of the car, beat him senseless, and destroyed his car. Seven men were indicted for assault and battery by a Hancock County grand jury, but the charges were later dismissed.[86]

SWOC failed to organize Weirton's steelworkers, and the drive ended in 1937 just as the NLRB opened up an investigation into charges of unfair labor practices. In April 1937, SWOC filed charges against Weirton Steel with the support of the NLRB, which alleged that the company fired 124 employees for union activity.[87] The NLRB held hearings in the New Cumberland courthouse beginning in August and listened to testimony from dozens and eventually hundreds of witnesses, whose names were frequently published in the newspaper along with summaries of their testimony.[88] As two hundred spectators sat in the courthouse wearing SWOC buttons, one worker testified that he was discharged for refusing to sign a loyalty oath. Another recalled how the 260-pound leader of the "Hatchet Gang" (the president of the Weirton Steel Employees Security League) intimidated him into signing a company union card, and others testified that the Hatchet Gang had viciously beaten them.[89] Over seventeen months, the board collected more than thirty-nine thousand pages of testimony. In the summer of 1941, the NLRB finally ruled that the Employees Security League was an illegal company union, but ten days later—before a union election could be held—Weirton Steel president Thomas Millsop signed an agreement with the newly formed Weirton Independent Union (WIU), which closely resembled the Employees Security League.[90]

Steelworkers in Weirton undoubtedly questioned the efficacy of SWOC and the ability of the federal government to protect them from company reprisals—even with new legislation, a new federal labor board, and a new national labor organization. The CIO opened an office on Main Street in downtown Weirton during World War II, and in February 1944 a gang of company thugs beat up CIO organizers outside the company gate to the point they required hospitalization. The next day, more CIO organizers arrived with a hundred union brothers from Youngstown and other steel towns in the area. In response, a hundred members of the Weirton Independent Union met them on the street. Hancock County sheriff Dick Wright ordered both groups to disperse but allowed the WIU to distribute literature. When CIO members also tried to pass out handbills, Wright promptly arrested them.[91] Governor Matthew M. Neely sent the West Virginia state police to take control of the situation and issued a proclamation that the police were there to prevent "various persons" from being "unlawfully deprived of their liberty and the Constitutional right peaceably to assemble."[92] While Weirton Steel tolerated the CIO organizers passing out literature, the company discharged more than a dozen workers for union activity during 1944.[93] This, it turned out, would be the last year that the company used violence and illegal discharges to maintain a nonunion workplace. After 1944, the company's strategy focused on propaganda, a variety of enticements, and its legacy of punishing union supporters to prevent unionization.

A Tentative New Deal Coalition among Hancock County Workers

Industrial workers in Hancock County found that while the new labor laws may have revolutionized labor-management relations in other places, locally the new technologies often undercut their ability to effectively challenge management. Just as local labor relations were evolving in the 1930s, so too were politics. Because two-thirds of the county's workforce was employed in either the mills or the potteries, the working class represented the majority of the county's votes. For decades, Republicans' support for high tariffs had attracted large majorities of farmers and craftsmen in Hancock County, but the Great Depression of the 1930s turned the issue of free trade on its head. Many Democrats in Congress and even some Republicans blamed the high import duties of the Hawley-Smoot Tariff of 1930 for bringing international trade to a halt. Over the next two decades, the State Department and other free trade proponents liberalized American trade by winning narrow victories over the protectionists within the federal government. In 1934, secretary of state Cordell Hull urged Congress to pass the Reciprocal Trade Agreements Act (RTAA), which gave the president the authority to negotiate tariff reductions with individual nations to encourage international trade and boost the American economy.[94]

National labor leaders had ambiguous feelings about free trade. They routinely fretted about "how lower wages in foreign countries might affect American employment," what labor economist John R. Commons called the "pauper labor argument."[95] Yet throughout the 1930s, because many labor leaders agreed that the Hawley-Smoot Tariff and the retaliatory tariffs from other countries exacerbated the Great Depression, both the AFL and CIO championed free trade as a way to boost employment in the United States. In 1934, William Green, president of the AFL, said his organization had no general tariff policy, but he supported the RTAA, believing it would benefit the majority of American workers.[96]

Pottery workers and owners opposed the RTAA and continued to support high tariffs and protest cheap imports, just as they had for decades. In the East Liverpool pottery district, which included Chester and Newell, West Virginia, union leaders consistently fought against free trade and increased imports. In 1932, the American Legion started a "Buy American" campaign, and industry executives as well as union officials quickly joined the effort. This would be the first of many campaigns that blamed the industry's troubles on Japanese imports.[97] NBOP president James Duffy wrote to William Green expressing disappointment that he would support the RTAA, which would put them in competition with low-wage workers in Japan. As it turned out, because AFL leaders had long considered Asian workers to be inferior and a threat to the American standard of living, they could set aside their support for free trade when it came to Asian countries. The AFL and the NBOP passed resolutions calling for the boycott of Japanese products.[98]

The "Buy American" campaign was one of several efforts that decade to combat Japanese ceramics imports. In the mid-1930s, many local potters took notice when inexpensive Japanese ceramics appeared on the shelves of many retail stores in the area, and the union went door to door asking East Liverpool residents to boycott "Jap" goods, as they disparagingly called them. On December 13, 1937, an enormous bonfire on a hill over East Liverpool consumed some $20,000 worth of Japanese products, and a parade wound its way through town featuring signs that read "We Can't Live on Rice—Buy American" and "Keep the Home Kilns Burning." During the 1930s and 1940s, West Virginia potters and glassworkers joined an organization called America's Wage Earners' Protective Association. Created by disaffected unions within the AFL, the association protested cheap imports, opposed the RTAA, and questioned the constitutionality of the president's making treaties (even trade agreements) without congressional approval. Executives often worked with union officials on the issue of tariffs and free trade. Joseph M. Wells, co-owner of the Homer Laughlin China Company, became one of the nation's most vocal opponents of free trade. In May 1935, he criticized New Deal leaders for continuously promoting increased imports when in his estimation increased imports meant job loss (not to mention profit loss) in the United States. In 1938, Wells and Duffy joined forces in an attempt to prevent a reciprocal trade agreement with the United Kingdom, their longtime rival. When that effort failed, the Columbiana County Republican Club charged Franklin Roosevelt with throwing American potters out of work.[99]

Through the 1930s, the potters of Hancock County stood by the Republicans. In 1932, 67 percent of voters in the Grant District, where most of the potteries were located, opted for Herbert Hoover, and New Cumberland's district, home to only one pottery, was evenly split. Potters did not tend to see Republicans as a threat to unions. The *Weirton Daily Times* reported that W. L. Smith, a Republican pottery manufacturer from Chester, who had been "dealing with organized labor for over a quarter of a century," was the favorite over the incumbent.[100]

While potters remained loyal to the Republican Party during the 1930s, steelworkers experimented with supporting the Democratic Party despite their employer's wishes. In the 1930s, Weirton Steel founder and chairman Ernest Weir, a lifelong Republican, tried to impose his politics on the citizens of Weirton. In 1932, Weirton Steel paid employees to drive voters to the polls and tell them that they had better vote for Hoover.[101] Greek steelworker John Alatis remembered that "you weren't allowed to put Roosevelt's picture in the window" and that the company threw "a big parade for Hoover." Nevertheless, Weirton voters chose Franklin Roosevelt two-to-one over Herbert Hoover.[102] Roosevelt won 51 percent of Hancock County's votes even though he was outvoted two-to-one in the Grant District and broke even in the Clay District. In the Butler District, where so many steelworkers and the majority of the county's population lived, Roosevelt enjoyed a twenty-eight-point victory.[103] Many in the Greek community became loyal supporters of FDR and the Democratic Party. One Greek man was so overjoyed by Roosevelt's victory that he named his son Franklin Delano Manios.[104]

After the 1933 strike in Weirton failed, one of the strike leaders, Billy Long, entered local politics as a Democrat. Born in Pittsburgh in 1897, the son of English immigrants, Long started working in the mills when he was fourteen, married at age seventeen, became a skilled tinplate roller, and moved his family to Weirton sometime between 1918 and 1920.[105] The Longs moved to California in 1923, where Billy helped start up production at a new steel mill, but they moved back to Weirton by the end of the decade. Unlike fellow roller William Reardon, who became a business booster, Long became a labor activist in the early 1930s and ran afoul of the vehemently antiunion management at Weirton Steel. He helped organize Weir-Cove Lodge No. 30 of the Amalgamated Association of Iron, Steel, and Tin Workers and was elected lodge president. In September 1933, he became a voice for thousands of striking workers who had become Democrats.[106]

In the mid-1930s, a cadre of skilled steelworkers as well as thousands of unskilled steelworkers turned to the Democratic Party in hopes of securing support for their unionization campaign and breaking company domination over the social and political life of Weirton. In 1934, Long ran against John Hertnick, owner of a local funeral home, for a seat in the West Virginia House of Delegates but lost a tight race. Hertnick received overwhelming support from voters everywhere but Weirton.[107] In 1936, Long ran again for the House of Delegates on the Democratic ticket along with Robert L. Ramsay, who ran for U.S. House of Representatives. Together they championed working-class causes. At an October 1936 rally, Long praised Ramsay as being "one of four men in Congress of 534 who have had a 100 percent labor record during the past two terms." Ramsay took the stage and declared the National Industrial Recovery Act to be labor's Magna Carta. He also called the Social Security bill "one of the greatest pieces of legislation in American history" and pledged to continue to support Roosevelt's legislation. Clinton Golden, regional director of the Steel Workers Organizing Committee, also made an unscheduled speech in which he criticized local efforts to defeat the CIO organizing drive.[108]

Ernest Weir and local Republicans made certain that Weirton residents learned about the dangers of voting for Democrats. At a 1936 Republican campaign rally, one speaker told the Pan-Slavonic League of Weirton to vote Republican because the communists were "working for the re-election of Roosevelt" and "these godless Bolsheviks" wanted to undermine by "violent means ... that Constitution which guarantees you the right to worship and talk as you please."

Then a "grim-jawed, 200-pound Strip worker" named John Gulas suggested that his fellow steelworkers had a lot to lose if they did not vote Republican: "The majority of the Slavs own their own homes here. . . . Don't sacrifice them. Don't let your emotions decide your vote." After Gulas finished speaking to the Slavs, Andy Zagula and Eli Yannin spoke to other eastern European workers.[109] Republicans candidates accused the Democrats of "making labor the issue in the campaign" and argued that Republicans had a favorable voting record on labor issues and "friendship with working men throughout the county."[110]

The Republicans had reason to be confident in 1936. First, registered Republicans outnumbered Democrats in Hancock County by about six to five (or 8,700 to 7,200), and second, they were "supremely confident "of their ability to win the Grant District, where potters remained faithful supporters of the Grand Old Party. The Butler District would be the "real battling ground," according to the *Weirton Daily Times*, because steelworkers were shifting their allegiance to Democrats whether they were registered as Democrats or not. The *Times* reported that the campaigning by rival parties for offices in Congress, the State Senate, and the county courthouse was "the most heated in the history of the county."[111]

When the ballots were cast, the steelworkers, who now greatly outnumbered the potters, pulled the county into the New Deal coalition. The incumbent Franklin Roosevelt won more than three-quarters of the votes of the Butler District where Weirton Steel was located, but potters were more hesitant. Roosevelt won 61 percent of New Cumberland's votes and only 53 percent of Grant's votes. Contests in the Grant District were tight, as pottery workers gave a slight majority to the Republican W. L. Smith and were evenly divided between Democrat Long and Republican incumbent Hertnick. Long garnered 64 percent of the Butler District's voters, Ramsey 73 percent, and both were "swept into office with the huge Democratic landslide which engulfed the entire Panhandle region."[112]

When Long went to Charleston and took his seat in the House of Delegates, he championed working-class causes. In January 1937, he introduced House Bill Number 49 to increase penalties on corporations for interfering with elections, undoubtedly in response to Weirton Steel officials meddling with local voters, a subject that came up in testimony at NLRB hearings at the time. In February, he introduced a bill to outlaw "yellow dog" contracts, agreements that forbade employees from joining unions, which had plagued the labor movement in West Virginia for the previous twenty years. Only his first bill appears to have been brought before the house for a vote, and it passed with the support of sixty-seven delegates. Long also took the floor to express his support of building better roads to help the "many thousands of our citizens who live in the rural districts" and to denounce another bill that by forcing bars to close at midnight would deprive men on afternoon shifts of "partaking of beer in a regular licensed establishment" and lead to bootlegging.[113]

The representatives that Hancock County voters sent to the U.S. Congress and the West Virginia House of Delegates in 1936 championed working-class concerns, and Hancock County voters continued to give Democratic presidential candidates majorities and elect local Democratic candidates over the next three decades. Weirton's district gave wide majorities to Democrats, and, being the most populous district, it overshadowed the rest of the county. Yet the Democratic victory in the county was never complete, and local working-class voters did not generally have the same values and goals of national labor leaders. As chapter 6 explores in more detail, the politicians Hancock County voters sent to Charleston and Washington D.C. were not typical New Deal Democrats.

The story of working-class hero Billy Long may demonstrate the rise of the New Deal coalition and class politics in the county as well as the relative weakness of class politics locally. Instead of seeking a second two-year term in the House of Delegates, Long ran for county clerk. Perhaps he did not have the impact on state politics that he had hoped and now merely wanted to win an office to earn a livelihood. Long failed to win a majority in any of the county districts, lost the race, and disappeared from the historical record.[114] George Loucas, a Republican lawyer and leader of the Greek community in Weirton, took the seat in the House of Delegates that Long vacated. Loucas barely eked out a 51 percent majority in his hometown and even struggled to get votes from his fellow Greeks. John Alatis recalled that Loucas tried to win Alatis's mother's vote, but she replied, "You want me to vote for you? You change to Democrat, and I'll vote for you."[115] Loucas had no problem winning sizable majorities in the other districts, and more than two-thirds of the voters in the pottery district gave him their votes.[116] When he returned from Charleston, Loucas started a successful law practice in Weirton and remained a community leader for years to come. At the peak of Roosevelt's popularity, Republicans were still able to win office.

Conclusion

At the end of the 1930s, the last big wave of migration to Hancock County was coming to an end and the contours of life for the rural-industrial workers in and around the factory towns were defined. New production technologies limited workers' ability to challenge management on fundamental issues, even in the potteries, where the union had five decades of history behind it. The emerging labor relations in the steel and pottery industries gave unskilled and semiskilled workers limited control over production and working conditions. Solidarity in the NBOP was weakened by a growing divide between skilled workers on one side and helpers and semiskilled operatives on the other. In Weirton, many steelworkers were disillusioned with national unions after the Amalgamated Association abandoned them and the federal government failed to safeguard their rights. While many of the new workers aligned themselves with the Democratic Party, this was not the beginning of unequivocal support for labor liberals but was instead the beginning of a tenuous entry into the New Deal coalition.

In other parts of the United States in the 1930s, organizers brought together working-class communities, influenced their understanding of class and political economy, helped create structures for democratic unionism, and laid the groundwork for dramatic social changes in the coming decades. In some cases, industrial workers were radicalized by their experiences standing in breadlines and on the picket lines and dedicated themselves to the class struggle. These things did not happen in Hancock County. The only similar organizing efforts in Hancock County withered on the vine, failing because of powerful employers, conservative unionists, and lost strikes. Faced with these constraints, rural-industrial workers held onto older strategies for improving their quality of life, pursuing a family economy and self-help activities during their "leisure time" at home. These activities did not confront local power structures and flourished in a place where workers had access to land and rural traditions of "making do."

CHAPTER 4

PROSPEROUS, INDEPENDENT RURAL-INDUSTRIAL WORKERS

By the early 1940s, semiskilled operatives and unskilled laborers did most of the production work in the potteries and the mills of Hancock County. They were not steeped in craft traditions, had no rare set of skills or knowledge, and usually had little experience with unionism. During the 1940s and 1950s, they used a variety of methods to improve their working conditions and to extract better wages and benefits from their employers, but—unlike millions of urban-industrial workers—they did not join truly national labor organizations and participate in national strikes. Instead, they relied on a system of local negotiations, often informal, occasionally invoking state and federal agencies to influence the outcome. Because this system delivered many of the same material benefits that American Federation of Labor (AFL) and Congress of Industrial Organization (CIO) unionists won in these decades, local steel and pottery workers saw no need to make fundamental changes to their systems of collective bargaining, and they came to value the local nature of labor relations.

Examining the history of these steel and pottery workers' culture and values is complicated by the extensive campaigns of the local employers to influence their employees' ideas about unionism and to maintain the status quo. These workers did not join the CIO, even though they had the opportunity to do so. The steelworkers lived in a town that had a history of brutality and intimidation, and the potters accepted relatively low wages and meager benefits and only went on strike once, a three-week walkout in 1959 that ended in mediation. Because these workers did not participate in the kinds of national strikes that captured headlines in this era, they might appear to have been passive, acquiescing to their employers' schemes, but that was not the case.

Steelworkers in Weirton and pottery workers in Chester and Newell often made decisions based on family security, seeking stable employment more than good wages and benefits, let alone less tangible goals. They made decisions within a world of limited possibilities and judged their wages and benefits in comparison to past compensation and to what other workers earned. By these standards, they earned an excellent living. They also carefully considered their employers' ability to pay higher wages and more generous benefits, and when potteries faltered in the 1950s, workers accepted less but still made enough to support their families. They did not focus on the balance of power between labor and capital, instead privileging material goals within an established system of local negotiations.

The localized system of labor-management negotiations differed by industry. Through their grievance procedure, the International Brotherhood of Operative Potters (IBOP), as it was known after 1951, offered rank-and-file members unparalleled access to the national union officials as well as top company officials. The grievance procedure enabled them to affect working conditions even though their negotiators accepted relatively low wages in this period. While the IBOP was unquestionably an autonomous union that bargained collectively with employers, the three different unions at Weirton Steel between 1940 and 1960 were dominated by the company. Nevertheless, Weirton steelworkers applied pressure to the company through a variety of formal and informal means, in ways that reminded management that unionization was but one NLRB-election away. As a result of this pressure and the changing political climate, Weirton Steel expanded its obligations to employees time and again, ensuring that they were paid as well as any American steelworkers. In short, both steel and pottery workers were able to meet their material goals while maintaining a local system of negotiation with companies. A by-product of this arrangement was a fair amount of company loyalty among the workers.

Semiskilled Operatives in the Factory

When R. H. Markham, a journalist for the *Christian Science Monitor*, visited Weirton in 1945, he encountered what seemed at first to be an anachronistic world of fire and brawn: "Smoke poured from the factory chimneys 24 hours a day, red flames leaped from boiling vats, thousands of persons toiled in this gigantic, powerful, seldom resting machine, drab houses lined many uninviting streets." Then he began to notice that machines did "all the heavy work, most of the dirty work, and practically all of the hot work." Workers pushed buttons, pulled levers, operated motor vehicles, and rode around "near the roof in stupendous, rapidly moving cranes that swoop down and pick up things like an eagle." As the workers tended their machines, the magic of the steel production came to life: "They press buttons and enormous kettles of liquid metal are poured steaming into molds, the molds are carried to other enclosures, forceps take them off, pincers grab the 10-ton square sticks of half-congealed steel jello and gently place them in furnaces beside other sticks, all standing erect as soldiers at attention."[1]

But new technologies did not eliminate the need for brawn and stamina nor did they eliminate danger. Alex Zucosky started working in the Strip Steel department as a sweeper in April 1945. He soon graduated to work on the slitter, where circular disc-like blades trimmed steel down to strips of various widths as specified by the customers. As the slitter trimmed the excess off the sides of the strip, Alex dragged the scrap over to the scrap hole. Down below "an old Polish fellow" operated a baler. With the slitter and both cutters operating, the amount of scrap steel going down the hole would keep the old fellow "hopping," and Zucosky would go down and help him at every opportunity. Asked to name the good part of his job, he thought for a while, laughed, and said, "There ain't no good part."[2] The most dangerous part of his job was banding the three-thousand-pound coils with metal straps. He said, "You had to be careful that some of them didn't fall on you" because sometimes the "vibration from the mill" would knock one of the coils over and ten or twenty would fall like dominos. Workers in his department could only pray that they were not banding the coils in those rare times they tipped over.[3]

Walter Danna worked several jobs at Weirton Steel. He started in the coke plant as a door cleaner, a laborer's position. Danna cleaned up the debris around the doors of the oven with a push broom and a shovel. Every time they quenched the coke with water, a huge mist would roar out. He said, "You'd get them fine particles of coke in your eyes, in your ears, in your taste, in your clothes, and everything."[4] Not too long after starting in the coke ovens, Danna got laid off, and when he was recalled, he got a job as a mason's helper. The masons relined the ovens with firebricks, and Danna spent a lot of his time cleaning out the flues, removing soot and debris.

> You cleaned flues on midnight turn.... They'd put us way down in this hole. And we'd climb down and load this big barrel that was on a cable, and the machine would hoist it out. They'd take it up and dump it. Put it back

down. . . . When you was digging down there it was red hot. It would even melt your tool. We had to have shoes on, wooden shoes, two, three inches thick. Sometimes you'd see them catch on fire. But you were down in that hole, and you stayed there until the man told you come up.[5]

Relatively few production jobs required highly skilled workers, but Weirton Steel still depended on a cadre of skilled tradesmen—millwrights, iron riggers, electricians, and welders—to maintain equipment and to expand the mill's facilities. Danna eventually became a welder, an important position in the mill that required training, practice, and certification tests. Bad welds could keep the production line from starting back up promptly, and in some cases bad welds on ladders and other structures could be a hazard to coworkers. Even skilled tradesmen like the welders accepted that injuries and discomfort were virtually part of their job description. Danna said that anyone who became a welder could "count on going up to the dispensary" to be treated for "flash burns" on their eyes, which resulted from working with another welder in their peripheral vision. "It wasn't pleasant," he remembered. "It'd keep you up all night." An old-timer told Danna to pour canned milk in his eyes because it cools and soothes them. He also remembered that there were "sparks all the time. . . . Seemed like all the time when you got a good hot spark that went down in [your shirt or your shoe], you were up in the air about two hundred feet hanging on with one arm, and you . . . just had to grin and bear it." Danna's arms still show scars from decades-old burns.[6]

Unlike the steel mill, automation did not take over the potteries entirely. Because pottery companies needed to remain flexible to meet ever-changing fashions and tastes, they only mechanized certain production processes. Ware still had to be touched by human hands at multiple points.[7] Male and female finishers using tools like paring knives scraped off clay "flash" or excess material from formed ware. Decorators applied decals by hand or silk-screened pieces of ware individually. Slip casters still filled molds individually. While modern tunnel kilns took virtually all of the "guesswork" out of firing ware, kiln placers still loaded the saggars—ceramic boxes filled with ware—onto the cars, and kiln drawers unloaded the cars all by hand. Brushers still brushed dust off bisque ware by hand. Warehousemen inspected all the ware individually for defects, and though by the 1950s they no longer packed ware into barrels of straw, packers still loaded it into boxes with cardboard dividers that they called "straw."[8]

Many of the jobs in the pottery were quite monotonous, which could be boring and could take a toll on workers' bodies. Lula "Pug" Rigdon silk-screened patterns onto mugs for nearly all of her thirty years in the pottery. She rolled a cup in a single motion to transfer the decoration, put the cup on a rack, and picked up the next cup. But the monotony never bothered this intelligent woman, who would later become the union president. In talking about her job, she said, "I worked in underglaze. I was a decorator, and I loved the job." She continued: "Of course, my hands prove it with all them crippled-up knuckles."[9] Linda Dickey, who started working at Homer Laughlin in the 1970s, observed that "every job over there is the same old, same old, same old." Describing the repetitive nature of the work, Dickey transitioned quickly into the health effects of repetitive motion:

> You're constantly doing this or doing this, moving your arms. You can tell by the way my elbow—they're both shot. Everything over there [at the pottery], you just have to use your hands. That's why we have carpal tunnel. I pray to God I don't get it. After all these years, I must have really strong wrists because I don't have a problem with my wrists. My elbows? Yes. But not my wrists, and, God forbid, because those hands is everything, every job you do over there.[10]

The camaraderie of pottery workers often overshadowed the monotony of the work. Fay Haught, who started working in the potteries during the 1940s, always found new ways to liven up the workplace. She enjoyed putting "loads" in her coworkers' cigarettes so that when they lit them the cigarettes would blow up in their mouth. She laughed as she remembered playing that prank on one young woman, who, when yet again her cigarette exploded, yelled, "Son of a bitch! You got me again!" Haught also brought firecrackers to work that had pull strings on them. She would tie off the strings so that when the other women opened a drawer or cupboard the firecracker went off.[11] Needless to say, work was rarely boring for the people at the bench next to Haught.

Speed remained an important factor for job performance. Linda Dickey explained that the union and company worked to make sure that older workers kept their jobs. She said, "As you get older, you're not as fast, and you can't work like you did when you were twenty years old." But she argued that employees should always have a job "as long as you can still give them a fair day's work for a fair day's pay." Dickey also observed that older workers were not as a rule the slowest. "They've just done it all their lives," she said. One sixty-five-year-old finisher could outwork almost anyone. "She lives in that clay," Dickey said, and "works all the overtime she can."[12] In 1950, Homer Laughlin discharged Ada Swearingen for not being able to produce "a day's work." She worked as a finisher of the ware coming off the automatic jigger in Plant No. 6. The company found that she finished 30 percent less ware than the rest of her crew. Swearingen and the union said that she was a "careful finisher rather than a speedy finisher."[13] The company contended that it was unfair to pay one finisher in the department the same wage for two-thirds of the work.[14] The arbitrator decided that the discharge was just but that he did not "intend that any stigma should be attached to Mrs. Swearingen" because she appeared to be "a fine, well-intentioned person who is probably well qualified to perform work requiring great care rather than dexterity."[15] It is easy to imagine the potters' stress as they tried to keep up with daily quotas.

Far from Hancock County: National Unionism among Urban Workers

While the experiences of factory work among Hancock County's steel and pottery workers mirrored those of industrial workers all across the United States, their experience with unionization was distinctive. In industrial centers like Pittsburgh, Detroit, and Chicago, workers joined national unions and participated in nationwide strikes, which encouraged them to see their interests as tied to the interests of workers far beyond their local communities. Even in cities like Chicago, though, industrial workers were not predisposed to identify with workers in other departments, let alone other cities. In the 1920s, Chicago's factory workers lived in small, isolated communities primarily defined by ethnicity. To help them through frequent layoffs, injuries, and the loss of a breadwinner, they had developed survival strategies that relied heavily on community institutions such as ethnic churches, ethnic fraternal organizations, and ethnic insurance companies.

These strategies reinforced the fragmented nature of the city's working class, but large historical forces transformed the workers' relationships to local institutions. First, national corporations socialized ethnic workers into large workforces and offered them a variety of welfare capitalism programs that could replace their reliance on ethnic institutions. Second, mass culture—though interpreted through various ethnic lenses—began to provide workers with shared experiences. Finally, when the Great Depression bankrupted their ethnic institutions and forced employers to eliminate welfare capitalism programs, working families increasingly turned to the Congress of Industrial Organizations, the Democratic Party, and the federal government to help them achieve security and stability.[16]

While their local or ethnic identities were not eradicated, working people began to form broader, more inclusive identities. CIO organizers worked tirelessly to form bonds across ethnic divisions and build solidarity even with workers in other cities fighting for the same advances. Building on this culture of solidarity, the largest trade unions won their biggest gains for workers during the late 1940s and throughout the 1950s. They did so by employing what Jack Metzgar called "disciplined collective action," the ability of unions to call hundreds of thousands of their members out on strike and the certainty that they would stay out until union officials told them to return.[17] Not only did thousands of frontline shop stewards preach the gospel of unionism to the rank and file, strikes themselves bred solidarity because workers realized that they were making sacrifices for one another. By the end of such strikes, workers more strongly identified with the working class.[18] They also experienced the rewards of higher wages and better benefits as a result of participating in nationwide collective action, further reinforcing national solidarity. The United Steel Workers of America (USWA) went on strike in 1949, 1952, 1955, and 1956, and during that period doubled the average hourly rate for steelworkers and won new benefits including a health insurance plan, paid vacations, paid holidays, an automatic cost-of-living-adjustment to wages, and the supplemental unemployment benefit (known as SUB pay), which made up the difference between their unemployment checks and their regular pay.[19]

Workers appreciated the wage increases and new benefits enormously. Jack Metzgar, whose father Johnny worked for U. S. Steel in Johnstown, Pennsylvania, a city of about sixty thousand people in 1950, explained that even a benefit as seemingly mundane as SUB pay gave workers a "security and predictability" in a "brutally cyclical" industry, allowing them to pursue long-term goals and investments such as buying a house, adding on to their house, or saving for their children's education. After Jack's mother suffered a heart attack in 1952, Jack's father told the family again and again that without health insurance their lives would have been "wrecked." Jack concludes, "If what we lived through in the 1950s was not liberation, then liberation never happens in real human lives."[20] The Metzgars, especially Jack's father, credited the union with these vital benefits and improved wages.

Experiencing such improvements in their standards of living as a result of membership in national unions not only strengthened many workers' commitments to unionism, but it also transformed their politics. During the 1930s and 1940s, working families gave enthusiastic support to Democratic politicians who shared their commitment to unionism. The New Deal coalition also delivered benefits the working class greatly appreciated: union protections, social security, home loan subsidies, a minimum wage, and the GI Bill. At the end of World War II, many labor liberals hoped they could continue to extend the welfare state and strengthen unions. It is no wonder that many working families had framed photographs of Franklin Roosevelt and John L. Lewis hanging in their homes when the Democratic Party and the CIO had been vehicles to an improved standard of living.

In the 1950s, however, the New Deal coalition fractured on the shoals of racial division. Economic insecurities still plagued blue-collar whites, many of whom had invested their life savings in modest homes and feared declining property values. In northern cities, blue-collar whites who had been the backbone of the coalition began to elect candidates on the basis of their commitment to racial segregation, not to unionism or the welfare state. Labor liberals' dreams of making more fundamental reforms and changing the balance of power in American society were not realized.[21] Nevertheless, historical forces had reoriented millions of industrial workers in northern cities from their neighborhood ethnic societies toward national politics and national unions. Unions like the United Auto Workers and the United Steel Workers became institutions that rested on nationwide solidarity and disciplined collective action.

A Negotiated Loyalty and Localism in Weirton

The rural-industrial workers of Hancock County had very different historical experiences from the urban-industrial workers in northern cities. The steel and pottery workers of Hancock County did not belong to truly national unions and they did not participate in national strikes. No CIO organizers preached a culture of unity to them, and neither their employers nor their community institutions went bankrupt during the Great Depression.[22] Instead, they had experiences that tended to strengthen their commitment to local institutions and to value local control. This, in turn, allowed them to preserve a localism that was consistent with many of their inherited rural ways.

In Hancock County, employers' campaigns to influence their workers dominate the historical record and complicate the historical analysis of workers' goals and values. This is partly because industrial workers who joined the CIO have often been considered liberated, gaining greater control over their worlds through unionization, whereas industrial workers who remained dominated by companies were not free to speak their minds or shape their worlds. Thus, analyzing workers' goals and values in a company town requires that their actions and rhetoric be differentiated from the company's influence. Discerning workers' true goals and values becomes yet more complicated if they overlapped with company schemes and propaganda.[23] This is especially true in examining the history of Weirton steelworkers. Weirton Steel thwarted several unionization campaigns and often portrayed the CIO as outsiders who would disregard local concerns and call strikes recklessly. Previous histories of Weirton have focused on company domination of the town and the workers, which fits into the broader labor history narrative that portrays workers who were unable to unionize—especially those employed by the so-called "Little Steel" companies—as living in fear and denied the right to choose their collective bargaining agent.[24]

On the surface, the divergent histories of Weirton and Aliquippa, Pennsylvania, seem to support this reading of mill towns in the mid-twentieth century. Both began the 1930s as notorious company towns on the Ohio River, with roughly the same population, located some thirty miles apart. Aliquippa earned the nickname "Little Siberia" because the Jones & Laughlin (J&L) Steel Corporation employed many of the same coercive antiunion tactics that Weirton Steel used, including intimidation, violence, firings, blacklists, and surveillance.[25] The histories of the two towns diverged when the Steel Workers Organizing Committee (SWOC) successfully organized J&L. In fact, the 1937 U.S. Supreme Court decision that declared the National Labor Relations Act to be constitutional, *National Labor Relations Board v. Jones & Laughlin Steel Corporation*, emerged from the unionization of steelworkers in Aliquippa. For decades, labor activists declared that democracy had come to Aliquippa while Weirton was now "Little Siberia." In 1944, Weirton Steel only reinforced that view when it fired more than a dozen union supporters and sent the Hatchet Gang to brutalize CIO organizers outside the company gate.

The violence and illegal firings of 1944 were the last recorded incidents of coercion in Weirton, but for many labor activists and USWA officials for decades to come, Weirton would be the "last company town" in the steel industry, a place where the company still dominated every aspect of residents' lives.[26] In 1958, Aliquippa steelworker Dominic Del Turco wrote to the *Pittsburgh Post-Gazette*: "In Weirton you are not allowed to speak your mind. The reason is fear. And as for striking, they wouldn't dare." He went on to say that Weirton was what Aliquippa had been before unionization: "The Siberia of the United States."[27]

By the late 1950s, however, Weirton steelworkers and their families did not think of themselves as slaves living in Siberia. When one Weirton steelworker's wife read Del Turco's letter, she responded with her own letter to the editor. The history of the union at Weirton, she wrote, was a history of independence and "workers' efforts to preserve that independence." Furthermore, they received many benefits as Weirton Steel employees. She explained that two thousand workers had recently been laid off, including her husband, but they were all laid off and recalled according to a "strict" seniority sequence. Moreover, during the five-month layoff, she and her husband received $450 in state unemployment insurance, $492 in SUB pay, and $228 of vacation pay. Plus they enjoyed hospital and surgical benefits, life insurance, a pension, and an annuity retirement plan. She concluded, if Weirton "is Siberia, I'm a Russian bird dog."[28]

That letter to the editor was sent anonymously and theoretically could have been propaganda written by a Weirton Steel public relations executive, but there are two reasons why it likely represented the views of many Weirton steelworkers and their families. First, it emphasized the material goals that many industrial workers held dear. Even during the unionization drives of the 1930s, many sought power primarily to achieve job stability and regularity in their lives and the lives of their families, not power to accomplish revolutionary goals. To workers primarily concerned with job security and steady wages, whether or not they exercised control and power in the workplace was secondary to concerns about family stability.[29]

Second, for those who criticized Weirton Steel from CIO union halls around the region, it would always be 1936 in Weirton. In other words, Weirton in 1958 was what Aliquippa had been before they unionized in 1936, and labor activists failed to recognize that much changed in Weirton between 1936 and the late 1950s. The changing political climate had opened up a space for workers to engage in informal negotiations. Workers increased the pressure on Weirton Steel management by inviting union organizers to town and keeping the possibility of unionization in front of managers. This led the company to change its strategies and rely less on coercion and more on incentives like higher wages and better benefits. Indeed, previous studies of labor relations in Weirton have noted that management's union-avoidance strategies shifted from violence and intimidation in the 1930s to a legal maneuvering, propaganda, and welfare capitalism in the 1940s.[30]

The company's concessions to workers were an important part of a "negotiated loyalty." Some workers who did not have militant, independent unions still used "formal and informal strategies" to force employers to expand their obligations to the employees and arrive at a negotiated loyalty.[31] Between 1940 and 1960, Weirton steelworkers renegotiated their loyalty in multiple ways and at key moments. By testifying in court about unfair labor practices and lending support—even marginal support—to USWA organizing drives, they kept the threat of unionization alive and applied pressure to the company. Weirton Steel, under scrutiny from the NLRB and with CIO organizers at the gate, made numerous contract concessions, providing members of the Weirton Independent Union with many of the same material benefits that CIO members enjoyed. WIU officials also negotiated for a grievance procedure and seniority clauses, eliminating many of the abuses of the old "foreman's empire."[32] By focusing on workers' choices, rhetoric, and oral history testimony, it is therefore possible to discern workers' values while still acknowledging the power of the company.

Official negotiations between the WIU and Weirton Steel appear to have been little more than theater. Union officers closely cooperated with Weirton Steel management. While the first WIU–Weirton Steel contract signed in 1941 technically had no expiration date—likely to avoid NLRB elections—negotiations still took place annually, for the sake of appearances, at which the WIU would ostensibly win concessions from the company such as increased wages and benefits. In reality, beginning with the second contract negotiation in 1942, Weirton Steel began a policy of signing wage agreements that were equal to or better than the so-called "Little Steel" contracts that the USWA won under National War Labor Board oversight.[33] As a result, the average hourly wage for West Virginia steelworkers stayed slightly above those for the nation through the 1950s and 1960s, sometimes just one penny more.[34] WIU officials never missed an opportunity to remind workers that there was no need to strike for their good wages. While USWA members were participating in the massive 1946 strike wave, WIU president Larry Lafferty pledged that the strike would "in no way affect Weirton workers" and that Weirton Steel employees would still receive wage and benefit increases.[35]

Sometimes the WIU took positions that seemed to come straight from the executive boardroom. In the early 1940s, WIU officials criticized the USWA for basing promotions on "seniority instead of upon a basis of reliability, originality, and merit," which discriminated against "superior workmen." Yet many industrial workers valued seniority clauses because they ended the favoritism of the old system that so many foremen had exploited. Despite WIU officials' criticism of seniority, the 1945 WIU–Weirton Steel contract added a seniority clause similar to the clause in USWA contracts. The same 1945 contract also included a grievance procedure, which, like many other union contracts, specified stages of grievance negotiation, with the American Arbitration Association being the final arbiter.[36] Such provisions began to change the reality of life on the shop floor. One foreman, Alex Fiedorczyk, noted that "in the old days, if they didn't want you to work, if he didn't like you, they'd tell you to get out," but by the early 1960s, Fiedorczyk had to carefully document employee conduct to be able to fire them. He also remembered that when it came to promotions, "you had to go by the rules. There was all kind of seniority. You had departmental seniority, company seniority. It could get complicated a little bit."[37] The days when foremen demanded bribes and abused workers without fear of reprisal had ended.[38]

During the late 1940s, Weirton Steel and the WIU produced an enormous amount of propaganda to try to influence employees and defend their position in a political environment that favored collective bargaining. CIO organizers were now able to freely distribute literature, but J. C. Carroll, a USWA staff representative in Weirton, said that he had "little hope of getting into Weirton Steel at the present" because the company was spending a million dollars on propaganda, lawyers, and welfare schemes to keep the CIO out.[39] Weirton Steel, which had almost always been involved in some welfare capitalism programs, boasted about its employee activities now more than ever. The Industrial Relations Department published the *Weirton Steel Employee Bulletin*; sponsored company baseball, basketball, and bowling leagues; created the Twenty-Five Year Club to recognize long-term employment; held an annual Twenty-Five Year Club banquet; and organized the Weirton Men's Chorus, the department's "most widely publicized activity."[40] Such activities were consistent with the "human relations" theory of the postwar era, which asserted that a company needed to cater to workers' "non-economic needs" to build "company consciousness" among employees.[41] Such activities also made social life in Weirton more varied and pleasant for working families.

The WIU continually advertised its advantages over CIO unions: members did not have to attend dull monthly meetings; WIU dues were $4 a year compared to the USWA's $24; and the WIU offered free income tax service, free notary service, the "biggest Christmas parties in the Ohio Valley," and $50 in the event of a family member's death. The WIU also worked with all of the "42 nationalities in the community," hosted the Spring and Fall Festivals as well as dances down at their Colonial Hall, and sponsored local high school football teams. Finally, WIU officials frequently noted that—unlike the CIO—all the officers and stewards lived in the area and participated "actively in every community event."[42]

The company and its independent union claimed to have a well-functioning system of collective bargaining, but on July 25, 1950, the National Labor Relations Board ruled otherwise. The NLRB found that the company had "steadily increased its interference in WIU affairs," including paying union stewards overtime and, in 1944, assaulting CIO organizers at the company gates and discharging at least eighteen men and women for seeking to join the union of their choice. The NLRB ordered the WIU to dissolve immediately and prohibited Weirton Steel from recognizing any labor organization for three months, during which time it was to provide "all their employees reasonable protection in their plants at all times from physical assaults or threats of physical violence directed at discouraging membership in or activities on behalf of any labor organization."⁴³ At the end of the three-month waiting period, the NLRB would supervise a new election.

Those three months were filled with propaganda aimed at winning the workers' hearts and minds. Anticipating the court decision, Weirton Steel and the WIU had already worked together to organize an "Americanism Week" to reaffirm the town's commitment to free enterprise and denounce collectivist social programs and government interference in the American economy. The events of the week employed sometimes subtle, sometimes blatant propaganda to equate the CIO with socialism and communism. Weirton Steel president Thomas Millsop cautioned that the expansion of government regulation represented "creeping socialism." During the week, thousands of Weirton residents attended and participated in patriotic parades, listened to guest speakers celebrate individualism, and enjoyed family picnics and baseball games. Merchants even used their storefronts to compare their prices to those in communist nations.⁴⁴ Meanwhile, a group of local merchants and businessmen hired Donald Ebbert, a labor lawyer with the Pittsburgh firm that represented Weirton Steel in its NLRB trials, to create the Independent Steelworkers Union (ISU). According to one journalist, Ebbert designed the ISU "to be ineffective, compromised, and self-lacerating," and in some ways it became all of those things.⁴⁵

During the three-month campaign leading up to the union representation election, the debate over health care illustrates how the company and its company union felt threatened into offering benefits equal to the USWA. In 1949, just months before the NLRB declared the WIU to be an illegal company union, the USWA went on strike until major steel producers agreed to fully fund pensions and jointly fund a health insurance plan.⁴⁶ USWA officials used the new pension and health insurance as a selling point to steelworkers in Weirton. William Huff, the temporary chairman of the ISU, warned local steelworkers not to listen to this propaganda. He wrote that "outsiders who WANT TO CONTROL WEIRTON" were using "lies and misrepresentation" by trying to make "an issue out of insurance." He assured Weirton steelworkers that insurance was "only one of many things" that the ISU would address at the first negotiating conference. More importantly, he concluded, "your independence—not your insurance or some other detail—is the REAL issue at stake."⁴⁷ A vote for the ISU, officials like Huff repeatedly insisted, would keep control over Weirton jobs in local hands.⁴⁸ On October 27, 1950, Weirton steelworkers ultimately voted 7,291 to 3,454 in favor of the ISU, and they got the same health care benefits through ISU contact negotiations.⁴⁹

"Independent" was a word that resonated with local steelworkers. One ISU ad during the 1950 representation election declared, "Stay Independent for yourself—your family—your community."⁵⁰ ISU officials for the next decade would equate independence with local unionism and contrast local control with the outsider domination of the CIO. The editors of the *Independent News*, the ISU journal, frequently portrayed the CIO as outsiders intent on "wrecking" independent unions. If they succeeded, Weirton steelworkers who asked "for anything beyond routine action on a grievance" or complained about paying high dues would face a "gang of thugs" who would "break an arm or a leg."⁵¹ During the 1959 USWA organizing drive, the *Independent News* asked readers who would make the best union leader: a man who worked his way up through the ranks, was active in the Weirton Community Service Council, coached a Weirton Little League baseball team, and belonged to the New Cumberland Masonic Lodge, or a man who only worked six weeks in a steel mill, "ramrodded" his way to the union presidency "when his boss died," belonged to one of Pittsburgh's "ritziest country clubs," and toured the country with a bodyguard. Like many articles in the *Independent News*, this comparison of ISU president Malcolm Graham and USWA president David J. McDonald equated "local" with honest and democratic, while "outsider" meant corrupt and threatening.⁵²

The ISU also emphasized the material benefits that Weirton steelworkers enjoyed. During the heated 1950 representation election, one "old timer" wrote to the *Independent News* to express doubt that workers would vote for a CIO union. "The men and women in this town aren't fools, or crazy," he wrote. "They are not going to sell their birth right for a mess of porridge. They know they have been treated more than fair. All they have to do is count their blessings, and take stock of how they and their children have prospered through the years." He concluded that people in Weirton had nice homes, drove good cars, wore good clothes, "set good tables," and had savings in the bank and surely were not "going to bite the hand that's feeding them, and been feeding them for a long time."⁵³

At the same time Weirton Steel was granting concessions to its workers, the company also provided more amenities to the city of Weirton as both its largest taxpayer and occasionally as its largest donor. In 1947, executives encouraged the incorporation of what was then the nation's largest unincorporated city, probably to avoid the appearance of a company town. Residents voted more than three to one to incorporate and elected Thomas Millsop, president of Weirton Steel, to be their first mayor.⁵⁴ The newly incorporated city took over many responsibilities from Weirton Steel such as utilities, maintenance of the streets and street lighting, and operation of Weir High's football stadium, and it used massive donations from Weirton Steel to build Weirton General Hospital, twenty playgrounds, Weir Memorial Park and Swimming Pool, the Millsop

Community Center, and a public library.[55] Weirton Steel also continued its long-standing policy of sponsoring community events—part of Ernest Weir's vision for the ideal American community—and subsidizing ethnic institutions. For example, the company provided a new auditorium and gymnasium to serve the African American community and donated stainless steel to cover the roof and tower of the All Saints Greek Catholic Church.[56] These are classic examples of paternalism, but to Weirton steelworkers they represented an improved standard of living and a local system of bargaining.

As glorious as strikes may have been to labor activists at the time and as effective as they may have been in encouraging a broader sense of class consciousness, Weirton steelworkers—like many industrial workers—feared that lengthy work stoppages would drain their savings accounts and force them to sell their homes. While national strikes were the only way to get concessions from large corporations in the 1940s and 1950s, Weirton steelworkers were able to reap the benefits of a strike without suffering the loss of income. This infuriated J&L steelworker Dominic Del Turco, who said that the steelworkers in Weirton "never had any guts to organize a union" and were "riding on the coat tails of a real free and democratic group of employees," the United Steel Workers of America.[57]

Through the 1950s, Weirton Steel and the ISU continued to deliver the material benefits of unionism to Weirton steelworkers while stressing the local nature of their negotiations. In 1956, half a million steelworkers went on strike and won a wage increase, a seventh paid holiday, a new automatic cost of living adjustment (COLA) mechanism, and the new supplemental unemployment benefit, or SUB pay.[58] The next month, the ISU also touted its 1956 contract, which included the same pay raises, a seventh paid holiday, COLA, and SUB pay.[59] While Weirton steelworkers were often called rats or "free riders," it made little sense to them to risk their job and the life they had made for themselves in this company town for what must have seemed an abstract measure of power.[60] During the 1959 USWA strike, Donald Anderson, a thirty-one-year-old crane operator, told one reporter, "We don't have strikes at Weirton Steel. When there are layoffs, they are easier here than at other places, too. I haven't missed a day's work for four years."[61]

Weirton steelworkers worked within this localized system of negotiations to achieve many of their goals. They focused on their families, social activities, and saving money to own their own homes and send their children to school. Louis Truax, the farm boy who wandered up to the factory gates in 1919, declared, "All the employees of the Company, I am sure made a very good living." He retired in 1965 after a forty-six-year career, and his gratitude to Weirton Steel poured out as he remembered all the years he spent in different departments, raising eight children who "never went hungry"; buying his home, appliances, and cars; paying doctors' bills; buying clothes for himself, his wife, and their children; and enjoying a "very good pension." He concluded, "I cannot express my appreciation and gratitude enough for what the Weirton Steel Co., has done for me."[62] Many workers were similarly grateful to Weirton Steel for providing them and their family with a livelihood.[63]

Local Unionism in the Potteries

The potters had a long history of being conservative unionists. In the 1890s and early 1900s, skilled potters had been reluctant to join a union in the first place. They had had the opportunity to join a CIO pottery union in the late 1930s but opted to remain with the more conservative National Brotherhood of Operative Potters, an affiliate of the American Federation of Labor. As one historian of the pottery union observed, the tableware ceramics industry "remained a small town phenomena dominated by the East Liverpool district," and since both the NBOP and the United States Potters' Association (USPA)—the employers' organization—had their headquarters in that town, the union's leadership "despite their national orientation seemed to have remained provincial in outlook."[64]

Because the potteries had to remain flexible to meet the production needs of ever-changing fashions and designs, there were continuous conflicts on the shop floor over wages and working conditions. When workers had problems with wage rates, safety issues, seniority, abusive supervisors, or wrongful termination, they took their grievances to the standing committee. The standing committee was made up of the national union president and pottery owners who heard grievances from every pottery in the East Liverpool district. Thus, rank-and-file potters were assured that their grievance would be handled by the most powerful individuals in the generalware industry, a benefit of unionism they valued greatly.

The standing committee was important to pottery workers because piece rates needed to be adjusted for each new line of ware. In 1955, for instance, when Homer Laughlin began production of "Epicure" china, it precipitated conflict over the rate. Edna Brereton, a member of the shop committee at Homer Laughlin's Plant No. 5, started working on the new handles for the Epicure cups on a day rate. After the trial period, she went from a day rate to a piece rate of $3.30 per hundred dozen. Brereton told her foreman that "the handles was worth more than that," more in fact than even the day wage they had paid her. Brereton and two other female coworkers were brought before their foreman's boss, General Superintendent Cartwright, who dramatically held up the cup and said, "This is what we are referring to?" Cartwright said he could not understand Brereton's attitude—that she refused to work on the cup for piece rate or day rate. When she retorted that that was not true, Cartwright would have none of it. Brereton recalled, "For at least ten or fifteen minutes he did nothing but belittle and ridicule me. . . . All Mr. Cartwright wanted to do was belittle me in front of the girls." Edna stood her ground, said that the handle was worth $4.20 per hundred dozen, and that even the fastest handle finisher, Mary Spurlock, could not produce two hundred dozen per day, the quantity on which the company had based their rate.[65] When such heated conflicts arose, it was no doubt comforting for union members to know that the president of the International Brotherhood of Operative Potters (IBOP), as it became known after 1951, would represent their grievance in the standing committee meetings.

But the standing committee struggled to keep up with the ever-expanding number of grievances, and union officers searched for ways to reduce their involvement in shop floor disagreements. Frank Hull, elected president of the IBOP in 1953, complained that national officers spent too much time and energy attending to the frustrations of a small group of members that had not gone through their shop committees. Instead, he said, officers should be spending more time staying informed about politics and economics.[66] Hull's successor, Edwin Wheatley, entered office with visions of creating a powerful and truly national union. The son of an East Liverpool jiggerman, Wheatley joined the union in 1915 as an apprentice kilnhand at Homer Laughlin's East End plant, was elected first vice president in 1933, and moved to Trenton, where he represented the sanitary branch of the industry, which included porcelain bathroom fixtures.[67] Wheatley was credited with reinvigorating that branch of the organization between 1933 and 1941, and this inspired him to imagine the IBOP as a truly national organization. As president, he hired several full-time organizers and instructed them to organize plants from the ground up in places like Corona, California; San Antonio, Texas; and Evansville, Indiana.[68] Many of Wheatley's reforms moved the union away from its traditional craft structure, which caused resentment among the ranks in the East Liverpool district, where they clung tightly to potters' traditions.[69]

Rather than building a national union, Wheatley found himself spending most of his time dealing with individual grievances. It was not unusual for members to drop by his office with individual complaints, such as when IBOP member John Siddall stopped by the president's office and talked to him for more than an hour about the history of craft jurisdictions. Wheatley explained to Siddall why the dishmakers and jiggermen had set up separate jurisdictions when the union was first created. In a letter to Siddall dripping with frustration, Wheatley noted that this was the second time he had "personally endeavored to enlighten" Siddall about which jobs he could bid.[70]

Like Hull before him, Wheatley wanted to reform grievance procedures to free up national officers. Just three months into his presidency, Wheatley created master committees to act as grievance boards in every pottery. The twenty-three local jurisdictions at the nine or ten separate generalware potteries in the district would file grievances first with their plant-wide master committee. This added another layer of bureaucracy between the shop committees and the district-wide standing committee, which, Wheatley hoped, would reduce the number of grievances the national officers had to handle. The *Potters Herald* explained that "many minor grievances have developed into serious situations when no real efforts have been made to settle them at the bench levels when they arise." The new master committees would "expedite" grievances and settle them in a "harmonious manner."[71]

When the rank and file resisted this new organization, Wheatley had to explain to some locals that that it would be "impossible to find enough International officers to service all the various jurisdictions." Feeling the pressure of dissent, he added that any "potential Executive Board politician" who said otherwise was a "phony" in his book. He hoped that locals would refrain from taking grievances to the district-wide standing committee because most would end up in arbitration, and pottery workers would have "schoolteachers, politicians, and etc. [who served on the arbitration panels] ... writing [our] tickets."[72] And presumably these arbitrators would have little knowledge of the pottery industry.

The fight to reform the grievance procedure proved to be a difficult task. When master committees had to make decisions between different craft locals in the same pottery, the losing parties turned their anger toward Wheatley and the union. The kiln firemen of Local Union 130 sent a letter to the *Potters Herald* condemning the new plant-wide committee for siding with the company to benefit another local. Wheatley chose not to print the letter in the journal and explained to Local Union 130's recording secretary that it would be difficult for him "on the basis of one grievance objection, to endeavor to charge any plant-wide committee with collusion with the company that will lessen the benefits of another trade or craft." He also cautioned that this method of processing grievances was new, and if they publicized their divisions, the manufacturers would "have an opportunity to play it back into our teeth."[73]

No grievances were more important to pottery workers than those that sought to redress unhealthy working conditions, and one such grievance spanned the presidencies of both Hull and Wheatley. Dust was a long-standing concern to potters. In the late nineteenth century, observers noted that potters' lives were "the shortest in all the trades and professions." The deadliest hazards were lead poisoning and—worst of all—potters' asthma or potters' rot, a form of silicosis.[74] During the 1910s and 1920s, pottery workers and companies became more conscious of the need for better ventilation, fans, respirators in some occupations, and wet processes, but the problem of silicosis persisted. Pottery workers feared the deadly disease, which felled many of their comrades during the first four decades of the twentieth century. In one case in the 1930s, a twenty-six-year-old woman worked in the potteries for five years as a finisher, where she was exposed to more than two hundred million dust particles per cubic foot. She developed a cold and began coughing up "grayish clay-like material similar to the dust in which she had worked." Over the next year she lost 41 pounds, continued coughing and wheezing, and was placed in a sanitarium. In the sanitarium her weight continued to fall from 103 to 92 pounds, and after fifteen months she suddenly became short of breath one night. Doctors discovered her lungs were collapsing and attempted to aspirate them. Their efforts failed, and she died minutes later.[75] Such cases were rare by the 1930s, but they were a terrible reminder of the danger of silica. Doctors and industrial hygienists in the late 1930s studied causes and incidence rates of silicosis in the pottery industry and took further measures to reduce workers' exposure to silica dust.[76]

By the 1950s, combating silicosis was on the minds of many company officials and workers.[77] The finishers of Local 53 at Homer Laughlin China tenaciously pursued a grievance because of the dust created by a new process called "dry finishing." Instead of finishing greenware with wet sponges, dry finishing used machines with whirling abrasive pads, which created more dust. The episode reveals their access to national union officers, pottery owners, and state agencies, and it illustrates the nature of their local control. In 1953, the finishers instructed the IBOP to contact the West Virginia State Department of Health to alert them of the possible dust hazard created by the introduction of dry finishing on the automatic jigger at Plant No. 6.[78] An industrial hygienist found that the pottery dust was "well below the limit" of four million particles per cubic foot of air and that while dry finishing produced more visible dust, the local exhaust system effectively removed the "fine particles which can get into the lungs."[79] This satisfied IBOP officials, but not the workers. A week later, worker-correspondents to the *Potters Herald* accused Homer Laughlin of jeopardizing "the health of clay workers" by introducing dry finishing and trying to have silicosis removed from the list of compensable industrial diseases at the

FIGURE 11. A finisher, Homer Laughlin China, ca. 1950s
Source: Homer Laughlin China Company

last session of the West Virginia legislature.[80] The next month, Local Union 53 asked that a state inspector return to take samples at both Plant No. 5 and Plant No. 6 with a union official accompanying them, which happened in June 1954. According to the inspector, the tests revealed little difference between the various situations, but because the average dust concentration did slightly exceed the threshold of four million particles per cubic foot, he advised the company to strive to improve air quality.[81]

Next, the finishers contacted their national union president, Frank Hull, and asked him to inform Arthur Wells, the plant manager whose family owned the business, that they would like to meet with him personally to discuss dry finishing.[82] In other words, the finishers contacted two of the most powerful men in their industry to handle their grievance personally. After the meeting with the finishers, Wells continued to argue in favor of the dry finishing method because it required "less time and effort than the standard wet finishing method."[83] Nevertheless, the finishers displayed a trust in Wells when they asked to meet with him personally, which was not uncommon at Homer Laughlin China.

In 1956, in the third year of this grievance, Wheatley took office and tried to reform the grievance procedure. He apologized to Vesta Phillips, the recording secretary of Local 53, for not getting to their grievance sooner, but he explained that there was an "enormous number" of complaints stacked up in his office because of the "improper functioning of the grievance machinery at the shop level." He asked Phillips to take another grievance through all the steps to the new master committee at their plant, which they did.[84]

Homer Laughlin expanded its use of dry finishing to Plant Nos. 4, 5, and 8 in 1957, and the finishers continued to complain to the union and request more samples be taken.[85] As late as January 1960, the Bureau of Industrial Hygiene was continuing to test air quality at Homer Laughlin.[86] Dry finishing became a standard procedure in the industry, but Homer Laughlin and other companies first installed more fans to remove dust from the shop and then installed dust collectors to avoid simply blowing the dust onto the surrounding area.[87] The finishers' level of vigilance was undoubtedly one of the reasons why the rate of silicosis among pottery workers decreased during the 1940s and 1950s, and it was only possible because of a grievance system that gave workers access to top union and company officials, both of whom were anxious to settle the issue quickly. This incident illustrates the close contact workers on the line had with union officials and management and their willingness to rely on government inspectors and expert consultants (although not blindly). And at the height of the controversy in the mid-1950s, they wanted to meet with the pottery owners to express their concerns directly to them. This was very much a localized system of negotiation at work.

Union officials and rank-and-file potters continued to disagree about how much direct contact union officers should have with members. In 1959, union leaders devised a plan to build a new headquarters complex several miles outside of East Liverpool, likely to avoid the many unscheduled visitors who had complaints they wanted to bring directly to officers. Not willing to give up easy access to the officers, some dissidents brought suit against the IBOP to prevent them from moving the headquarters, but they withdrew their case when the new facility opened with George Meany making a keynote speech at the opening ceremony.[88]

Wheatley also tried to reduce the number of grievances by reducing the number of craft locals. He counted the number of craft unions that were represented at each pottery and determined that there were more than two hundred potential sources for grievances in the East Liverpool district. Between 1956 and 1961, he merged twenty-four locals into eleven. Some officers believed that merging the locals would not only streamline the grievance process but might also dilute the influence of some particularly disgruntled locals.[89] At the same time, Wheatley and his officers resisted attempts to divide the existing locals. In 1959, one union representative notified Wheatley that Homer Laughlin wanted a new division in finishing that would make cup finishing, hand jiggering finishing, and automatic jigger finishing different jobs, presumably to pay different finishers different rates, but the finishers and the representative argued that "a Finisher is a Finisher period."[90] Yet, two years later, finishers at Taylor, Smith & Taylor (TS&T) wanted to split their local into four or five to gain an advantage through seniority. Wheatley advised them that they needed to be "united in their thinking" regarding seniority and warned that "some unscrupulous plant management" would start "singling out these minor groups" and "disintegrate" their trade completely.[91] He also had just finished streamlining the locals to cut down on the number of grievances. By merging locals and establishing master committees at the plants, the IBOP took steps toward becoming a more hierarchical organization with larger, consolidated locals and more layers of bureaucracy.

Like the steelworkers, pottery workers enjoyed steady advances in pay and benefits through the 1940s and 1950s, but IBOP leaders and members were well aware of the shaky financial ground upon which the pottery companies rested in the 1950s. Pottery wages had already fallen behind other industries. In 1938—a strong year for pottery workers—they made 90 percent of what the average steelworker earned each week, but by 1944 they were earning only 65 percent.[92] After World War II, American potteries faced fierce competition from English, Italian, and Japanese potteries. Between 1948 and 1952, American potteries saw their share of the domestic market drop from about 30 percent down to 16 percent as imported ceramics poured into the United States. In the East Liverpool district, employment declined rapidly. Between 1945 and 1955, the payroll at Homer Laughlin dropped from 3,200 to 1,400, and nine American companies went bankrupt.[93]

Walking a tightrope, union officials pushed for what wages and benefits they believed companies could afford, considering that several were on the verge of bankruptcy. The pottery workers often looked to the United Steel Workers of America negotiations as the ideal for the wages and benefits they should be receiving from their employers. In 1946, the NBOP demanded that the pottery companies give workers the same across-the-board eighteen-cent raise in their hourly rates that the USWA had won in recent contract negotiations, and the United States Potters' Association conceded.[94] When Weirton steelworkers based their contracts on USWA negotiations they were called "free riders," but it was not unusual for autonomous unions like the NBOP/IBOP to follow the lead of successful union negotiations in other industries.

The year 1946 proved to be a good one for potters, but their average weekly earnings still rose to only 80 percent of the steelworkers'. After 1946, potters fell further and further behind as the gap in hourly wages between the two industries widened steadily from thirty-one cents in 1947 to fifty-nine cents in 1953 and eighty cents by 1957.[95] In 1950, the average annual earnings of blast furnace, steel works, and rolling mill employees in West Virginia was $3,612, compared to the $2,345 potters made.[96]

West Virginia potters could not count on the same steady workweeks and large paychecks that the steel industry offered, but the industry still attracted thousands of local workers. Tom Rector, who worked at Homer Laughlin, knew steelworkers made more money: "The average potter had a nice little home and everything, but the guy who worked in the mill, you could tell he had a nicer car and a nice big home." Rector quickly added that the steelworkers "didn't have any more food on the table though." He chose to work in the potteries most of his life because he believed that potters had safer working conditions and he personally had better job security.[97] Even though each potter worked fewer hours at a considerably lower hourly rate, the potteries employed married women, meaning both husband and wife often brought home paychecks, which often evened out the difference in household incomes between the two industries.[98] In the steel town of Weirton, only one in five women worked outside the home, but in and around the pottery towns, fully one in three women worked for wages. And more than half of the 1,198 employed women in the pottery towns were factory operatives (54 percent) with the rest being divided among clerical (12 percent), sales (9 percent), professional (7 percent), service (5 percent), and private household workers (4 percent).[99]

When it came to winning new benefits for pottery workers, the sanitary branch—not the tableware branch—led the way in the late 1940s. The workers at the Mannington Pottery Company, which manufactured porcelain toilets and tanks in central West Virginia, actually won pensions and health insurance one year before the steelworkers. The 1948 contract at Mannington included the industry's first pension plan and a health insurance program paid on a 50–50 basis with the workers, but it would be many years before most other potters won those benefits. The NBOP and USPA held a series of meetings in August 1950 to discuss the possibility of adopting pension and welfare plans like those the USWA had just won, but manufacturers repeatedly argued that meeting the costs of those benefits would mean raising prices to a point that would kill the industry. The union agreed to table the demands.[100] A long six years later, IBOP president Wheatley appointed a pension committee and retained an actuarial expert to strengthen the case for pensions and health plans, but it was not until September 1957 that the USPA, representing nineteen potteries, finally agreed to contribute $3.19 per employee toward a health insurance plan, simply because so many other industries had already adopted health plans. In 1962, the IBOP won pension plans after a dozen years of negotiations.[101] Pottery workers—though they had an autonomous union that could call strikes—were willing to accept less compensation and leaner benefit packages than steelworkers because of the threat of bankruptcy their employers faced.

The 1958 recession devastated the potteries and resulted in massive layoffs and four business closings. West Virginia pottery workers averaged only twenty-seven hours a week and brought home about $52 compared to the thirty-eight hours and $110 a week of steelworkers.[102] When business conditions for the remaining pottery companies improved the following year, IBOP negotiators demanded a wage increase, but the USPA refused and insisted they resort to binding arbitration. The IBOP membership voted to strike, and twelve IBOP-USPA potteries shut down on April 15, 1959. A U.S. Mediation Service official brokered a deal on May 7 when the USPA agreed to a six-cent hourly increase, three additional paid holidays, and elimination of the 10 percent fee for operating the dues check-off.[103]

More significant than the strike or its outcome is that it was only the third industry-wide generalware strike in seventy years of negotiations between the IBOP and the USPA. Collective bargaining and a localized grievance process served potters and pottery companies well. Lula "Pug" Rigdon, one of the union's presidents in the 1980s, commented on the union's relationship with the company: "I feel we went overboard for them [the pottery companies]. I'd listen to them, and I'd go back to the people. Some of them didn't like it, but the majority did. They felt I was fair. I had two foremen tell me—they would argue with me—but they told me I was fair."[104] Linda Dickey, who became the local union president in the 1990s, considered "closeness with our owners" one of the advantages of working at Homer Laughlin. She said that she could "always go to management, and if I needed something they would usually give it to me."[105] Furthermore, the union leadership in the 1950s and 1960s accepted lower wages and fewer benefits than steelworkers received because pottery companies in Hancock County teetered on the verge of bankruptcy, with many going out of business. Undoubtedly, many pottery workers believed that being fair to local companies was an important aspect of being part of a localistic economic system.

State and Local Labor Politics

In the years after World War II, leaders of the American labor movement set their sights on ambitious political reforms, especially to strengthen unions and extend the welfare state. Both the AFL and the CIO created lobbying organizations to screen and endorse candidates and educate union members. In 1947, the political climate changed and the hopes of labor activists and labor liberals turned to fears. After an unprecedented wave of strikes in 1946, Republicans took control of Congress and passed the Taft-Hartley Act the following year. The act curtailed union power by outlawing closed shops, limiting union shops, and giving the president the ability to end strikes for reasons of national emergency.[106] Reeling from the effects of Taft-Hartley, labor leaders renewed their efforts to influence national politics, but during the 1950s they found themselves simply trying to hold on to the gains they had already made and prevent any further weakening of the legal protections for unions. When the AFL and CIO merged in 1955, AFL-CIO officials created the Committee on Political Education (COPE) to inform their members which candidates voted "right" or "wrong" on bills important to labor.[107]

When the state-level branches of the AFL and CIO merged to create the West Virginia Labor Federation in 1957, they also created a state-level branch of COPE as well. COPE in West Virginia endorsed the same national candidates as its parent organization but also sent questionnaires to all West Virginia's candidates to ascertain the candidates' positions on right-to-work laws, the minimum wage, unemployment compensation, workers' compensation, and other labor issues. Then a COPE committee made a final determination on which candidates to endorse and communicated that to union locals and members across the state.[108] West Virginia COPE also lobbied for new legislation and changes in state policies. Delegates at COPE's 1957 convention called for pension plans for the twenty-one thousand state employees; a larger budget for the State Department of Labor; improvements in public education; tax cuts for the lower class; increased Social Security payments to the elderly, the disabled, and dependent children; creation of a national unemployment compensation program; and a cost of living increase in the state's workers' compensation benefits. Most importantly, the delegates vowed to prevent the passage of a right-to-work law, which would return West Virginia to the "evil days of the open shop wherein workers would be at the mercy of unscrupulous employers and the entire economy of the country would be controlled by selfish, privileged interests."[109] Like the platform of national labor liberals, most of these proposals sought to extend the welfare state and protect union rights.

During the late 1950s and early 1960s, COPE in West Virginia managed to protect the gains labor had made in the 1930s and 1940s but accomplished little more.[110] The inability of West Virginia COPE to realize broader goals in some ways mirrored the troubles organized labor faced nationally. One factor was the lack of success that COPE-endorsed candidates had in elections. In their examinations of major northern cities, historians have found that white working-class voters abandoned labor's candidates and voted for conservatives who, in effect, promised to maintain racial segregation and protect white homeowners' property values. Such a shift in political allegiance often followed battles over public housing projects and the erosion of racial segregation.[111] Hancock County residential areas were largely segregated by race during these decades, but there were no battles over public housing, no race riots, and no credible threats to the color line as there were in cities like Detroit and Chicago. COPE had trouble harnessing the votes of Hancock County's working class, but not for the same reasons it lost voters in Detroit and Chicago.

Even within West Virginia, Hancock County's steel and pottery workers had a lot in common with workers in other industries, and there were many reasons for them to form alliances to influence politics and for mutual support during negotiations and strikes. Industrial workers in Hancock County and those all along the Ohio River had similar experiences and grievances. Pottery workers, for example, had a lot in common with glass workers. Like the potters, the glass workers had been steeped in craft traditions and had structured their union around skilled crew leaders, only to be stripped of their authority and influence by new production technologies.[112] While steel and pottery workers had very different work lives from coal miners, there were many miners in the northern panhandle in nearby towns that held similar values and attitudes. Admittedly, the miners of the southern West Virginia coalfields had little in common with the factory workers of northern West Virginia, but the United Mine Workers of America was the most powerful union in the state and a powerful ally for any union member.

Yet for all they had in common and might gain from alliances with other workers in the region and in the state, the steel and pottery workers of Hancock County in these decades had few formal connections with workers in other industries or places. For example, the West Virginia State Federation of Labor's annual convention had long been a meeting place for industrial workers throughout the Mountain State. In 1919, steelworkers from Wheeling and Follansbee (just a few miles south of Weirton) attended the convention, as did pottery workers from Wheeling, Cameron, Mannington, Grafton, Clarksburg, and Huntington, but neither the steel nor pottery workers of Hancock County attended, and that held true for decades. The Independent Steelworkers Union, created in 1950, appears to have stayed out of statewide labor organizations and out of politics altogether through the 1950s and 1960s.[113] The first formal ties between Hancock County's workers and union members in the state occurred in the mid-1940s, when potters of the East Liverpool district began to pay more attention to the work of the federation. In 1946, potter E. C. Armstrong of Chester was elected a vice president of District 1, and a potter from the East Liverpool district held that position for the next several years.[114]

It was not until the 1947 Taft-Hartley Act that the potters' union embraced political education, endorsed prolabor candidates, and lobbied for favorable legislation.[115] In early 1948, union officials urged members to send voluntary contributions that would be donated to the AFL as well as to the State Federation of Labor and the Central Labor Union. One letter explained that the "failure of the present Congress to do anything in the interest of the workers of the nation, its complete subservience to the reactionary antilabor lobbies, the wave of legislation against labor in the various States throughout the country have made it imperative that the workers of the nation create a solid and effective organization for political action." To get the union more involved in politics, secretary treasurer Charles Jordan accepted the position of deputy treasurer in the AFL's Labor's League for Political Education.[116]

Still, Hancock County's working-class politics reflected a desire for local control, and voters often opted for more conservative politicians who favored limits on union power and put greater emphasis on restricting imports, which stood in stark contrast to the political agendas of state and national labor organizations. The election of Republican Arch Moore to the U.S. House of Representatives demonstrated the degree to which Hancock County voters diverged from COPE's endorsements. Moore entered politics in 1952, winning a seat in the West Virginia House of Delegates. In 1954, he made a bid to represent West Virginia's First Congressional District in Congress, won the primary that spring, but lost in the general election to a Democrat who was part of the statehouse machine.[117] Two years later, he hired a Weirton Steel public relations executive to write press releases and won the election.[118] That would be the first of six terms Moore spent in the U.S. House of Representatives before serving three terms as governor of West Virginia, two from 1969 through 1977, and one from 1985 through 1989.

In 1954, the majority of Hancock County voters opted for the Democrat, much like the rest of the First District, but over the next few campaigns, Moore won them over. In 1960, he finally won a majority—56 percent—of Hancock County's votes and built on that support, winning 61 percent in 1962 and 62 percent in 1964.[119] The 1962 election was an important test for Moore because the loss of population in West Virginia resulted in the consolidation of two of the state's congressional districts and pitted him against one of the biggest labor politicians in the state: Democratic representative Cleveland Bailey. Not only did COPE endorse Bailey in the 1962 election, but President John F. Kennedy also came to West Virginia to speak on his behalf. Bailey had an excellent voting record on labor issues and was the second highest ranking member of the House Committee on Education and Labor. Despite Bailey's endorsements and labor record, Moore defeated him by 97,556 votes to 65,328, a margin of 19 percent, and by more than 22 percent in Hancock County.[120]

A Republican, Arch Moore was an unlikely victor in a working-class stronghold. He was a corporate lawyer who represented national chemical companies that had plants just south of his hometown of Moundsville (forty miles south of Weirton). He had to tread lightly when it came to labor issues because the First Congressional District of West Virginia was one of the most heavily unionized districts in the state—Hancock County being only one of seven counties in the district at the time—and Republicans rarely received union endorsements. He often emphasized that he had been a union member during high school when he had worked at the U.S. Stamping Company factory in Moundsville and belonged to the Enamel Workers Union.[121] Despite his past union experience, his voting record in Congress led West Virginia COPE and the USWA to endorse his Democratic opponents in all the elections he ran in up through 1964. The UMWA endorsed him in only two of those six elections. Obviously, he would not have won those elections if rank-and-file union members had voted faithfully for COPE's candidates.[122]

Moore's success left several labor leaders in West Virginia dumbfounded. Mary Goddard Zon, a research director for COPE in West Virginia, believed that even though Moore rarely supported their platform, his "personal services" to constituents overshadowed his voting record. Political scientist Larry Sayre agreed, observing that Moore's "conquest of the rank and file" was accomplished by bypassing union leaders and campaigning directly to the rank and file through numerous personal services and personal mailings, a strategy

CHAPTER 4

FIGURE 12. Arch A. Moore
Source: West Virginia Archives and History

Sayre termed the "Moore method." Providing services to individuals—whether it was helping a steelworker's sons get into the Naval Academy, sending flowers to funerals, or helping a voter get a visa for a family member—proved effective, Sayre argued. Services were "tangible things" that laborers could "see and feel" and therefore seemed "more valuable to him than his union organization's endorsements." Moore also avoided taking strong stances, often left "Republican" off his campaign literature, and used his personal services rather than his political views to win votes. As proof of this, Sayre noted that fewer than 20 percent of his survey respondents could evaluate any of Moore's congressional actions specifically and only 10 percent who thought they knew his voting record could accurately identify Moore's position on four major bills before the House.[123]

What West Virginia's political scientists and labor leaders did not understand was that when working-class voters in Hancock County elected Arch Moore, they did not elect a candidate whose views were at odds with their own. His concerns about distant labor bureaucracies and overly powerful union bosses matched those of the rural-industrial workers he represented. Weirton steelworkers viewed the USWA leadership as distant and divorced from local concerns, such as when to strike and why.[124] Pottery workers appreciated local control over labor issues, easy access to national union officials, and the absence of a large and dense union bureaucracy. Potters also believed that however contentious negotiations with management may get, working for family-owned businesses was preferable to dealing with a large, impersonal corporation.

On the whole, union members in Hancock County used their unions to improve working conditions but did not fight for great federal protections for unions. A closer look at their attitudes toward two important labor bills in the U.S. House reveals that when working-class voters lent their support to Arch Moore, they elected an official that reflected their values. In 1959, Congress passed the Landrum-Griffin Act that required secret ballot elections, inspection of ballots, and scheduled elections for officials at least every five years. Landrum-Griffin also included a "bill of rights" for individual union members and required unions to provide accounting reports to the secretary of labor. While supporters of the act argued that such measures were necessary to keep dictatorial labor bosses in check, labor leaders saw the new restrictions and requirements as an attempt to further complicate union activities, making it difficult to perform routine duties.[125] Working-class voters in Hancock County thought that the Landrum-Griffin Act was in workers' best interest. Ralph Powell of New Cumberland told Moore to support the "legislation to control the power of gangsters and thugs in labor-management relations" and correct this "shameful situation."[126] Weirton Steel employee John Crow and his wife asked Moore to vote to "curb union racketeering," to support "secret voting in unions for or against strikes," and to return control to "individual members instead of the gangsters who control from the top of the pile."[127] Mrs. Robert L. Doughty of Weirton said that there was a time when she "truly believed that it was strictly up to the union membership to wash their own laundry," but she was now convinced that the members were "almost powerless without Congressional legislation." She urged Moore to vote for legislation to "stop the ever growing menace."[128]

Regardless of what Hancock County wanted, Moore listened to the rest of his heavily unionized district and voted against the Landrum-Griffin bill. As a result, the following year the UMWA endorsed Moore for office.[129] Many businessmen expressed their disappointment in Moore, including one Wheeling man who accused Moore of being a "hillbilly" and a "traitor" because of his vote. Moore received hearty congratulations from his union supporters, few of whom lived in Hancock County.[130]

In 1965, Lyndon Johnson announced his opposition to section 14 (b) of the Taft-Hartley Act that allowed states to pass "right to work" laws. Among other things, right to work laws prohibited the union shop and, in effect, stopped union organizing in those states. Ardent unionists, like pottery worker Dorothy Mayles of Chester, sent a form letter to their congressional representatives stating, "I am a union member and proud that our state has never had the blight of a 'right-to-work' law. But I believe we would be even better off if our entire nation was rid of these laws."[131] Some workers, like John Major of Chester, told Moore unequivocally that right to work laws were "anti-labor" and that 14 (b) should be repealed on that basis alone. Major stated that the repeal was "vitally important to myself and other working people."[132]

While some in Hancock County called for the repeal of section 14 (b), many more constituents sent letters to Arch Moore asking him to preserve 14 (b). Some framed the issue as a question of individual freedoms, not of union protections. Mrs. William J. McConnell of Weirton explained that she did not "believe a person should be forced to become a member of any organization against their wishes" because that was "contrary to our basic heritage and the American way of life." She explained, "Whether or not we believe in labor union is not the question. The vital question is 'should the American working man be forced to become a member of a labor union in order to keep his job?'"[133] Moore proceeded cautiously and replied to correspondents, "I am confident that this Congress will take affirmative action right away."[134] Privately, he agreed "one hundred percent" with Frank Rich, president of Wheeling Steel, that it was, in Rich's words, "un-American and immoral to deny any person the freedom of choice whether or not to join or not to join any organization" and "absolutely wrong to force a person to join any organization to get or to hold a job."[135] On July 28, 1965, perhaps listening to those voters who wanted to check union powers, Moore voted against repealing section 14 (b). Nevertheless, the House passed the bill to repeal section 14 (b), but it did not become law because the Senate did not allow it to come to the floor for a vote.[136]

The concerns of working-class voters in Hancock County about the possibility of corruption in unions and the abuse of power by union leaders suggest that Moore was indeed a candidate who represented their desire for local control and not just a smooth-talking politician (although he was that as well). When they wrote to Moore, they asked him to take positions that stood in opposition to the visions of labor liberals. Clearly, the conservative unionism of workers in Hancock County after World War II dovetailed with Moore's politics despite the low rating he received from COPE during his tenure in office. Moore also listened carefully when industrial workers asked that he help their industries compete with foreign imports, which is discussed in chapter 6.

Conclusion

In 1959, some five hundred thousand USWA members across the nation went on strike, their fifth national strike in ten years. The steelworkers exhibited remarkable collective discipline, walking out together and coming back together after 116 days. Two decades of shop stewards preaching the importance of solidarity, two decades of improvements in wages and benefits, and repeatedly walking the picket lines with their fellow workers had welded them into an effective organization that recognized the value of unified national action.[137] While USWA members were making withdrawals from their savings accounts and deferring payments on their mortgages, Weirton steelworkers continued to receive regular paychecks and were grateful.

During the 1940s and 1950s, the historical experiences and the values of the rural-industrial workers of Hancock County diverged from their urban counterparts in the CIO and national unions. While industrial workers in cities like Chicago and Detroit turned to national unions and Democratic Party politics, participated in national strikes, and reaped the benefits of disciplined national strikes, the rural-industrial workers in Hancock County had little contact with national labor organizations. After experiencing defeats and setbacks in the 1930s, these steel and pottery workers began to work within a largely local system of negotiations. They appealed to state inspectors and took advantage of new federal labor laws, but they also exhibited a preference for local control and a suspicion of distant bureaucracies. Such views overlapped with the positions of employers, who portrayed distant labor bosses as corrupt and dictatorial, but local companies did not dictate the values and choices of their employees. Working within the localized system and using formal and informal means, the industrial workers of Hancock County exacted better wages and benefits from their employers. They recognized limits to what companies—especially the potteries—could afford, but their wages and benefits compared favorably with those of industrial workers around the country, which helped them achieve a modest but comfortable standard of living. Finally, they elected officials that struck a balance between supporting collective bargaining while placing limits on the strength of unions and union leaders.

Yet the rural-industrial workers of Hancock County were still motivated by economic insecurities, as were their counterparts in major northern cities. In Chicago and Detroit, industrial workers had replaced older survival strategies—ethnic churches and fraternal organizations—with unions, national strikes, and mass politics. During the 1940s and 1950s, new white, working-class homeowners in major cities turned to their unions to protect their privilege in the workplace, waged street battles over racial integration, and elected politicians who were sensitive to working-class concerns about property values. In Hancock County, the rural-industrial workers—who faced no racial integration in these years—turned to self-help activities in and around the home to safeguard their standard of living, the same survival strategies they had used on farms. In the rural-industrial environment, that meant "making do," which encompassed a myriad of rural skills that helped them stretch their earnings and do for themselves. The next chapter explores these rural self-help skills, which reinforced a culture that looked inward rather than outward, strengthening rural-industrial workers' localism.

CHAPTER 5

WORK AND IDENTITY IN THE FACTORY AND AT HOME

By the end of the 1940s, steel and pottery workers in Hancock County had had very different experiences from urban-industrial workers. Workers in big cities who belonged to locals of the Congress of Industrial Organizations (CIO) became incorporated into the national labor movement through participation in national strikes as well as through the CIO's culture of unity. They looked to the Democratic Party to strengthen labor rights and to create federal programs that would be their safety net in hard times. After abandoning their old survival strategies such as relying on local ethnic charities and fraternal organizations, many CIO families now credited unionization and the Democratic Party for their improved standard of living. The changes they experienced were so dramatic that many working-class homes in cities across the country had photographs of John L. Lewis and Franklin Roosevelt hanging on the living room wall. Industrial workers in Hancock County were lucky enough to keep working through most of the 1930s, did not participate in national strikes that resulted in better wages and benefits, and often focused on their old strategy of "making do" to improve their standard of living. The work experiences of families in Hancock County strengthened a rural-industrial culture that privileged place and localized community over national unions and distant bureaucracies.

Although the experiences of these rural-industrial workers diverged from the experiences of urban-industrial workers in several ways, one important commonality was that work, whether at home or in the factories, tended to be organized by gender. Because gender was so fundamental to the organization of work, it provides an important lens onto the daily experiences of Hancock County's rural-industrial workers. The gendered division of labor in the factories evolved in the 1940s and 1950s. Potteries hired increasing numbers of women to fill more and more roles in the production process. The fact that pottery wages fell behind steel wages in these decades contributed to the declining percentage of men in the potteries as they sought a family wage. At the same time, Weirton—where the mill was "no place for a woman"—became a town of steelworkers and housewives with few job opportunities for women, especially married women. At home, women and men fell back into more familiar gender roles as they produced their own food, made their own clothing, and built their own houses. Rural-industrial workers believed in "making do" to stretch their family income, performing self-help activities that harked back to older work patterns on the farms that many of them had left behind. Thus there were two gender divisions of labor operating in parallel: one at home and another in the factory, one derived from rural self-sufficiency and the other from industrial production.

Neither the gendered patterns of work nor the rural-industrial workers' adaptations to them were unique in America at this time. In cities across the nation, factory managers replaced male workers with female workers, and the urban working class experienced a gender division of labor at home. What was different in Hancock County compared to places like Detroit or Chicago was that rural-industrial workers relied far more on self-help activities to achieve a comfortable standard of living, and far from drawing them into a national network of unionists or into national politics, these survival strategies emphasized the importance of workers' families, their local community, and the land around them. By adapting rural habits to the dictates of industrial capitalism, many working families in Hancock County maintained an important connection to their rural past, complicating their entry into the New Deal alliance in which urban-industrial workers played such a central role.

Shifting Gender Lines in the Potteries

During and after World War II, the mills and potteries of Hancock County pursued two different employment strategies. Weirton Steel hired large numbers of women during the war, but after the war, managers once again restricted women to clerical work and the assorting room. The pottery companies, on the other hand, increasingly relied on female labor. For working-class women, pottery jobs paid far better than housecleaning, waitressing, or other service industry wage work available to them. They worked variously to achieve specific financial goals, permanently increase household income, or sometimes because they liked working and earning their own income.[1] In an industry where profit margins were thin and labor costs represented half of the overall production costs, companies wanted to hire more female potters because they historically made lower wages. And because the potteries were located near thriving steel mills, they struggled to attract men, who could earn much higher wages in the mill. Finally, the percentage of female potters increased because, whether by design or chance, new production technology like tunnel kilns, iron horses, and automatic jiggers eliminated the jobs of once highly paid, skilled workers, most of whom were men.

In the early 1940s, the head of a jiggering crew might still hire his son to be his mold runner, a nephew his batter-out, and his wife the finisher, but craftsmen no longer exercised unquestioned authority as they once did. With the installation of automatic jiggers in 1941, the National Brotherhood of Operative Potters (NBOP) and the United States Potters' Association (USPA) decided that female finishers would be employees of the company, not of the jiggermen.[2] That year at Hall China Company in East Liverpool, some women still worked for jiggermen while others worked directly for the company. One woman wrote anonymously to NBOP president James Duffy to complain about the poor wages of female helpers who reported to jiggermen. A "person starting at any trade," she wrote, was entitled to 20 percent below the minimum, but if a jiggerman hired a finisher she started on a piecework basis. As a result, some of "these girls" who were hired by jiggermen made $4.83 for eighty hours of work. Such arrangements were once the norm, but they no longer made sense to this anonymous complainant. In a union shop, why did it make a difference whether the company or a jiggerman hired a woman, seeing how "one has to live the same as the other?"[3]

During World War II, gender structures of factory work changed dramatically across the country as companies scrambled to replace the men who had gone off to war and keep up with increased demand. Because the pottery industry had long hired women, the changes in the potteries were more subtle than in nearly-all-male workplaces like automobile plants or steel mills. Sterling China of Wellsville, Ohio, was the first local pottery to secure a defense contract to produce thicker and heavier hotelware, which would stand up well to frequent use in army mess halls. Because they had one of the few companies already producing hotelware, Sterling's owners found themselves trying to keep up with extraordinary demand. One owner's son, Bill Pomeroy, recalled that potters joked that "even if it was only half a piece, if it still held gravy you could pack it and ship it."⁴ When Sterling could not keep up with the Department of Defense demands, Homer Laughlin won a contract and converted to producing hotelware for the first time. Between 1942 and 1944, Homer Laughlin produced one million dozen all-white dishes: saucers, unhandled cups, handled mugs, and jugs. Interestingly, the war effort resulted in one other change: the company discontinued production of its brilliant red Fiestaware. To achieve its coloring, the company had used uranium now needed for the Manhattan Project.⁵

The new defense contracts and the dramatic decline in imports during the war resulted in a tremendous boom for the pottery industry, and company executives were anxious to keep up with demand. In October 1941, even before America entered the war, the *Weirton Daily Times* reported that the ceramics industry—the county's "second greatest industry"—was experiencing one of its "greatest periods of prosperity." Joseph M. Wells, secretary treasurer of Homer Laughlin, said that his company was "turning out more in dozens and dollars than ever before" largely because their raw materials were not essential to defense industries. He thought that at some point they might be faced with a shortage of railcars "because of the demands for troop movements and transportation of defense goods," but for the time being they were turning out three hundred thousand pieces of dinnerware per day. And he noted, "We can sell more if we could make it."⁶

The problem was finding enough workers to keep up with demand. Of a total adult male population of a little more than twelve thousand, a third of Hancock County's men—4,356 to be exact—served in the armed forces during the war, leaving numerous vacancies in the county's industrial plants.⁷ By 1943, Wells reported to the United States Potters Association convention that no pottery had three-quarters of the workforce it had had just two years earlier. The potteries had always employed women, but during the war they began to rely on women even more. Companies also hired high school students during the summer even though they would have to quit when school resumed in the fall.⁸ Fay Haught began her long career in the potteries as one of those high school students during the war. When she was sixteen years old, she got a job at TS&T in Chester in the brush room, where she brushed the dust off of bisque ware. At the end of the summer, she decided not to go back to school for her senior year but to work full time at nearby Harker Pottery. She brought her paychecks home to help her parents pay the bills and raise the younger children. After three years at Harker, she quit to get married and start her own family, but she would eventually return to the potteries.⁹

As in other industries during World War II, women were hired into jobs that they previously had not worked. A 1937 survey of pottery occupations in West

Virginia shows that there were no women in the generalware potteries working as batter-outs, mold runners, or hand truckers (ware movers). By 1944, there were forty-nine female batter-outs, six female mold runners, and thirty-five female hand truckers. There were other occupations women already had, and their numbers in these jobs increased significantly during the war. Before the war, few women worked as casters, injecting liquid clay into casts. In 1937, only four of the 312 casters were women, but by 1944 their numbers had increased to 60 of 418. Overall, the potteries of West Virginia in 1937 had a workforce that was 37 percent female. The 1944 survey of potteries in the East Liverpool district found that workforce to be 46 percent female, a 24 percent increase.[10]

At the same time that the percentage of women in the potteries was growing, women were also swelling the ranks of an NBOP reinvigorated by the Wagner Act. Their wages increased dramatically but not without their fighting both the companies and the union. In 1941, the mostly female finishers of NBOP Local 53 refused to accept their low wages and were equally disappointed with their union representative, Joshua Chadwick. Gladys Hartzell, the recording secretary of Local 53, explained to President Duffy that when Chadwick visited Hall China to help settle the hourly rate, he turned against the finishers, questioning the rate they thought they deserved. Hartzell demanded that Duffy "enlighten Mr. Chadwick on this matter."[11] The following year Chadwick arrived to settle a dispute for the finishers of Plant No. 7 at Homer Laughlin. The finishers believed they should be paid seventy-five cents per hour and were outraged when Chadwick investigated the situation but did not "take any of the finishers with him when he talked to Mr. Wells." Demanding that their voices be heard, Hartzell told Duffy to send another representative who would take a committee of finishers with him.[12]

After the U.S. entered the war, the National War Labor Board (NWLB) supervised labor contracts using the so-called "Little Steel" formula, which was designed to control inflation by restricting wage increases. As a result, the highest paid workers received small wage increases during the war. The 1942 agreement frustrated male unionists because it met few of the union's demands. Yet female workers benefited tremendously from the new contract because it established minimum wages for occupations that were mostly female, such as warehousewomen, women handle finishers, cup spongers, packers, and handle casters.[13] By the end of the war, they were enjoying far better wages as a result of working directly for the company and having a minimum wage established.

During the late 1940s and through the 1950s, men—especially highly skilled men—saw their numbers in the East Liverpool district dwindle while women made important gains. The number of male jiggermen declined from 284 in 1944 to 172 in 1953 and 99 by 1959. The number of male kilnmen, kiln drawers, and kiln firemen dropped from 643 in 1944 down to 427 by 1959, a loss of one-third in fifteen years. Even though between 1944 and 1953 the overall percentage of female potters in the East Liverpool district dropped from 46 percent to 42, that was still greater than the 1937 figure of 37 percent. Most female potters worked in the same trades they had for decades: warehousewomen, which included brushers and ware dressers (796), followed by decorators (531) and finishers (207).[14] Yet women increased their numbers in a handful of occupations like mold runner and batter-out. In 1944, 80 percent of the 243 batter-outs in the district were men, but by 1959 only 59 percent were (table 5).[15] Women saw their percentage of the operatives in the pottery industry increase from 42 percent in 1940 to 47 percent in 1950 and 43 percent in 1960. They accounted for only 10 percent of the laborers in the potteries in 1940 but 22 percent by 1960.[16]

Wages in the pottery industry had long reflected a hierarchy of skill and gender. In the Staffordshire potbanks in the nineteenth century, women had a separate wage scale from the men, and only the most skilled "paintresses" earned more than the least skilled male laborers.[17] Wage inequalities remained in the East Liverpool district after World War II. In 1945, the highest wage potteries in the East Liverpool district paid to newly hired women was $0.55 an hour compared to the $0.70 an hour that a newly hired male common laborer made. Furthermore, 90 percent of the women made between $0.52 and $0.75 an hour, which was considerably lower than most male potters, 66 percent of whom earned between $0.99 and $1.59 an hour.[18] The gilders and liners department had roughly an equal number of men and women, about 190 of each sex. These workers carefully hand painted lines of gold on the outer edges of plates or around the rims of cups. In 1944, it was also one of the highest paid jobs for men and women, but men made $1.55 an hour compared to $1.17 an hour for women.[19] Lula "Pug" Rigdon remembered that in the 1960s, men "always made more" than women no matter what their trade was. This point was dramatically illustrated to her when three male gold liners complained that they did not make enough money, even though gold lining was the highest paid female occupation.[20]

Because steel mills offered higher wages, potteries often employed men whose family had a long tradition of working the potteries or men who were unable to get work in the mills. In 1966, pottery owners Joe Wells Jr. and John Hall reported that the industry would face a serious shortage of skilled operatives as older workers started to retire and the only men available to become apprentices were "high school drop-outs and older men not hireable in other industries." Wells and Hall advocated hiring women to be apprentices because,

TABLE 5. East Liverpool–Chester–Newell District Locals by Gender, 1953, 1959

Local Union	Trade	1953			1959		
		Male	Female	Total	Male	Female	Total
4	Casters	255	12	267	156	5	161
9	Kilnmen	368	0	368	270	6	276
10	Turners and Handlers	115	0	115	88	0	88
12	Jiggermen	172	0	172	99	0	99
16	Saggermakers	124	0	124	101	0	101
17	Kilndrawers	105	0	105	79	0	79
18	Dippers	61	0	61	32	0	32
21	Clay makers	112	0	112	102	0	102
22	Mold makers	64	0	64	43	0	43
25	Packers	116	0	116	90	0	90
29	Dish makers	34	0	34	26	0	26
53	Finishers	6	231	237	0	207	207
86	Warehousemen	504	0	504	411	0	411
94	Warehousewomen*	0	569	569	0	459	459
124	Decorators, tinters, decorating kilnmen, liners, etc.	242	807	1049	148	531	679

TABLE 5. Continued

Local Union	Trade	1953			1959		
		Male	Female	Total	Male	Female	Total
130	Kilnfiremen	97	0	97	78	0	78
131	Mold Runners and Batter-Outs	196	60	256	117	80	197
132	Handle Casters and Finishers	22	83	105	11	59	70
133	Bisque warehousemen	290	0	290	264	0	264
140	Porcelain workers	81	43	124	70	41	111
141	Laborers and Oddmen	236	1	237	227	0	227
148	Color workers and waxers	82	148	230	49	123	172
155	Underglaze workers	0	107	107	0	61	61
163	Pottery supply workers	61	35	96	76	29	105
172	Maintenance men	95	0	95	161	0	161
186	Porcelain workers	102	30	132	52	19	71
195	Warehousewomen	0	484	484	0	337	337
Totals		3540	2610	6150	2750	1957	4707
		58%	42%	100%	58%	42%	100%

Source: IBOP Papers, Box 62, Folder 3 (lists trades and district locals) and Folder 5 (lists of local memberships, 1953, 1959).
*The 1953 list had 569 males and 0 females for Washerwomen, when clearly it should have been 569 females and 0 males.

in the experience of the Homer Laughlin plants, they were "entirely satisfactory in productivity and workmanship."[21] Their plan was consistent with changes the potteries had been making for decades: increasing the number of women on the job and placing them in previously all-male occupations.

Viewing the issue from a different perspective, male pottery workers and union leaders saw the prestige and pay of the potteries declining and in need of fixing. In the early decades of the twentieth century, potters were the aristocrats of labor, but by the 1960s young people looked for jobs in steel mills first and potteries second. Increasingly, local residents came to associate low-wage, low-prestige jobs with the potteries.[22] The growing number of women working in the potteries and the declining status of pottery work was no coincidence, as many industrialists and workers alike had long associated women's work with low wages. Some observed that it was a failing of the pottery industry to reach the high levels of productivity that would have enabled men to make high enough wages to support stay-at-home wives.[23] In the 1960s, IBOP president Edwin Wheatley agreed, arguing that the industry suffered from a lack of modern machinery and that automation would increase productivity.[24] In the 1950s and 1960s, automation in other industries sometimes led companies to replace multiple female workers with a single male worker at a higher pay rate.[25] Pottery union officials believed that technological advances in their industry would increase profits, enable companies to pay higher wages, and add to the prestige of the industry, no doubt increasing its percentage of male workers at the same time. In reality, new technologies had repeatedly led to greater percentages of women and that would not change in the coming decades.

The pottery workers' union had a long history of accepting women in the workplace and at times courting their support. During the 1940s and 1950s, the union needed the solidarity of female workers, and editors of the union journal, the *Potters Herald*, almost always used inclusive language and reminded readers of the importance of female participation. In 1943, one editorial read, "Women Are Here to Stay," explaining that more than nineteen million women were working, more than half of whom were married. It noted that women tended to receive less money, highlighting the need for "equal pay for equal work," which, the editor noted, was the "program of Labor Unions."[26] In 1955, when a newspaper columnist charged the labor movement with gender discrimination, the editor of the *Potters Herald* insisted that "nothing could be further from the truth." He said that it is "so clearly understood that the trade union movement is opposed to pay discrimination against women" that they did not even need it explicitly stated in the AFL-CIO constitution.[27] In the 1960s and early 1970s, the journalistic standards of the *Potters Herald* declined, and the articles seldom mentioned women—or any workers for that matter—but occasional stories focused on women workers, especially stories celebrating retirements. In 1972, the journal profiled the sixty-year career of Mollie McGown. The eighty-four-year-old started as a dipper's helper at Homer Laughlin in 1912, joined the union in 1933, held numerous positions in the union, and raised three daughters who also grew up to be potters at Homer Laughlin.[28]

The working women of Hancock County did not typically live in male-dominated households. Pottery worker Fay Haught recalled that her husband did not want her to return to work after the kids were all in school. She said, "He didn't want me to drive. Lots of things he didn't want me to do, but I did them anyways."[29] Pug Rigdon worked at Homer Laughlin China while her husband worked at a steel mill in Pennsylvania. For Pug, equality at home was perfectly natural. She and her husband shared equally in the responsibilities of paying bills and making financial decisions. Of course, she noted, they did not have much money to argue about in the first place.[30] Linda Dickey got a job in the pottery in the early 1970s and felt empowered by her union membership. She had just quit a job in a grocery store because the store manager sexually harassed her, and her coworkers advised her to either ignore him or quit; there was no other recourse. In the pottery, however, she soon learned that she was "not alone" because the union was there to support her and enabled her to stand up to male supervisors.[31]

Breadwinners and Housewives in Weirton

The Weirton job market for women contrasted starkly with the job market for women in the pottery towns. In the pottery towns, about one-third of the women had wage jobs compared to one-fifth in Weirton.[32] Furthermore, while women accounted for an increasing proportion of West Virginia pottery workers between 1940 and 1960, their proportion of the steel industry workforce decreased. In 1940, women accounted for 10 percent of all operatives in the state's steel mills, but that figure decreased to 4 percent in 1950 and to only 1 percent by 1960.[33] Because the potteries hired married women, women working in the pottery tended to have longer careers as evidenced by the age distribution of the two workforces. Whereas in 1950, 30 percent of female West Virginia steelworkers were under the age of twenty-four, only 16 percent of the female stone and clay workers in the state were that young. Furthermore, only 15 percent of female steelworkers were over the age of forty-five compared to 30 percent of the female potters.[34] In the potteries, married women gained acceptance, unlike in the steel mill, where female workers were expected to be single or widowed.

World War II proved to be an exceptional time for the gender division of labor in Weirton. In 1940, roughly 95 percent of steelworkers in Hancock County were men.[35] When the war began, Weirton Steel hired women as never before. The company secured defense contracts to produce eight-inch artillery shells for the war effort, and it employed mostly women in the new shell plant. It also struggled to keep up with the demand for steel while facing a labor shortage. In March 1942, the mill ran at 99.8 percent of total capacity and broke its record for steel ingot production with 153,823 tons that month.[36]

As more and more men joined the military, Weirton Steel, like many other mills, promoted and hired women into previously all-male positions. At first, steel companies transferred male clerks to production jobs and backfilled their positions with women. As the labor shortage got worse, they hired women to be cranemen, operatives at the rolling mills, stampers and metal fabricators, and maintenance workers. Only the strongest women could meet the physical demands of many labor gang jobs, such as wielding eighty-pound pneumatic jackhammers.[37] Some were also placed in more physically demanding labor jobs but often had to double up on particularly challenging tasks or simply leave some of the heaviest lifting to men. Some women who became crane operators found that work physically less challenging than sorting and inspecting tin—the only mill jobs previously available to women—and it paid considerably better wages.[38] A few steel companies even hired African American women for the first time, but only placed them in the jobs reserved for African American men: labor positions in coke ovens, blast furnaces, and sintering plants. Company and government literature during wartime often portrayed black women as being tougher or huskier, but after the war they were once again largely banished from these relatively lucrative mill jobs.[39]

When journalist R. H. Markham visited Weirton Steel in 1945, he witnessed the peak of wartime production. He was amazed to see "girls handle 10-ton sticks of red hot steel almost as easily as a powder puff." One "girl without the slightest confusion" sent her "magic crane" to pick up an ingot that had fallen off a conveyor belt "as easily as a cat might put an erring kitten back into the basket." Another woman he observed sat at a lever sending steel ingots into the rolling mills "as easily as an office girl types figures." Markham witnessed a mill mechanized to the point that men became "jinns" and women became "giants," as they shove steel around like "Jupiter was once reputed to handle lightning bolts."[40] To a large extent, mechanization had eliminated much of the logic of sex-typing jobs, which held that the physical nature of steel industry tasks dictated that men perform most of the work. *Life* magazine observed that in England and Russia, they had always accepted the concept of the "weaker sex" sweating away near blast furnaces or ladles of molten iron, but it was only because of the extraordinary wartime circumstances that American steel companies made this "revolutionary adjustment."[41]

During the postwar years, a combination of factors led to the reconstruction of the sexual division of labor. Some women readily stepped aside for returning veterans, seniority forced others out of their jobs, and many men and women renewed their commitment to the ideal of female domesticity. State legislators reinstated laws designed to protect women from hazardous working conditions after the war, which facilitated the return to male domination of steel mill jobs. Women who were unable to return to the life of a housewife had to accept low-wage and low-prestige jobs because of the renewed sexual division of labor, which insisted that the steel mill was "no place for a woman."[42]

After the war, women with the seniority to stay in the mill found themselves back in the assorting room. The technology in the assorting room had not changed since the 1890s, probably because it was one of the mill's few low-wage departments. Assorters still inspected the sheets of tinplate individually for flaws and sorted them by hand onto skids based on the nature of the defect. The *Weirton Steel Employees Bulletin* featured the "Women of the Tin Mill" in 1957, showing pictures of Helen Tonski measuring the height of a stack of tinplate and Catherine Victor holding up a "mirror-like" sheet of Weirite (sheet steel with a patented coating). Minnie Pirraglia, being a "safety-minded" employee, wore leather gloves and a heavy apron. The article boasted that the "skill of such veteran Assorters" as Helen Levenson and Merion Knell ensured that Weirton Steel would be synonymous with top quality.[43]

Working in the assorting room was not as pleasant as the *Employees Bulletin* suggested. The edges of those sheets, Ramona "Boots" Hines recalled, were like razor blades that left scars on many women's arms as they hustled to inspect their quota for the day, a stack of sheets forty inches high. The foreladies strictly timed the assorters' breaks and permitted only a fifteen-minute break in the morning and afternoon and a thirty-minute break for lunch. Flopping tin would really "take a toll" on girls that were not used to hard work, Hines remembered. Worse yet, after the summer canning months were over and demand for their tinplate dropped, the company laid off many assorters. Because of the layoffs, she could not buy a house until she turned fifty years old. She always worried: "Now if I should get laid off, I could feed the boys and take care of them. But if I lost my job . . . I couldn't make a big house payment and take care of everything. They were all big eaters." During layoffs, Hines cleaned houses for ten dollars a day and used five dollars to "feed the boys" and the other five to pay bills. Women tolerated the layoffs and unpleasant conditions because working as assorters was by far the most lucrative postwar job a woman could get in Weirton.[44]

After the war, Weirton Steel also returned to its policy of employing unmarried women only. Margaret Heaton remembered that "down at the tin mill, if you were married you did not work." She only knew of two married women for whom Weirton Steel made an exception (probably because of nepotism). Normally when supervisors discovered that a woman was married, they fired her. That was also the policy for the general office, or G.O. as most called it: "When you got married, you knew that you didn't have a job. That was just understood."[45] Boots Hines was married for ten years and also recalled, "You couldn't work at Weirton Steel if you were married." Some women would "sneak off" to another state to get married, she said, but there was "always somebody to squeal on them." Those who were discovered to be married would be "out of a job." After she divorced her husband, Hines was able to get a job working in the assorting room so she could raise her three boys.[46]

Outside of the mill, there also were comparatively few job opportunities for women, especially married women, in Weirton. Women could find jobs as secretaries for some of the professionals in town, cashiers at local grocery stores, schoolteachers, nurses at the mill, or as domestic workers cleaning houses. In Weirton, the leading occupational categories among the 1,683 employed women were clerical (26 percent), operatives (19 percent), sales workers (15 percent), service workers (14 percent), professional (including teachers and nurses) (12 percent), and private household workers (7 percent).[47]

The restrictive job market in Weirton may have made little difference to the wives of male steelworkers, but widows and divorcees competed for very few mill jobs. Those who could not get jobs in the mill struggled to make a living in the service sector. Alma Haning lived in Weirton, and in 1943, at the age of forty-nine, faced this unfavorable labor market when her husband died unexpectedly. Alma got a job as a nurse's aid making $4.00 a day. By 1957, after several raises, she was making $7.05 but still struggled to pay her bills. She said that though she earned much less, she still paid the same price for goods as people who made "Weirton Steel money." Haning observed that she was not alone; there were many other women who were struggling. Once married and now "too old or poor to further their education," these women were "forced to take any jobs in hospitals (laundries, dietary, aid) and restaurants, small offices and clerking jobs."[48] These service and retail jobs not only paid low wages but were sometimes degrading, as customers and supervisors treated women workers with contempt. This was not an uncommon scenario for women in postwar America.[49]

Many families in Weirton achieved the male breadwinner ideal with husbands working in the mill, wives staying at home, and children staying in school. In the 1950s, the *Weirton Steel Employee Bulletin* reinforced that family structure. For example, one article listed the many roles that "Weirton Steel Mothers" (whose husbands worked in the mill) played at home: meal planner, practical nurse, seamstress, and child psychologist. In photographs that accompanied the article, Mrs. James Ayers, whose husband worked in the Steel Works Stores Department, was shown cooking for her three daughters, and Mrs. William Davies, whose husband was a Steel Works mechanic, posed with her two small children, whom she had just dressed. Mrs. Frank Zablackas, the article noted, spent "many busy hours" sewing for her "Weirton Steel family of five sons and one daughter."[50]

Another article in the *Weirton Steel Employee Bulletin*, titled "Hobbies Keep Them Happy," showed that women who spent "their working days assorting or inspecting tinplate in the Tin Mill" pursued traditionally female leisure activities at home in the evening, knitting in a group, making colorful oil paintings, hand painting antique lamps, taking care of shrubbery, or collecting antique pitchers.[51] One page in the bulletin reserved for women called "Embracing All Women" featured recipes appropriate for the season, wedding photographs, fashion tips, and photographs of women's clubs.[52] These articles suggested that women steelworkers retained their femininity despite working in such a masculine workplace.

Blue-Collar Wages and Self-Help Activities

Between 1940 and 1960, rural-industrial workers in Hancock County—just like their urban counterparts across the country—enjoyed dramatic wage increases that helped them rise above the poverty line and achieve what the Bureau of Labor Statistics called the modest budget for a family of four. On that budget, they could afford to rent a three-bedroom apartment, eat cheaper cuts of meat several times a week, go to the movie theater every three weeks, and buy two pairs of pants and three shirts every year for each growing boy. But they could not afford to own a car or take a vacation. It was in 1953 that the average American steelworker was first able to afford the minimum standard of living set by the BLS and 1958 when the lowest-paid steelworkers achieved it.[53] Their annual income would have been about $42,000 in 2014 dollars.[54] That would have been when steelworkers could afford to become a single-income household. The wages of Hancock County steelworkers, as discussed in the previous chapter, kept pace with average wages for the industry nationally—so they were no poorer than steelworkers in Pittsburgh or Chicago—but like those urban counterparts, they too struggled to achieve the minimum standard of living through the 1940s and early 1950s. Most potters could only achieve the minimum standards throughout these decades by having two incomes.

The gap between blue-collar wages and a comfortable standard of living encouraged rural-industrial workers to engage in self-help activities, many of which were habits of a rural existence. In the 1940s, this was not unique to rural-industrial workers, as urban-industrial workers also pursued some "make do" strategies. In 1949, journalist David Dempsey spent a week with steelworkers in Pittsburgh and found that only by "meticulous budgeting, making many of the children's clothes, keeping a garden, and 'making out the grocery order with a pruning knife'" would they have enough left over for an occasional trip to the movies or a ball game.[55] In Johnstown, Pennsylvania, Johnny Metzgar, like other steelworkers, could "build, fix, or grow all kinds of things in and around the house" and his wife, Irene, could can "all manner of fruits and vegetables" and make low-cost casseroles.[56]

As densely populated cities passed increasingly restrictive zoning ordinances, there were limits on self-help activities. One study of South Gate, a working-class suburb of Los Angeles, found that in the 1920s it was a "borderland between rural and urban life," but by the 1950s it was no longer a "suburb of ratty owner-built homes, unpaved roads, kerosene lamps, and yards overgrown with fruits, vegetables, and small livestock. Now it looked more like its middle-class counterpart: paved streets, orderly rows of matching homes, yards of lawns and flowers, and plenty of street lamps."[57] During the 1940s and 1950s—two decades of great national strikes—urban-industrial workers abandoned many rural habits and put tremendous faith in the ability of unions rather than hunting or canning vegetables to continue to improve their lives. Johnny Metzgar might have been able to build and fix all kinds of things, but he preached the virtues of unionism to family and friends, not the importance of gardening or home repair. To him, history could be divided into two periods: "before the union" and "since the union." And although he might brag about filling his freezer with walleyes from his fishing trips, he credited the union with everything they enjoyed as a family right down to the curtains that hung in the living room.[58]

Thus, Hancock County and places like South Gate or Johnstown were not as different as night and day. Obviously some industrial workers in cities continued a variety of self-help activities, and not all of Hancock County's steel and pottery workers chose to raise their own food or keep livestock in the backyard. Some chose to focus their energies on living a frugal life rather than engaging in self-help activities. Those who lived in one of the few apartment buildings in Weirton and took the bus to work every day would have had little opportunity for any meaningful self-help activities. And there were migrants who came from major cities with few if any rural folkways. Francis Asfour, for example, left Haifa in 1948 when the Israelis took the city over, and she and her husband came to Weirton in 1955 when the Eisenhower administration distributed forty thousand visas to Arab refugees. Asfour's initial impression was that some homes in Weirton looked like "an army barrack" compared to the beautiful homes, churches, and scenic vistas of Haifa.[59]

Yet rural or "borderland" conditions persisted in Hancock County throughout the twentieth century, and better understanding the small towns and rural places where residents lived will help us gauge the extent to which they could have continued their rural ways. Doing that requires a careful examination of population statistics. By 1960, the county's population reached 39,615, and roughly 24,000 of them were part of the Steubenville-Weirton Urbanized Area, which the U.S. Census judged to have a population of 80,717. A city of 80,000 is hardly a rural or small-town setting, but this statistical area included Steubenville, Ohio, with a population about 32,000, Weirton with its population of 28,000, and another 20,000 who lived outside of those two cities, including the residents of Mingo Junction, Ohio (5,000), Follansbee, West Virginia (4,000), Wintersville, Ohio (2,700), and Brilliant, Ohio (2,100). Hancock County's remaining 15,000 residents were not part of the urbanized area. They were divided between Chester (3,700), New Cumberland (2,000), Newell (1,800), and rural areas in the county (7,500).[60] Thus the urbanized area was the compilation of two cities separated by the Ohio River and several small towns, and it did not include the pottery towns or the county's 7,500 other residents.

To be sure, Weirton in the 1950s was a far different place than the collection of dirt roads and company houses it once had been, but even the residents who grew up there in the 1940s and 1950s still recalled producing a significant amount of their food at home. Henry Burns remembered that when he was growing up, his family's company house on Sixth Street in the North End had a big backyard, big enough, he said, "to have a pig pen back there, a place for our goats, a place for the dog, chicken coop, everything." They ordered chickens out of a catalog. "In the wintertime," he said, "we'd have them in the house in a box with a light in it until they got big enough. We'd put them in the yard. And then, after they'd laid enough eggs for us, we'd kill them and eat them." They would keep some fifty or sixty chickens, and his job was to feed them, collect the eggs, and shoot any rats or snakes that tried to get in the coop. Because Weirton remained unincorporated until the late 1940s, there were few building codes and zoning ordinances, and working-class families could build outbuildings and fences and raise a variety of livestock.⁶¹ Frank Gregory's family, who came from Union County, South Carolina, also raised hogs and chickens in the North End. On one side of their lot, he recalled, a Greek neighbor had sheep and goats and on the other side an Italian family kept hogs. He remembered watching the Italian family bleed a hog out and collect the blood to make blood pudding.⁶²

Household production of food—while no longer critical to family survival—provided workers with more variety in their diets, a sense of accomplishment and self-reliance, and an additional layer of security. Workers who had greater access to the land could engage in these self-help activities on a larger scale, and in Hancock County, most residents, even in Weirton, had access to hunting grounds and a small patch where they could garden and raise livestock. During World War II, Weirton Steel set aside land near the river for workers to clear and cultivate. Those living on the outskirts of Weirton could have large livestock and cornfields.⁶³

Weirton's city code increasingly regulated the raising of livestock in the city limits. By the 1950s, the city required anyone raising domestic fowl or pigeons to follow strict guidelines, locating coops more than sixty feet from a house; keeping it dry, well-lit, ventilated, and whitewashed; cleaning it twice weekly during summer months; and keeping the yard free of all decaying animal or vegetable matter. The city also prohibited residents from slaughtering animals within the city limits except in places approved by the health department. Finally, the code declared it unlawful for people to keep any animals that "by barking, howling, squalling, crying or in any other manner whatsoever, disturb the comfort or quiet of any neighborhood within the limits of the city."⁶⁴ Such strict regulations made it more and more difficult for residents in the city limits to raise livestock for meat, milk, and eggs.

Even after the new codes were enacted, those living on the outskirts of Weirton continued to raise livestock. Frank Maslowski raised rabbits for food in a housing development in Weirton Heights. He recalled, "I had maybe twenty little bunnies at one time."⁶⁵ Alex Fiedorczyk grew up in the 1950s in what was called King's Creek Bowl over the hill from Weirton's North End. He said that the more popular name for his neighborhood was actually "Cow Shit Valley" because there were "all kind of cows down there in the fields." He remembered that in addition to their garden, his parents raised chickens, pigeons, and even rabbits one time, all of which they would butcher and eat.⁶⁶ By raising their own livestock, workers did not have to settle for only the "cheaper cuts," and they also supplemented their household income.

During the 1950s, many Weirton steelworkers bought land on the outskirts of town or beyond. At this time, the classified section of the *Weirton Daily Times* almost always advertised affordable farms. A steelworker could buy anything from a house foundation on four acres for $3,100 to a 70-acre farm with a five-room bungalow for $8,000.[67] By comparison, the *Chicago Daily Herald* advertised properties that were far more expensive. One two-bedroom house on a five-acre lot for anyone who had been "dreaming of a ranch in the country" cost $17,000. A 120-acre farm, likely being sold for a future housing development, went for $79,500. And 40 acres with a new two-bedroom ranch house only three miles from town went for $45,000.[68] Around 1952, Hugh Snider left rural Wetzel County, West Virginia, and got a job at Weirton Steel. He and his wife, Garnet, initially lived in an apartment above a beer joint in Weirton Heights, but after putting up with the noise and graphite-covered sidewalks for a few years, they bought land just on the other side of the ridge where Kings Creek meanders through a quiet and relatively rural valley. Because they preferred to be "out in the country," in Hugh's words, the rural setting fit the Sniders perfectly, and they planted gardens that were larger than the ones he had in Wetzel County.[69]

Outside of the Weirton city limits, rural-industrial workers faced no restrictions on their agricultural activities. Walter Danna, who worked at Weirton Steel for more than thirty years, grew up in the 1940s and 1950s in Cedar Grove, a small coal town just over the state line from Weirton in Washington County, Pennsylvania. Remembering how important gardens were to families when he was young, he said, "You lived off of that garden basically." He also remembered how older folks in his town would fertilize their gardens. They dropped a bucket down through the hole in the outhouse, brought up human waste, and spread it on the garden. Danna said the old-timers called that "honey-dippin." His family also had a chicken coop and a rabbit hutch when he was a young man. He remembered that where he lived everybody had a chicken coop, and he and his friend would steal eggs from some of the coops at night and boil and eat them. One time when they had leftover hard-boiled eggs, Danna had the idea of putting them back in the nest, and the old Italian woman who lived there found the hard-boiled eggs and thought her neighbor put a curse on her. Some people in the community raised hogs and nearly everybody raised rabbits for meat.[70]

Some factory workers even lived on full-fledged farms. In 1943, 75 percent of the roughly four hundred farms in the county were being operated only on a part-time basis. One survey noted that nearby industries employed a large percentage of local farm residents and that some farmers were evidently spending so much time in the factory that their fields were grown up with broom sedge, goldenrod, sheep sorrel, and second-growth woodland species like black locust and wild cherry trees. Still, these part-time farmers owned between fifty and one hundred acres and raised fifteen acres of hay, eight acres of corn, and six acres of oats. These small, part-time farms reflect the blending of industrial wage work with traditional agriculture.[71]

On their farms, rural-industrial workers planted wheat and corn and raised large livestock like cattle. The *Weirton Steel Employee Bulletin* showed a photograph of Joe Cross, a heater in the hot mill, as he walked behind his oxen and a hand plow in a field "way out on his farm."[72] One retired pottery worker wrote to the *Potters Herald* to praise the union's group insurance. In July 1949, he was mowing hay on his farm and his left arm got caught in the mowing machine. The policy paid him more than $600 for the loss of his arm.[73] Hugh Snider spent an entire career at Weirton Steel, and one of his friends, who had moved from Tyler County to work at Weirton Steel, asked Snider for help tending a herd of cattle on his farm just north of Weirton. The two men worked different shifts, which meant one would always be available to tend the herd. Hugh bought his own calf and cow to keep on the farm, and they sold the cattle at a livestock auction in Ohio.[74]

In 1958, the *Weirton Steel Employees Bulletin* ran a feature titled "Steel Men and the Good Earth" about the some three hundred Weirton Steel employees who went "back to the good earth" each day as they combined "industrial and agricultural lives," enjoying the advantages of both. James H. Pearcy, a slitterman on the tin mill cutting lines, raised Hampshire hogs on his 88-acre farm near New Cumberland, and Steve Chapko from the sheet mill general crew cultivated potatoes with his son on their 136-acre farm near Chester. Since farming often required help from friends and neighbors, it was an activity that could bring men together outside the mill or pottery. Dwight Wylie, who worked in the strip steel department, and his brother-in-law, Theodore Kokochak, who worked in the boiler house, raised hogs and Shorthorn cattle and fertilized fields together. Brothers Steve and James Takach baled hay on their dairy farm near New Cumberland.[75] The profile of these three hundred "Steel Men" obviously did not include the thousands who simply gardened, hunted, and raised food for their own consumption.

Working-Class Women and Self-Help Activities

As they were "making do" at home, families often organized their tasks by gender, and women in Hancock County played a key role in these tasks. Whether because they chose not to get jobs or because they could not get jobs in Weirton's restrictive labor market—where the majority of the county's women lived—many local women remained out of the workforce. In 1950, based on a comparison of data for Hancock County and the counties where Pittsburgh, Detroit, Los Angeles, Chicago, and New York are located, women in Hancock County were more likely to stay at home than their urban counterparts. While male labor force participation in those places ranged from 76 percent to 84 percent (with Hancock County having the highest figure), female labor participation ranged from 43 percent in New York County down to 24 percent in Hancock County (table 6). This may have resulted from the "family wages" in Weirton's steel mills as compared to the wide range of occupations, industries, and incomes that existed in major cities, which likely required two-income households. Nevertheless, because they could stay home rather than seek a second household income, many women in Hancock County engaged in a wide range of self-help activities that improved the family's standard of living.

In the 1940s and 1950s, many middle-class professionals prescribed self-help activities for working-class women, which often included thrifty shopping, a strong work ethic, saving money, and effective home and resource management, skills that rural-industrial women usually learned from their mothers. In 1945, George Strayer, who headed a committee to investigate the state of education in West Virginia, wrote that the state's industries and businesses employed "thousands of girls and women in sales, clerical, and semi-professional positions," but almost all of them would still at some time in their lives "have homes and families as a major life career responsibility," just like "farm women." Strayer declared that West Virginia's ability to train girls and women "as makers and managers of homes" would determine the "extent to which we are a nation of healthy bodies or weaklings, happy or dissatisfied in our daily work, our family resources conserved or frittered."[76] Strayer was one in a long line of professionals who wanted to use public schools to better train girls in home management. Home economics emerged as a formal profession in the early twentieth century as progressives sought to formalize training women in the skills of housekeeping, child rearing, cooking, and sewing, among others. Proponents of home economics saw themselves as "agents of modernity" who hoped that by disseminating the best practices of domestic labor they could improve standards of living for all families.[77]

From the beginning, home economics professionals focused as much attention on the housewife's role of consumer as they did on her role as producer. This was especially true of their efforts to train rural women, whom they often saw as being isolated and ignorant of labor-saving consumer products. In 1951, the West Virginia Extension Service started a "consumer marketing project" in the Weirton area aimed at the thousands of wives of industrial workers. The project sought to educate housewives on nutrition, "good buys" at local grocery

TABLE 6. Male and Female Labor Force Participation by County, 1950

	Females 14 Years and Over			Males 14 Years and Over		
County	Total	In the Labor Force, 1950	Percent	Total	In the Labor Force, 1950	Percent
Hancock, WV	12,355	2,975	24%	12,749	10,697	84%
Allegheny, PA	599,488	156,502	26%	567,497	447,448	79%
Wayne, MI	928,681	278,094	30%	931,245	775,543	83%
Los Angeles, CA	1,701,213	551,708	32%	1,542,328	1,205,701	78%
Cook, IL	1,820,741	657,997	36%	1,723,987	1,412,952	82%
New York, NY	869,264	373,307	43%	780,861	595,876	76%

Source: Historical Census Browser, from the University of Virginia, Geospatial and Statistical Data Center: http://mapserver.lib.virginia.edu, accessed on February 9, 2015.

stores, and family finances, all topics they undoubtedly thought relevant to the families of factory workers.[78]

As opposed to being good consumers, the women in rural-industrial Hancock County—as part of their strategy of making do—tended to focus on producing goods for the family and avoiding buying consumer products whenever possible. Just as they had on the farm a generation earlier, many women in Hancock County tended to small livestock and backyard gardens, raised children, attended to the family's health care needs, and cooked and preserved food, sometimes enlisting their children's help with these tasks. Pottery worker Fay Haught grew up on a farm in the countryside of Hancock County. Her father worked for a commercial apple orchard, Hillcrest Farms, and her family farmed on the side. After she got married, she and her husband, who also worked in the pottery, continued to raise a lot of their own food. She recalled that they grew cabbage, tomatoes, potatoes, and lettuce, and if they got snowed in, she had a cellar full of canned potatoes, green beans, and tomatoes. She said that their garden "helped a lot." The Haughts also raised chickens for eggs and meat and bought cows and pigs in the spring to fatten up and butcher in the fall. They would store all the meat in the "deep freeze" in their basement.[79]

These women were primarily responsible for food preparation, another important self-help activity. Creative recipes and cooking could turn inexpensive ingredients into beloved family meals. John Alatis said his family managed to get through the Great Depression because his mother "was a good cook and she knew how to take care of everything."[80] Through food preparation, women also became caretakers of rural traditions and ethnic heritage. West Virginia women devised many creative ways to prepare local game, braising venison steaks, parboiling groundhog, roasting pheasant, and stewing squirrel.[81] Margaret Heaton's mother, a Hungarian immigrant, made lots of soup with soup bones, beef, celery, parsley, potatoes, carrots, and "maybe a big wedge of cabbage." Her mother also made chicken *papricas*, a Hungarian favorite, and Hungarian dessert crepes known as *palicintas*.[82]

According to Theresa DeCaria, many of her family's traditions revolved around cooking and eating together. The DeCarias exemplified "making do" by preparing inexpensive meals like pasta with herbed tomatoes, which was best, she noted, when "using freshly-picked tomatoes and basil from our garden." Her mother baked four or five loaves of bread for the week and her father helped by making dandelion salad using the best dandelions from their lawn. DeCaria wrote, "From an early age, we learned to appreciate and care for nature's bounty. We reaped many benefits too. By growing our own fruits and vegetables, we were able to use the freshest of ingredients in our recipes."[83]

Frank Gregory, whose parents came to Weirton in the 1920s along with many other African Americans from South Carolina, recalled that his mother made "extremely southern food." The Sunday meal was a banquet with two or three different meats and many kinds of vegetables. "When I was growing up," he said, "we didn't have everything, but I was never without food, shelter, and clothing." His mother sewed clothing for the family, washed their clothes, and even made the soap that she used for the laundry. Gregory credited his mother for being able to cook and clothe him and his six siblings at the same time she worked as a domestic servant for other families. He added, "I don't know what it is to be poor."[84]

Homebuilding and Hunting

The men of rural-industrial Hancock County also performed a number of self-help activities. Some raised corn and wheat, tended to large livestock, hunted for local game, and built their own homes. Home ownership was probably the single most important material goal of steel and pottery workers in Hancock County during the twentieth century. Like working-class Americans in many parts of the nation, these potters and mill workers viewed owning a home and a small plot of land as their bedrock of stability in an era of unpredictable layoffs.[85] When *Christian Science Monitor* journalist R. H. Markham visited Weirton in 1945, he immediately recognized the importance of home ownership to working families there. He observed that most men and women of Weirton "own their own homes, which are furnished as well as the homes of most schoolteachers."

While Markham noted that workers' houses by the mill were "drab," on the hill he found a "city of pleasant new houses, belonging mostly to workers."[86]

Mr. and Mrs. Frank Kulbacki were among the many moving away from the mill to the hilltop developments. In 1941, they moved from Weir Avenue behind the open hearth furnaces to Marland Heights near the local country club. Their new home on Elwood Lane had a kitchen that featured a sink directly beneath a wide window, an electric vent fan, countertops of black linoleum trimmed in bands of chromium, and a black linoleum floor with a red feature strip. The home included a two-car garage, a sixteen-by-sixteen-foot master bedroom, two smaller bedrooms, and a modern bath with maroon linoleum.[87] Behind the romantic description of chromium and linoleum was a modest three-bedroom house that nevertheless was the pride of this steelworker's family, and the goal of many more. In a 1954 edition of the *ISU Independent News*, the Independent Steelworkers Union journal, the caption for one photograph of new homes in Weirton Heights declared (in an oblique reference to independent unionism): "Freedom Won It For You. The Highest Percentage of Home Ownership of Any City in the World."[88]

According to the U.S. Census, home ownership rates in Hancock County marched steadily upward from 50 percent in 1940 to 74 percent by 1960.[89] Given that most industrial workers in Hancock County could barely afford even the Bureau of Labor Statistics model budget, which called for a rented apartment, this level of home ownership was only possible because many of them built their own homes or at least did some of the work themselves. When Bob Rossell was growing up in Weirton Heights in the 1940s, plenty of steelworkers used a shovel and wheelbarrow to excavate for a foundation and then built a concrete or ceramic block basement. Families would live in those basements until they had enough money to build the first story of their house.[90] It was not uncommon for potters to build their own houses as well. Both Fay Haught and her husband worked in the potteries. When he built their house in the 1950s, they lived in her sister's basement while he dug out the basement with a team of horses and a scoop. Then they stayed in their own basement for about three years while he built the first story. She said that her husband was "one of these guys who could do anything. If something didn't work he could fix it."[91]

Many men in Hancock County came together to build and repair houses. Frank Maslowski, a welder in the mill, learned "a little bit here, a little bit there" about home construction and did not shy away from complex homebuilding techniques like hip roofs. He and his brother-in-law, who was also a welder in the mill, turned out finely finished homes with brick fireplaces, hardwood floors, and plaster ceilings for in-laws, brothers, and other relatives before finally building one for Frank and his wife.⁹² After Alex Fiedorczyk became a foreman in the mill, he spent a grueling few months working on his house in Bel Air Addition. When he got off work at 7 A.M., he would come straight to the building site and work until three or four o'clock in the afternoon. Then he would go home, eat, "lay down" for about three or four hours, and go back to work in the mill. It took him two years to move into the house because, as he said proudly, "we did most of the work ourselves. . . . I did all the finish work in here, period." The Fiedorczyks moved in before the house was finished, and he remembered that his daughter would roller skate through the house on the plywood subfloor. Financing self-built houses was just as simple as mortgaging a house already built by a contractor. Fiedorczyk recalled, "In them days, I went through the Bank of Weirton. . . . At that time, they had access to the records of Weirton Steel. So if you went down and applied for a loan, they'd check your Weirton Steel record and everything like that. If you were satisfactory, you had no problem getting a loan." Fiedorczyk hired a contractor on paper to satisfy the bank, who in turn hired him to build his own house.⁹³

Frequently, fathers and sons worked together to build their own houses. Paul Barkhurst's father originally came to Weirton in its early day around World War I to build houses for steelworkers but eventually started working in the mill himself. He passed his house-building skills along to Paul, an iron rigger in the mill, who in turn built his own house and then helped his son, a third-generation Weirton steelworker, build his house as well.⁹⁴ If they needed help, steelworkers like Barkhurst who were in the skilled trades could also call on many of their friends who were carpenters, electricians, and other tradesmen in the mill. Building their own houses helped industrial workers accomplish a lifelong goal and filled them with a sense of pride and accomplishment.

The men of Hancock County also carried on the hunting and fishing culture of rural northern West Virginia. Like the autoworkers of Lansing, Michigan, who "came to understand their own access to the land and its game as both a right of American citizenship and an emblem of a particular type of working-class masculinity," significant numbers of industrial workers grew up on farms in the region and often learned to hunt and fish from their fathers and their uncles.⁹⁵ During their transition to industrial work, these outdoor activities remained important cultural and pragmatic activities for working families that appreciated extra meat as well as the cash they could get for pelts. In the postwar years, hunting fit into a pattern of spending leisure time on self-help activities as well as maintaining a relationship with the land. One West Virginia hunter described the opening day of hunting season: "In the stillness of the morning hours, you find yourself sitting on a moss-covered log, far from civilization. The autumn air is cool and crisp. Your eyes and ears are alert to the fading symphony of thousands of night insects.... Suddenly, without warning, the morning sun breaks through the tree top openings and its brightness and beauty lighten up the whole forest community." This author also noted that hunting was an escape from the "crowded, complex work-a-day world," as well as a time to "mold a lasting companionship" with the son he brought along.[96]

In 1940, there were 2,719 resident, statewide hunting-fishing licenses issued to Hancock County residents, or enough for one in five males over the age of fourteen.[97] In a 1943 survey, 87 hunters reported that they bagged 508 rabbits, 108 gray squirrels, 65 fox squirrels, and 91 groundhogs.[98] By 1966, squirrels had become the most popular game of West Virginia hunters, as some 92 percent of hunters surveyed hunted for squirrel while 65 percent hunted deer and 62 percent rabbits.[99] Fay Haught's husband hunted deer, rabbits, and squirrels, so the deep freeze in the basement was always full of game. After Fay's sons caught three baby squirrels and made pets out of them, however, squirrels were taken off the menu.[100] Walter Danna, son of Italian immigrants, listed hunting as one of the many things he and his family and friends did to supplement their income.

> We hunted pheasant, rabbit, squirrel. Deer weren't abundant. If you seen one in your days back then you were lucky. In the fall we'd go pheasant hunting. And we made what was called "polenta," which was a cornmeal with a tomato sauce and we used the pheasant as the base of the sauce. So we looked forward to that. We hunted squirrels. We hunted rabbits. We trapped possum. We trapped weasel. Enough to sustain yourself. We picked May Apple roots. We dug 'em all by hand. Picked 'em out. Dried them. Took 'em down. And they supposedly make medicine out of 'em.

Walter and his friends trapped a lot, mostly muskrats, and sold their pelts for cash. "We had to stretch them out, cure them, hang them up, and we'd take them to a dealer. Back then it paid pretty good money." He also hunted groundhogs, which he said were good to eat as long as they were young and you waited a few weeks after they were done hibernating. Otherwise they are all flab and had a "mud taste." Walter even hunted groundhogs before he had a gun. He would spend hours digging up their holes until his dog could kill them. Danna said there was not anything wrong with eating groundhogs, and if "push came to shove" he would eat them again.[101] Groundhogs were a popular game in part because they were classified as rodents and could be hunted all year long, except for September, when all hunting was prohibited. In 1960, *West Virginia Conservation* magazine noted that a "young and plump woodchuck weighing three, four, or five pounds, offers excellent eating."[102]

In Hancock County, it was not uncommon for descendants of nineteenth-century settlers and farmers to live next to European immigrant families or African American families from the South. This setting sometimes encouraged cultural exchanges. For example, it is unlikely that many European immigrants like the parents of Frank Maslowski brought a tradition of hunting with them to the United States, but Frank became a lifelong hunter. After he got married and the couple moved into their own home, Frank used to travel to Elkins and other places to hunt deer, but said that he had the most success hunting deer "right out here on Lick Run on the Zagula farm." In fact, he got a doe and a buck about three years in a row there.[103] Since deer in Hancock County had become scarce, many hunters traveled to southern West Virginia, or "down hoopie" as they would say, or to hunting preserves in Pennsylvania or West Virginia's eastern panhandle.[104]

In the mid-1950s, Maslowski heard that if you did not belong to a hunting club, there would soon not be anyplace left to hunt. A group of Weirton Steel employees formed a hunting lodge called the Hancock County Sportsmen's Association, and he joined up. In the early days of the club, new members had to buy a $50 share and pay annual dues of a dollar or two. Maslowski helped them build the clubhouse and install a septic tank on the club's 155 acres off Wylie Ridge Road in the countryside just north of Weirton. But once they established the club, the members realized that it would not be feasible to open the land up to hunting for all of them because there would be too many hunters. Some members ended up planting gardens at the "Sportsmen's farm," but mainly it seems to have become a shooting range that hosted various outdoors events. Hunt clubs brought men together outside of work to socialize and form mutual aid networks. Members might come to the clubhouse to play poker, find somebody to help them put a new roof on their house, and exchange information about hunting and gardening. Such informal networks supported self-help activities and reinforced an older notion of hunting as a masculine activity.[105]

A Sense of Place and a Feeling of Independence

At the same time that various self-help activities like gardening, hunting, and raising livestock reinforced gender identities, they also had ideological implications. Late nineteenth-century farming families in the North embraced self-reliant independence and community autonomy and believed that the loss of control to a centralized bureaucracy was a threat to democracy.[106] This localism of rural culture persisted into the industrial era in Hancock County.

While steelworkers like Johnny Metzgar of Johnstown, Pennsylvania, attributed their improved standard of living to unionization, the rural-industrial workers of Hancock County—when they did not give credit to their employers—were likely to point to the house they built themselves or the food on their table that they raised in their own garden. By making do and closing the gap between a minimum and comfortable standard of living, steel and pottery workers maintained a mentality of self-reliance. These habits supplemented the incomes of rural-industrial workers, tied them to the land and their pasts, and conditioned their entry into the national labor movement and liberal politics in the post–World War II era.

Many twentieth-century Americans associated doing things for themselves with keeping government in check, and some—like Clay Tate, the author of the 1954 book *Building a Better Home Town: A Program of Community Self-Analysis and Self-Help*—believed that small towns and rural places were ideal settings for such self-help. Tate went so far as to argue that centralization would lead to fascism because, in the degrading conditions of big cities, people would naturally turn to "big government and big unions to protect them."[107] In Hancock County, self-reliance and local control were integral parts of workers' concepts of "independence," which in turn shaped their approach to unionism and electoral politics. As discussed in the previous chapter, they generally opted for local unions, preferring local control over jobs to becoming part of a potentially more powerful but distant bureaucracy, and they elected politicians like Republican Arch Moore who they hoped would place limits on union leaders' power.

Ideals of self-reliance also put the steel and pottery workers of Hancock County out of step with labor liberals' agenda of extending the welfare state. New Deal liberals in the federal government, after abandoning ambitious plans to fundamentally reform the economy, turned toward extending the welfare state to ameliorate the negative consequences of modern capitalism. In the late 1950s, delegates of the West Virginia Committee on Political Education (COPE) called for increased Social Security payments, a national unemployment compensation program, a stronger workers' compensation program, and pensions for government workers.[108] Not only did many of Hancock County's industrial workers—because of good benefits through their employers—never need the assistance of government welfare programs, such programs meant a more powerful distant bureaucracy and dependency.

In Weirton, the union promoted the Community Chest, a private, local charity, as the answer to poverty. One editorial in the *Independent News*, the journal of the Weirton steelworkers' union, asked, "Would you give a bum a dime?" The editor pondered how one could truly know he was in need or was simply "a slick character" who made his living by "mooching." Instead of giving money to panhandlers, the editor advised readers to donate to the Community Chest, where "skilled workers" would "serve the real needs of the people."[109]

The county's Democratic strongholds were in what was a bustling and crowded downtown Weirton, where residents would have been least able to engage in self-help activities. Between 1944 and 1968 in downtown precincts 18 through 22, Democratic presidential candidates routinely won by 80 and 90 percent majorities. In 1964, Lyndon Johnson won 98 percent of Precinct 19's votes.[110] The immigrants and African Americans who still lived in these downtown precincts were undoubtedly motivated by a variety of factors, but certainly one was that they had different experiences with self-help than voters living on the outskirts of town or in rural areas. New zoning laws increasingly made practicing self-help activities difficult and in some cases illegal, and by the 1960s they were tearing down houses in North Weirton rather than building new ones with their own hands like many steel and pottery workers outside of downtown Weirton. A mentality of self-reliance would have struggled to find expression in those precincts.

In Arch Moore's 1964 bid for U.S. House of Representatives, he netted 50 percent or more of the vote in every precinct in the county except 19, 21, 22, 23, and 25, all of which were in downtown Weirton. Those precincts certainly had low numbers of registered Republicans, between 14 and 30 percent, but so did other parts of the county. Only 22 percent of the voters who came to Kosciuszko Hall in Weirton Heights on Election Day were Republicans, but 60 percent of them voted for Moore. Similarly, only 41 percent of voters in the rural district around Pughtown School were Republicans, but 80 percent of them supported Moore.[111] Once in office, Moore received a letter from pottery worker Lawrence Savors of Chester, who advised Moore, "We do not need too much federal aid like unemployment doles."[112] Similarly, Weirton steelworker Myron Batson wrote, "I can remember when people took care of their own needs."[113] In his newsletter to constituents, Moore explained, "I am working to decrease Federal spending so that money is available to reduce the National Debt, and to give *you some tax relief.*"[114]

Hancock County continued to lend its support to Arch Moore in his bid for governor, giving him 66 percent of their votes in 1968.[115] By his own account, Governor Moore focused his administration on the state's welfare system, making West Virginia the "nation's yardstick and inspiration for welfare reform." He reduced the welfare rolls, he said, by a "judicious method" of caseload management, with "economic independence" as the ultimate goal of the programs.[116] Moore also claimed that more than 50 percent of the reductions in welfare rolls were the result of the employment of "welfare mothers."[117] By the 1970s, the phrase "welfare mothers" had taken on racial connotations as the white backlash against the civil rights movement and the Great Society was in full swing.[118] In major cities, African Americans mobilized through the National Association for the Advancement of Colored People (NAACP), Urban League, and CIO and made significant strides toward equality and social justice. Working-class whites often responded by forming conservative, grassroots political groups and becoming yet more racist. Defending their privileged position in their workplaces, neighborhoods, and governments eclipsed class concerns that once welded together the culturally, ethnically, and racially diverse New Deal coalition in major industrial centers.[119] While racial tensions never reached the same heights in Hancock County as they did in places like Chicago and Detroit, the relatively privileged position many whites in the county held within the working class began to crumble during the 1970s (see chapter 6).

Conclusion

In many ways, the end of the 1950s marked the end of an era for industrial workers. In the first week of January 1960, steelworkers around the country were relieved that the 1959 strike had come to an end as the United Steel Workers of America reached a settlement with industry negotiators. The strike had been a powerful demonstration of disciplined collective action. Across the country, rank-and-file members walked out together, went 116 days without a paycheck, and came back together. It was the culmination of two decades of work by shop stewards and rank-and-file activists to build a national organization that brought some of the most powerful corporations in America to their knees. Steelworkers would remember it as the "big one," the last of a series of national strikes by the USWA.[120]

The 1960s would witness a new era for labor. Labor leaders—no longer renegades fighting for legitimacy—were now the heads of massive organizations with access to the halls of power. Walter Reuther, president of the United Auto Workers, regularly met with President John Kennedy's Council of Economic Advisors to discuss wages, inflation, and economic strategy, even if the AFL-CIO's leadership routinely rejected Reuther's innovative ideas. In 1962, celebrating the twenty-fifth anniversary of the UAW's hallowed Flint sit-down strike, Reuther told union delegates, "A labor movement can get soft and flabby spiritually. It can make progress materially, and the soul of the union can die in the process."[121] Labor leaders like Walter Reuther and John L. Lewis had welded together industrial workers from towns and cities all over the nation into organizations that had reached maturity and had become institutions in their own right, helping to shape national policy in postwar America. Building these organizations transformed millions of industrial workers as they walked the picket lines, defiantly wore union buttons on the shop floor, and represented their locals at massive national gatherings.

But the steel and pottery workers in Hancock County were not part of those national industrial unions and had taken no part in those events. In the 1940s and 1950s, while autoworkers in Detroit, packinghouse workers in Chicago, and steelworkers in Pittsburgh took on industrial giants and voted on new contracts, the rural-industrial workers in Hancock County stayed on the job and participated in a localized bargaining system. They turned inward and spent much of their time on self-help activities that emanated from their rural culture to get through the hard times and attain a more comfortable standard of living in good times. This reinforced a local identity by underscoring their attachment to place, family, and community. Building their own homes, planting large gardens, raising livestock, and hunting local game filled them with a sense of self-reliance.

Beginning in the 1960s, the American labor movement faced a new challenge: demands for gender equality and racial equality. Women and African Americans waited many long years for union presidents to make good on their promises of equality, and the 1964 Civil Rights Act finally gave rank-and-file members the power to demand equal opportunity from their unions and employers. Their lawsuits chiseled away at white male privilege in the workplace in major cities across the country as well as in the mills and potteries of Hancock County.

CHAPTER 6

MOVEMENTS FOR EQUALITY IN A TIME OF INDUSTRIAL RESTRUCTURING

The global industrial restructuring of the late nineteenth century brought new industries and jobs to rural farmland in northern West Virginia, but in the late twentieth century, another round of industrial restructuring occurred in the steel and pottery industries with dire consequences for the factory towns of Hancock County. Foreign competition undercut the profitability of local companies, resulting in a steady loss of jobs. Initially, steel company executives and steel union leaders applauded the postwar shift in American policy toward free trade, while pottery executives and unionists protested its destructive effects on their industry. By the late 1960s, the steel industry too began to notice the adverse effects of foreign competition on their profits, and by the 1980s investors were moving their capital to other sectors of the economy, leaving many manufacturers paying "legacy costs" such as pensions and health care for retirees and searching for ways to achieve high levels of profitability to attract new investment capital.[1]

At the same time foreign competition and shifting capital threatened local jobs, historic national movements for equality, coalescing around black freedom and women's rights, played out at the local level. Locally, African Americans and women demanded greater access to factory jobs in the wake of the 1964 Civil Rights Act, which outlawed discrimination on the basis of race and gender. In the local potteries that had survived the 1950s, the workforce changed little, but pay scales and the sex typing of jobs changed in subtle but important ways. In contrast, workers at Weirton Steel experienced a radical redrawing of gender and racial divisions even while class-action lawsuits for discrimination were still working their way through the court system. Women and African Americans were finally making progress toward economic equality just as the industrial jobs that formed the foundation of these working-class communities were slipping away.

The View of International Trade from the Local Level

Before World War II, workers in Hancock County were continually concerned about cheap imports undercutting their way of life. World War II offered local companies and workers a respite from competition with imports, which potters especially appreciated. Joseph M. Wells of Homer Laughlin warned that after the war ended there would be a flood of cheap, imported pottery, but ideas about free trade differed sharply among national labor leaders, local labor leaders and workers, and company executives.[2] Steel executives and officials of the United Steel Workers of America supported free trade, but pottery owners, pottery workers, and many local rank-and-file steelworkers opposed free trade, seeing it as a threat to profits, the American standard of living, jobs, and the localized system of labor-management relations that seemed to them to be the linchpin of local prosperity.

Those who favored high tariffs, however, were increasingly in the minority. During and after the war, free trade proponents won victories over protectionists, and policymakers reduced import duties and even eliminated them in some cases. Labor joined with government planners during World War II to promote liberalized trade as a path to full employment and economic prosperity in the United States after the war. In 1946, the Office of Price Administration lifted price controls from a long list of imports including ceramics, noting that pottery was "of minor significance in the nation's economy."[3] In 1947, free trade proponents created the General Agreement on Tariffs and Trade (GATT), a multilateral trade organization with several member nations. Labor leaders supported an alternative, the International Trade Organization (ITO), which regulated trade more comprehensively because it included provisions for full employment and fair labor standards among the trading partners, but conservatives defeated the ITO.[4]

During the 1950s, the Eisenhower administration, at the urging of the State Department, promoted free trade with renewed vigor because of the new imperatives of the Cold War. Thomas C. Mann, assistant secretary for economic affairs, explained that with "the free world and the Communist bloc competing for the allegiance of vast numbers of people in less developed areas of the world, an expansionist foreign trade policy on the part of the United States has become more important than ever before." Mann continued, "We cannot deprive other nations of markets, encouraging ingrown, inward-looking regional self-sufficiency, and giving up the economic competition with the Soviets by default. We must cooperate to survive."[5] Eisenhower concurred and thought about foreign policy almost exclusively within the context of the Cold War. He believed that strengthening the capitalist nations of the "free world" would contain communism. In 1954, he said, "Japan cannot live unless something is done to allow her to make a living."[6]

Still believing that high levels of international trade were the key to high employment, many U.S. labor leaders at the national level supported free trade policies. UAW president Walter Reuther was among the most progressive of labor's free trade proponents at the time. Reuther and other UAW staffers supported free trade because their broader analysis of the postwar economic order envisioned a larger role for labor in shaping the global economy, forging international solidarity, raising the standard of living of American workers by lowering the cost of consumer goods, increasing employment in the United States, and helping to raise the standards of living in foreign countries. However well-intentioned free trade advocates like Walter Reuther were, most of their efforts to influence global trade proved ineffective, and American manufacturing workers increasingly found themselves in competition with "pauper labor."[7]

Occasionally labor leaders adopted the Cold War rhetoric of the Eisenhower administration. David McDonald, president of the United Steel Workers of America, testified before Congress, "Either we can continue as a full-fledged member of the family of free nations and trade with them or we can retire into a shell of imagined self sufficiency and take the consequences. With the world divided as it is between communism and freedom the consequences of the latter course are not pleasant to contemplate."[8] McDonald shrugged off concerns that cheap labor would undermine the steel industry, saying, "We in the steel industry, in the metal-manufacturing industries, are still able to 'skin' almost anybody pricewise, competitionwise, because of our skills, our techniques, because of what some people call know-how, our sales ability, our imagination, general resourcefulness. We could even 'skin' the sweatshops."[9]

Pottery owners and workers were already suffering the effects of cheap imported ceramics. Between the end of the war and the mid-1950s, nine American companies went bankrupt as a result of foreign competition, putting some 2,400 potters out of work.[10] In just a four-year period between 1948 and 1952,

American potters saw their share of the domestic market decline from 30 percent to about 16 percent. Between the end of the war and 1955, the payroll at Homer Laughlin dropped from 3,200 to 1,400, and jobs continued to vanish at an alarming rate after that. Between 1953 and 1963, pottery employment in the district as a whole decreased from 6,191 to 3,075.[11]

Pottery company executives and union leaders joined forces in their opposition to free trade. Leaders of the International Brotherhood of Operative Potters (IBOP) often opposed renewal of reciprocal trade agreements and tariff reductions. The *Potters Herald* reported that the union was "putting forth every possible means and effort at their command to try and head off a further reduction in tariffs which would make it impossible for domestic producers of dinnerware to compete with low-wage foreign producers." The journal encouraged every member of the brotherhood to play their part by urging their representatives in Congress to support "a fair and just tariff on imports of ceramic products."[12] Joseph Wells of Homer Laughlin testified before Congress and the United States Tariff Commission about the injurious effects of imports on his industry. He said that increased tariffs would no longer save the potteries and that only import quotas could help now. Even though potteries had mechanized to a great degree during the previous twenty years, they simply could not compete with the cheap labor costs of Japanese firms.[13] Robert Boyce of Harker Pottery argued that the imports were only part of the problem and that the "sloppy Joe generation" no longer believed in the formalities or keeping china as an heirloom. Sometimes they just bought plastic dishware.[14]

By 1955, Wells had finely honed his anti-import testimony. Appeals to Congress to save American jobs failed because, as an oft-quoted statistic held, fourteen million jobs depended on exports and only 100,000 would be lost to cheap imports. So Wells appealed to the patriotism of Congress and the American public. He told the Committee on Ways and Means,

> We find ourselves facing a situation so fantastic it has all the elements of a nightmare for those of us in the pottery business. Here we have an American industry older than the Nation itself that has always maintained an honorable position in the family of business. An industry that in all our wars, and particularly in World War II, has supplied not only its share of young men for the Armed Forces, but essential materials for the conduct of those wars. An industry that, during the past 8 years of unprecedented national prosperity and industrial production, has steadily lost ground and its home market to rapidly increasing imports of competitive products from the aggressor nations of Japan, Italy, and Germany, in each of which countries the pottery

industry is flourishing and expanding. And yet, in the face of those facts, our own Government is demanding the passage of legislation that will still further increase the foreigner's share of our home market and correspondingly reduce our production and our employment of American citizens at American wages.[15]

He acknowledged that his "feeble protest" would likely have no effect, but he wanted to "prophesy that the successful pursuit of this policy will mean an unemployment problem in our country within the next 5 years, far in excess of anything we have experienced in the last 20 years."[16] Louis K. Friedman, vice president of Homer Laughlin China, testified that he went to Japan in October 1954 and found eight well-equipped factories but "literally hundreds of small ill-equipped factories in bombed-out shacks" that paid "exceedingly low wage rates." Japanese potters averaged $1 a day compared to American wages of $1.70 per hour. Friedman said that American potteries had "no recourse" to meet such competition.[17]

In 1958, Roy Rowan, the Chicago bureau chief of Time-Life, and George Bookman, a New York correspondent, did a story for *Life* magazine on the effect of imports and free trade on the upper Ohio Valley. Joseph Wells told them, "Japanese competition is forcing some pottery firms to the wall. People say letting in foreign pottery stimulates our economy, but you don't think a Japanese pottery worker is going to buy an American car, do you?"[18] The reporters arrived at a different conclusion. They reported that Japan exported nearly the exact dollar amount in pottery that it imported in steel. "Here is reciprocal trade in microcosm: lowered tariffs enable Japan to make money on pottery which she thereupon spends in the U.S. on steel."[19] They noted that John A. Jones, a Weirton Steel executive, toured Japan and stood dockside in the "busy seaport" of Yokohama. Jones saw "the familiar Weirton trademark on shining boxes of Weirton Tin Mill products being unloaded from two big transpacific freighters." Ten days later, he saw Weirton Steel tinplate being fabricated "into an interesting variety of products in the plants of Weirton customers in Japan." He added that trade with as many as forty countries "of the free world" was "important to every Weirton Steel employee for it helps to provide steady work at good pay."[20]

Workers in Hancock County equated the appearance of foreign products in their retail stores with the decline of employment in Ohio Valley factories. In 1958, when Hancock County's congressman, Arch Moore, asked constituents if they favored a tax cut "as a means to stimulate buying during an economic slump," Ruth DeLong, who identified herself as a "potter," responded, "We could buy if the work was better and if the market weren't full of foreign made goods." She explained, "I know this is not how you would answer but when only one pay check is coming in (part time) I would like for Washington to know how we live."²¹ Dale Highfield, a steelworker who lived in Chester, captured some of the complexities of working-class politics in the pottery towns when he wrote to Moore. He noted that he was a veteran of World War II and a lifelong Republican like his father and grandfather before him. As a working man, however, he did not like the way his party was "trying to tie labor down." Highfield was disturbed by companies that "put on a propaganda campaign out of this world" to turn workers against unions. The most important issue to Highfield, however, was that of tariffs. He explained, "Thank God I am working . . . but the pottery industry here is dead and our stores are filled with foreign ware."²²

Despite the confidence of steel industry executives and leaders, the economic shock wave worried steelworkers. During economic downturns in 1958 and again in the early 1960s, steelworkers wondered if they too might be suffering as a result of cheap imports. Frank Blaskovich, who lived just outside Weirton, responded, "I believe that foreign made products are causing some unemployment, but if we are to have world relations, we must have reciprocal trade. I think that there should be some fair adjustment or compromise made on this subject."²³ Despite support of free trade by Weirton Steel executives and even the president of the United Steel Workers of America, steelworkers in Hancock County fully supported protective tariffs. In fact, little support could be found among these workers for the free trade policies of the Eisenhower administration or their own leaders. In one poll Arch Moore conducted, his supporters favored not just higher tariffs, but 77 percent of them also favored legislation to restrict imports.²⁴

Arch Moore responded to his constituents and broke ranks with his party and the Eisenhower administration to protest reciprocal trade agreements with low-wage nations. In his 1957 newsletter to his constituents, Moore wrote, "Protection of our workers and industries. This is a matter of most <u>serious concern</u> to the <u>glass</u> and <u>pottery workers</u> and <u>coal miners</u> in our District and for the industries for which they work. The invasion of the American market by foreign-made goods and crude oil has made a threat to the livelihood of so many people in our part of the State." Echoing Joseph Wells's assertion that tariffs were not enough, Moore said that he supported bills to establish "<u>IMPORT QUOTAS</u>," which he emphatically wrote in all caps and underlined.²⁵

Just as they preferred to keep control of labor-management relations in local hands, rural-industrial workers in Hancock County hoped to insulate themselves from the pressures of the global economy. They viewed free trade with low-wage nations as a threat to the system they had shaped and protected over the years. The recession of the late 1950s demonstrated that their local companies, local unions, and the economic foundation upon which they had built their lives were more fragile than they thought.

African Americans Demand Equality

At the same time that workers in Hancock County watched foreign-made goods fill the shelves of local stores, historic national movements for equality unsettled the local system of patriarchy and white privilege. In the early 1950s, African Americans still lived separate lives from white families in the county. Public schools were segregated by law, and many public facilities in Weirton, including pools, parks, and movie theaters, were segregated by local customs and police harassment. For the Fourth of July, since they could not visit the white parks, Weirton's black community held a celebration at the Colored Community Club picnic and at Washington Playground in North Weirton. The Margaret Manson Weir Pool, built in Marland Heights in 1934, refused to admit African Americans in the 1950s.[26] At the local movie theaters, African Americans had to sit in the balcony. Cecelia Arnett remembered being required to enter the theater through a separate door and going up the back steps to the balcony. She did not think anything of it until she got older and realized they were being segregated.[27] Furthermore, West Virginia schools were segregated by law, and Weirton's were no different. Dunbar School opened its doors in 1917 to forty-three African American grade school students, and Washington School had an enrollment of about two dozen.[28] Many of Dunbar's teachers and administrators became influential leaders in Weirton, but the school suffered from underfunding, old textbooks, and poor facilities. Henry "Tex" Burns, for example, remembered playing football with shoddy equipment on a field full of cinders.[29]

Weirton Steel played an important role in race relations in the community during the decades after World War II, but the company often sent mixed messages to employees and residents. President Thomas Millsop praised Weirton's black steelworkers in 1945 for their "dependability, loyalty, and contributions to the advancement of the industry."[30] And Tex Burns recalled that Millsop was "the kind of guy that would come down through the mill and speak to you whether you were black or white."[31] The company continued its long-standing policy of cultivating loyalty among African Americans through generous donations to churches and close cooperation with church officials. For example, when the Morningstar Baptist Church built a new church on Weir Avenue,

CHAPTER 6

FIGURE 13. Three-legged race on Fourth of July at Washington Park
Source: Weirton Area Museum and Cultural Center

Rev. Dr. Peyton Henry Johnson secured a large donation from Weirton Steel to help pay for its construction.[32] In some ways, the company brought white and black workers together, such as when it honored African Americans for longtime service by including them in the Twenty-Five Year Club along with whites. In others, the company segregated black and white workers in many of its social programs. It kept the teams in the interdepartment basketball league segregated, and though African American jazz bands were included in the Festival of Nations, they always appeared last in the show. Similarly, the Weirton Steel men's choir gained acclaim touring the country, but African Americans had to form a separate singing group known as the Jubilee Singers.[33]

More importantly, Weirton Steel continued to discriminate against African Americans in its hiring and promotions. Until the 1960s, the company placed almost all African Americans on the general labor gangs, especially around the blast furnaces and coke ovens, which limited them to many of the lowest-paying, hardest, dirtiest, and most dangerous jobs in the mill. Whites routinely started out on the labor gang but moved into other departments and sometimes into the skilled trades within a few years. Meanwhile black steelworkers languished on the labor gang for decades, often for their entire careers at Weirton Steel. Tex Burns spent twenty years on the labor gang. He was born in Weirton on August 20, 1935. His parents had migrated from Georgia to Weirton in the 1920s, and the family encountered a mix of hostility and acceptance. One of Burns's earliest memories was of his whole family laying quietly on the living room floor while a Ku Klux Klan march went past their house on Sixth Street. Yet he also remembered basketball games at the Christian Center where black and white kids played together. After high school, Burns started working at Weirton Steel, where most African Americans found themselves trapped on the labor gang doing some of the hottest and dirtiest jobs in the mill. One of the worst jobs was hauling ashes out of the flues. "It was like going to hell," Burns remembered. "You stick your shovel in there and it was red as fire."[34]

As late as the 1960s, Walter Danna, a white steelworker, recalled working with African Americans in the coke ovens of Weirton Steel and learning about their plight. He had attended a racially integrated school across the state line in Pennsylvania and was surprised to learn about the segregated schools of West Virginia. His coworkers also told him about the discrimination they faced at Weirton Steel. After he put in his time on the labor gang, he planned to bid on better jobs in other parts of the mill, but he learned that despite having many more years of service, most black steelworkers like Tex Burns were trapped on the labor gang.[35]

Foremen and line supervisors were instrumental in keeping many departments all white. Walter Danna recalled how one black worker, Lewis Titus, learned about the welding department from taking the labor gang's broken tools there to be fixed. The head of the welding shop, who made no secret both about not wanting any blacks to work there and his "power to keep them out," insisted that Titus go back to the labor gang rather than wait in the shop so he would not "see what's going on, on the other side of the fence."[36] Another reason black steelworkers struggled to gain equal access to good-paying jobs in the mill was because of departmental seniority. Once they had been placed in the blast furnaces or the coke ovens, it became difficult for African Americans to get jobs in other departments. And the longer they were trapped in those job categories, the more they would have to give up to start at the bottom of a seniority ladder in another department. In 1950, as a result of discriminatory practices, 52 percent of the town's black working men were laborers and about 25 percent were operatives, which included blast furnace work. Only 9 percent were foremen or craftsmen, which included the heads of the labor gangs, compared to 28 percent of white workers. Their employment conditions improved by 1960, but African Americans in Weirton still lagged behind white workers in every category except service workers and laborers, where they outnumbered whites by at least two to one.[37]

African American women faced an even more restrictive labor market. In 1960, out of every three black women who worked outside the home in Weirton, one worked as domestic servant and one as a service worker. A small number also worked in retail and as schoolteachers.[38] Cecelia Arnett remembered, "My mother graduated valedictorian of her class, and when she went to the employment office they told her the only thing that they could offer her was a job cleaning people's houses. And that's what my mom did."[39] Two-thirds of the African American women in Weirton remained out of the labor force altogether.[40]

Racial discrimination in the local job market resulted in income inequalities. In 1949, African American families in Weirton were disproportionately poor. They were more than twice as likely as the average Weirton family to make less than $2,000 annually. They were also considerably underrepresented in the top income categories. While some 28 percent of Weirton families earned more than $5,000 a year, only 14 percent of nonwhite families made that much.[41]

Weirton's immigrant families may have been moving "up the hill" and building new homes, but black residents could not. As the sons and daughters of immigrants moved out to exclusively white neighborhoods on the ridges surrounding downtown Weirton, white residents, realtors, and policemen conspired to keep African Americans in the neighborhood that locals called "Calico Hill," behind the open hearth furnaces. Black residents were restricted not only in where they could live but even where they could walk. Tex Burns recalled that if any African American went below the bus terminal on Main Street, the police would "chase you back uptown."[42] Burns's daughter, Karen Williams Harris, explained that it was just "unheard of" for blacks to live in Weirton Heights or Marland Heights. She also believed that whites in Weirton Heights seemed more racist than whites in her neighborhood and even seemed to look down on the whites that lived near blacks. In stark contrast to Weirton Heights, Harris remembered that on Weir Avenue, "everybody kind of looked out for everybody." She said that "there was a lot of love there within your community. . . . We never looked at color."[43]

Living outside of Weirton was not an option for African Americans; racism was even more entrenched and more virulent in the rest of the county, not surprising given the unchecked growth of the Ku Klux Klan in the pottery towns during the 1920s. Tex Burns remembered that many of the white steelworkers who drove down from the pottery towns to work at Weirton Steel tended to be more racist. And as late as the 1980s, one of Burns's black friends bought a house outside of Weirton only to have it "mysteriously" burn down shortly thereafter.[44]

African Americans had few opportunities to challenge racial discrimination in Weirton. In cities like Detroit, the local chapter of the NAACP allied with the CIO to expand job opportunities for black workers.[45] In the late 1940s and 1950s in Youngstown, Ohio, black steelworkers and a cadre of white radicals worked through their United Steel Workers of America local to force U.S. Steel to open up production jobs to African Americans.[46] Such activism paved the way for renewed civil rights struggles in the 1960s, and community leaders often emerged from the labor movement. In Hancock County, however, there was no local chapter of the NAACP, and the CIO failed to organize the steel or pottery workers. Black steelworkers in Weirton had little hope of an impartial hearing of their grievances. Tex Burns remembered times when he was pushed to the brink of violence by cruel and racist foremen. When one boss used the "N word," he said, "I jumped across the ditch ready to kill him, and that's when I thought about, 'Oh, I better not. I've got a wife and a kid.'" He reported such incidents to his Independent Steelworkers Union (ISU) representative, who replied there was nothing the union could do about it.[47] Walter Danna recognized the racial discrimination in the ISU in the 1960s, noting that black steelworkers could not even bid on other jobs. They did not have a union steward, he explained; they had "what was called a representative," a single official to represent all black workers.[48]

At the Wheeling Steel plant across the Ohio River in Steubenville, African Americans did have a local of the United Steel Workers of America and had more opportunities in the 1960s. Frank Gregory worked at that plant but left a higher-paying job to come to Weirton Steel hoping for more stable work. In Steubenville, he said, they were having "strikes and things like that, unrest. . . . It was just something I didn't want to be part of." In the USWA-organized plant, there were black bricklayers, electricians, motor inspectors, railroad engineers, and other craftsmen, but at Weirton Steel, he said, he "worked continuously without stoppage." He hired into Weirton Steel in plant security, making more than a laborer but less than a boilermaker, and he spent the rest of his career there.[49]

African Americans in Weirton formed a small, tight-knit community and looked inward, focusing on family and community. Within the confines of segregation, black steelworkers and their families built a rich social and cultural life. Cecelia Arnett, who grew up in Weirton during the 1950s, recalled, "We had this world—our own community world—that was all black." At school, the teachers were black, her classmates were black, and the people in local shops were black. She did not "really venture that much into the other world," she recalled, because they could not go to white stores or other businesses or even most public buildings.[50] Even though they were often relegated to the lowest-paying jobs in the mill, black steelworkers made considerably more money and enjoyed a higher standard of living than had sharecroppers in the South before World War II or even blacks in other parts of West Virginia. In 1960, African American men in Weirton earned more than their counterparts in any of the other major cities in the state, bringing home 40 percent more than black men in Fairmont, the second highest-paid group. The handsome wages that black steelworkers earned enabled them to better provide for their families.[51] At work, they relied heavily on the friendships they formed with other black steelworkers to endure the hostile environment. Tex Burns explained, "We'd go to work and it would be hard, but we would find something to rejoice about or something pleasant to talk about, even though the working conditions were horrible-like at times, but we would find some sort of camaraderie with one another."[52]

In some rare instances in the mill, steelworkers consciously broke the color line. Tex Burns recalled one instance in the late 1950s when a white steelworker bought a lemon drink off the canteen and offered some to him. Burns assumed that he had intended for him to drink the rest of it since white and black steelworkers never drank from the same container. In fact, Burns recalled how black steelworkers would use that to their advantage when the company brought out whiskey during the holidays. They would open the bottle first and take a drink and, he recalled, "We'd have all the whiskey we wanted." On this occasion, however, the white steelworker cussed Burns out for trying to drink the whole thing, but his profanity masked a generous act. He took it back and started to drink out of the same container. Burns recalled that after that "white guys and black guys started drinking out of the same canteen."[53]

The end of racial segregation in Weirton began when the Supreme Court declared in its 1954 *Brown v. Board of Education* decision that segregation in schools was unconstitutional, but it was the Civil Rights Act of 1964 that enabled African Americans to challenge racial discrimination in the mill. Title VII of the act explicitly banned racial discrimination in employment, and companies around the country began to change their policies, often making discrimination more subtle and unofficial. For some black steelworkers, persistence paid off. As Lewis Titus took broken tools to the welding shop, he learned what was happening "on the other side of the fence" despite the foreman's efforts to keep him out. He became increasingly interested in welding and eventually became one of the first black welders at Weirton Steel.[54] In 1968, Weirton city fathers, in response to the civil rights movement nationally, established a Human Rights Commission, and the Ohio NAACP posthumously honored Thomas Millsop's commitment to racial equality.[55] Between 1950 and 1970, the percentage of black residents who were craftsmen or foremen increased from one in ten to one in six. Still, fully one in four African American men remained trapped on labor gangs compared to one in ten white men.[56]

According to the Civil Rights Act of 1964, victims of discrimination had to file their complaints in federal court to seek justice. Charles Williams, with the help of a court-appointed attorney, filed his complaint against Weirton Steel and the Independent Steelworkers Union in the fall of 1969, but then spent the next three years looking for a qualified attorney to take the case. He eventually found a black attorney named Franklin Cleckley more than two hours' drive away in Morgantown, West Virginia. Cleckley spent three years as a U.S. Navy JAG officer in Vietnam and earned his master of laws degree from Harvard University before becoming a professor at West Virginia University's College of Law.[57] Cleckley saved Williams's case from dismissal and litigated it through the early stages of its becoming a class-action lawsuit.

In 1974, a federal judge issued a consent decree that forced nine of the major American steel producers and the United Steel Workers of America to institute affirmative action plans to redress decades of racial discrimination, but Weirton Steel and the Independent Steelworkers Union were not part of that lawsuit. Black steelworkers in Weirton would have to wait several more years for a ruling.[58] In 1982, the ISU voted to change its seniority structure to make it easier for racial minorities to advance, but the program still did not offer company-wide seniority, which would have made it easier for African Americans to escape the coke ovens and the blast furnaces, two departments where jobs were withering away.[59] Company-wide seniority not only would have enabled them to bid on jobs in more desirable departments but also would have brought many laid-off African Americans back to work.

In 1983, Judge Charles H. Haden II approved a six-year plan to satisfy his consent decree. The plan included financial compensation for the now 1,300 African Americans named in the suit and an affirmative action program that sought to boost black employment in the skilled trades and first-level plant management positions to 4.2 percent and 7.1 percent within five years. Many of the plaintiffs did not want affirmative action but instead wanted company-wide seniority based on original hire dates rather than department or job dates.[60] One plaintiff, Willie McKenzie, said he did not mind the time that had passed since the suit was filed, saying that "if justice needs to be served by a few more years, then I will wait.... I would be willing to wait another 10 years if need be."[61] Judge Haden responded that McKenzie had "very eloquently" stated his position, but unfortunately "one cannot achieve one's imaginative idea of what perfect justice would be for any of the class members."[62] Haden's statement seems to suggest in a condescending tone that the plaintiffs' idea of "perfect justice" was unobtainable because it was impossibly lofty and unrealistic. Haden explained that he was bound by a body of law that "in recent years has become more and more restrictive."[63] But what the judge did not say was that what the plaintiffs were asking for was nothing more than a nondiscriminatory system of hires, promotions, and layoffs, which seniority was supposed to accomplish in the first place. Still, after several decades of discrimination and segregation, African Americans' right to access to the most lucrative jobs in the mill was recognized by the courts.

Women's Rights Movement and Rural-Industrial Workers

World War II revealed the extent to which women could participate in the industrial workforce, but the male breadwinner ideal, which held that men should work in factories while women raise children and do housework, led most companies to return to the prewar gender division of labor. As discussed in the previous chapter, gender structures evolved in the postwar era in Hancock County. The percentage of the women in the potteries dropped after World War II but never returned to their prewar levels, and while pottery managers eagerly employed more women in more jobs, union leaders fretted about the declining wages and prestige of their industry. Weirton Steel, on the other hand, came close to achieving the male breadwinner ideal. Many Weirton Steel families in the 1950s and 1960s relied on the father's income from the steel mill. At home in Hancock County, it was common for men and women from both industries to engage in household work to improve the family's standard of living.

In the 1950s and 1960s, more and more women in the United States took jobs outside the home as their percentage of the workforce increased from 29 percent in 1950 to 35 percent in 1965 to 40 percent in 1975. While the postwar American ideal envisioned working fathers and stay-at-home mothers, the reality was that many working-class families depended on two incomes, and divorcees and widows had to work to survive. Working women became increasingly insistent on equal pay and equal opportunity.[64] In the 1950s, women around the country began campaigning for equality in the form of the Equal Rights Amendment, and in 1955 the *Weirton Daily Times* editor supported their movement. He noted that one could hardly pretend that women enjoyed equal rights as many states legally favored men in custody suits, contractual agreements, and labor regulations. He argued that women deserved "equality with men" and that women had earned that right by proving themselves to be responsible voters and workers, keeping production at full capacity during the war.[65]

Regardless of the occasional supportive editorial in the local newspaper, women workers continued to face numerous barriers, including unequal pay, discriminatory promotion practices, and harassment on the job. Married women also faced the "second shift," meaning that a greater portion of the household work tended to rest on their weary shoulders.[66] Single mothers like Boots Hines struggled to make ends meet and keep up with parenting responsibilities. Once she got into the mill, Hines was lucky to find an apartment near her parents so that her mother could sometimes watch the boys when she went to work. When her mother could not be there, she hired a babysitter. Working shifts, however, wreaked havoc on her sleep schedule. She swears that one time on midnight shift, she was literally standing and flopping tin in her sleep. Shift work also interfered with her parenting. The three-to-eleven shift was the worst because she got up in the morning and sent them to school and they would be asleep when she got home from work. The midnight shift was actually the best because she could come home and get them off to school before going to bed. Then, when she woke up, they would be coming home from school, and when she was going to work, the babysitter would arrive to stay with the boys while they slept.[67]

It was not until 1964, when Title VII of the Civil Rights Act finally prohibited employment discrimination on the basis of gender and lawsuits mounted, that many companies felt increasing pressure to change their discriminatory hiring and promotion policies. Weirton Steel changed its policy in 1969, according to Hines, so that if a woman could "do a man's job, they could work at it." She jumped at the opportunity and bid on a job in the shipping department, where she worked for the next sixteen years. A woman working in the shipping department did not go unnoticed, and the men did not welcome a change to their all-male workplace. Hines recalled that it was "just one of those things that it just had always been that way, and a lot of the men weren't too happy to have those women come in and work with them."[68] Many women found that there were other jobs in the mill that were not as demanding as they had been portrayed. Hines joked that she discovered how some men could work so many doubles: by sitting around for four hours. She actually found her new job in the shipping department was less physically demanding than working in the assorting room.

For most women in the steel industry, however, change did not come until 1974, when a federal judge found nine of the largest steel companies, including National Steel (Weirton Steel's parent corporation), guilty of gender discrimi-

CHAPTER 6

nation. A court-ordered consent decree instituted one of the largest affirmative action programs in the country, requiring the steel producers to hire greater percentages of women into the skilled trades, production, maintenance, and management.[69] The consent decree opened the steel industry to more women (although not to the level they experienced during World War II). After 1975, the percentage of women in each occupational category in the industry increased steadily. The proportion of women in sales, clerical, and professional jobs increased by about 20 percent, and their numbers in labor, service, and technical jobs grew by about 10 percent in each category. By 1977, the number of women at National Steel had increased to 636 out of 10,352, about 6 percent, at a time when overall employment in the industry was shrinking.[70]

The increased presence of women on the shop floor created tensions. Perhaps fearful that women would drag down wages or replace family men, many male steelworkers tried to defend the "family wage" they had worked so long to achieve. Some were simply unwilling to give up the exclusively male work culture that had developed in the mill, which actually contributed to the notion that a steel mill was "no place for women." Indeed, many men refused to modify their behavior or stop using offensive language, sometimes shocking their new female coworkers. Boots Hines said that when men used "that word," it actually made her ears tingle.[71] Even relatively banal male culture alienated most women, who had little interest in discussing sports, fishing trips, and cars in minute detail.[72] Some women, like Hines, eventually gained acceptance in the mill. She said that her hard work won her the respect of the men on her crew, and she learned to stay away from the men who resented women for being in the mill. They may have also been swayed, she believed, by knowing that she was raising a family on her own. She even shamed one man into cleaning up his foul language.[73] Other women in the steel industry faced long periods of sexual harassment, discrimination, and obstinacy, even in their own union.[74]

Beginning in the 1950s, as local potteries were losing market share to imports and going out of business, female potters demanded their fair share of hours and wages. They filed a series of grievances to combat what they saw as unfair labor practices. For example, in the late 1950s managers at Homer Laughlin scheduled the finishers for Saturday work but then scheduled them for fewer hours the following week to avoid paying overtime. Local 94 did not accept this treatment for long. They refused to show up one Saturday and then showed up for work even though they had been suspended without pay. More than once, the company terminated women who refused to work Saturdays, but when the whole department stood firm and the IBOP supported them, management rescinded the terminations and worked out a compromise. In the 1950s and 1960s, these union women, like many across the country, boldly used the grievance procedure to challenge more and more aspects of gender inequality on the shop floor.[75]

Female potters' efforts to achieve equality on the job culminated in 1966 and 1967 with a series of grievances over unequal pay. As early as 1957, the IBOP and USPA agreed to a clause that stipulated that men and women receive the same minimum pay rate when doing the same job, but this clause was poorly enforced and openly defied on multiple occasions. In January 1966, female dippers' helpers at Hall China notified IBOP leadership that they did not receive the same wages as male helpers, which they noted was now a violation of federal laws. The union's attorney pointed out to the officers that if they did not represent the women on this case that they, too, would be in violation of the law. The company and the USPA contended that although they had the same title, the men actually had heavier jobs than the women, justifying the difference in pay. Handle finishers at TS&T then made a similar demand for equal pay, charging that their separate pay scale was illegal. In February 1967, outside arbitrators agreed with them. Wet handle finishers at Homer Laughlin then filed a similar grievance, which was followed by grievances from Homer Laughlin's dry handle finishers, cup finishers, strippers, and female clay laborers. Their results were mixed. The wet handle finishers won the male minimum rate, but the lack of male workers in the other trades complicated those cases and only the strippers enjoyed a partial victory. The 1967 grievances proved to be the beginning of the end for separate pay scales for women and men, and female union activists continued to use the grievance procedure to open up new jobs to women and reduce gender inequalities in the potteries. But even today, women continue to be clustered in lower-paying jobs in the potteries.[76]

The Long Decline

Most of the potteries in Hancock County that weathered the storm of the 1950s and early 1960s did so because they were the most modern facilities with popular lines of ware. Homer Laughlin devised a winning formula for profitability by selectively adopting mass-production technologies while remaining flexible enough to cater to changing tastes and fashions. Cost savings from Homer Laughlin's automatic jiggers and fuel-efficient tunnel kilns proved vital for the company's survival during the highly competitive postwar decades. Equally important were its popular designs, particularly those created by the world-renowned designer Frederick Hurten Rhead, including Fiestaware.[77] Some of the other local potteries followed Homer Laughlin's formula for success.[78]

But the pottery industry as a whole continued its decline. In 1962, the Edwin M. Knowles China Company shut down its facility in Newell after more than fifty years of operation, and eight hundred potters were thrown into a labor market already glutted with potters.[79] By 1963, the surviving potteries of the district employed 3,389 people, with Homer Laughlin being the leading employer (1,350 potters) followed by TS&T (650), Sterling China (420), Hall China (302), Harker (260), and Wellsville China (120). Harker was bought out by the Jeanette Glass Company in 1969 and suspended operations in 1972. Its Chester plant enjoyed a brief revival in the mid-1970s but was soon shut down permanently. By 1980, there were 1,371 ceramic workers living in the East Liverpool district, with only 148 living in Chester and 201 in Newell.[80]

Homer Laughlin China remains in business today, producing its ever-popular Fiestaware line. In 1993, Joseph Wells III pledged to keep their production facility in Newell even after the much-anticipated North American Free Trade Agreement went into effect. He wrote, "Even though the chinaware industry is labor-intensive and some of our U.S. competitors have moved their facilities to Mexico, I am convinced that keeping Homer Laughlin in Newell is the right thing to do, both for economic reasons and for reasons that have little to do with economics." He went on to argue that investing in new technologies was a better strategy than relocation. In 1992, for example, Homer Laughlin invested one-third of its revenue in "new computer-operated, fast fired kilns" that cut the time ware spent in the kilns from seventy-two hours down to nine. Innovation and investment in U.S.-based manufacturing would continue to pay dividends over the long term, but the substitution of cheap Mexican labor for U.S. labor was a "one-time, short-term fix." Beyond economics, he wrote, "American companies have a responsibility not to abandon the towns where they have thrived in years past. Homer Laughlin has been in Newell since 1907. Its loss would devastate the town." He concluded that while Homer Laughlin was a "vigorous, healthy company," GATT talks could lower tariffs worldwide and that new investments in Mexico from the Pacific Rim "could make survival impossible."[81]

By contrast, the steel industry thrived in the 1960s. In 1964, Weirton Steel embarked on its first modernization program in more than fifteen years when the company announced plans to build the "mill of the future." It invested $400 million in the new facility, which it completed in 1967. The mill of the future included new technology such as the basic oxygen furnace and continuous casters, making Weirton Steel one of the most technologically advanced American steelmakers. Yet Weirton Steel actually lagged behind European steel producers in adopting basic oxygen furnaces and continuous casters.[82]

MOVEMENTS FOR EQUALITY

FIGURE 14. The Weirton Steel can in front of the Millsop Community Center
Source: Weirton Area Museum and Cultural Center

In the 1970s, the American economy struggled in the face of foreign competition and shrinking markets, and the "malaise" resulted in massive layoffs and plant shutdowns. In the steel industry, companies desperately searched for solutions, adopted new technologies, and reorganized their business structures. Between 1974 and 1989, production of American steel dropped from 125 million tons to 70 million, while employment at steel mills dropped from 512,000 employees to 168,000. Eighteen of the twenty-one steel companies left the steel-making business, merged, reorganized under bankruptcy, or simply closed their doors forever.[83] At the time, many industry executives blamed their troubles partly on the handsome wages and benefits companies paid to steelworkers, while others blamed the short-sightedness of management. In the 1980s, despite hefty wage concessions from the workers, investors shifted much of their capital investment from steel to other, more promising sectors of the economy.[84]

Struggling to remain profitable, National Steel, the parent company of Weirton Steel, closed down its Hanna Furnace Company and shut down part of Great Lakes Steel before turning its attention to the Weirton plant. In 1975, the Weirton plant's profits stood at a shaky $5 million, followed by a $6 million loss in 1976 and a $32.5 million loss in 1977. The company was still a leading producer of cans for Campbell Soup, Del Monte, and Heinz, but the aluminum can took over more and more of the market share, especially for canned beverages. The company had invested $150 million in the facility in recent years, but that investment was overshadowed by declining revenues, high wages, and a growing number of retirees collecting pensions and health care benefits. National Steel's consulting firm, Bain & Company out of Boston, recommended severely cutting labor costs. Jack Redline, the president of Weirton Steel, reduced the workforce from 9,371 in 1977 to 5,397 in 1982, but when it posted a $1.1 million in profit in 1981, management deemed that the cuts still were not enough.[85]

The National Steel Corporation no longer saw steel as its future, and the company began diversifying by acquiring a wire producer, an aluminum smelter, and a financial services company.[86] National then began to divest its steel-producing capacity. Bain & Company believed that getting concessions from steelworkers would be difficult and recommended that National try to sell its Weirton division to the employees, as they might be willing to "make concessions to themselves."[87] On March 2, 1982, Howard "Pete" Love announced that National Steel would either sell the Weirton plant to the employees under an Employee Stock Ownership Plan (ESOP) or it would shut the plant down. Love had the reputation of being a rich playboy who rose to the top of National Steel because his father had been chairman of Chrysler. Because of his diversification attempts, he also had the reputation of having little allegiance to steel making. When Love made his announcement in 1982, ISU president Richard "Red" Arango, viewing the situation through a local lens, said to him, "You've always hated Weirton, haven't you Pete?" Love replied that that was not true.[88]

After the announcement, union and management representatives formed a joint study committee (JSC) to determine the path forward. They hired consulting firms to study Weirton Steel's viability, the financing of the ESOP buyout, the ESOP's bylaws, and employee concessions to pay for the buyout. When they announced that employees would have to give up 32 percent of their wages and that laid off employees could not vote on the plan, a rank and file committee (RFC) formed, which included black steelworker Willie McKenzie and Staughton Lynd, a labor lawyer and activist from near Youngstown, Ohio. The RFC demanded to see the studies the consulting firms produced, and they challenged the JSC at every step.[89] Glenn Beamer, who studied the ESOP period of Weirton Steel, found that "many Weirtonians recalled being skeptical of the RFC because Lynd was from outside the community and because his efforts in Youngstown had not forestalled mill closures in that community."[90]

The stakes were high in Weirton during the ESOP negotiations. Among the major concerns were the pensions that hung in the balance. While the pension fund was valued at $350 million, there were potential liabilities valued at $770 million should the mill shut down, and National Steel would be bankrupted by the $420 million in unfunded liabilities. Some employees argued that they should be able to obtain the mill for nothing because National was so desperate to unload it and the unfunded liabilities. The RFC raised concerns about the amount of debt the ESOP was going to have by paying National and assuming its debt. While the RFC called for the workers to make greater demands, new ISU president Walter Bish argued that the ESOP plan had to be approved in the first election or they would scare off potential investors, which created the feeling that the first vote was a "do or die" moment for the mill. The editors of the *Wheeling Intelligencer* came out in favor of the ESOP, writing that there was "no choice" but to vote "yes" to save the mill and the community. In the end, employees agreed. On September 23, 1983, they voted seven-to-one in favor of the ESOP provisions, and the new Weirton Steel formed on January 11, 1984.[91]

The new employee-owned Weirton Steel enjoyed a brief period of profitability but struggled mightily to stay afloat during the 1990s. Already saddled with the costs of pension and health care liabilities for retirees, it also incurred enormous debt when it attempted to further modernize its steel production. The company's problems were compounded, at best, by mismanagement, and at worst, by the greed and corruption of executives like Harvey Sperry, a New York attorney who acted as an advisor during the ESOP negotiations, and Herb Elish, the CEO who presided over several missteps such as investing heavily in an online sales system.[92] Hoping to make the company leaner and more profitable, workers consented to further reductions in force as the company cut one-quarter of its remaining 6,800 workers between 1993 and 1995 and offered early retirement to many of these longtime employees.[93] On top of all this, steel producers in South Korea, Russia, and Brazil began exporting steel to the United States at the same time they were suffering currency crises. As inflation raged out of control in their home countries, manufacturers were able to export below-cost steel, a practice known as "dumping," which was supposed to be outlawed under existing trade agreements. American steelworkers grew frustrated by the federal government's failure to enforce those provisions. The Stand Up For Steel campaign united steel unions and management, and busloads of steelworkers traveled from Weirton to Washington, D.C., to protest the federal government's inactivity on the issue.[94] President George W. Bush eventually offered the steel companies temporary relief from dumping, but it was too late to save Weirton Steel.[95]

In 2003, the company entered bankruptcy, and in 2004 the International Steel Group bought out the employees. Shortly thereafter, Mittal Steel, an India-based steel manufacturer, purchased the mill and continued cutting back production, converting it largely into a finishing mill, which is how it had begun in 1909. By 2006, employment at Weirton Steel stood around 1,200 employees, less than one-tenth of its peak employment of 13,000 (as late as 1974) and one-seventh of its pre-ESOP buyout level.[96]

Economist Glenn Beamer argues that while the ESOP never achieved the level of worker democracy that many labor progressives had hoped it would, the ESOP nevertheless provided workers with the ability to make decisions during critical moments such as softening the blow of job loss through early retirements, which enabled many younger workers to keep their jobs longer.[97] Historian Judith Stein has observed that the architects of the Civil Rights Act presumed that a robust economy and a labor market free from bigotry would correct the past ills of discrimination. They had not imagined a sharp decline in the economic sectors that disproportionately employed members of racial minorities.[98] Weirton Steel's consent decree hardly lasted a decade before the company experienced massive reductions in force.

Economist Don Goldstein found that because of the exodus of investment capital from the steel industry, the jobs that the Weirton ESOP saved were "ultimately, mostly unsalvageable in the context of global overcapacity, competition, and consolidation." By the late 2000s, Weirton Steel had been reincorporated as a "bit player in a fully consolidated and globalized industry," and the "financially-driven corporate restructuring in steel and other basic industries" had decimated industrial unions and working-class communities. In the world of finance, where short-term profitability took precedence over longevity, labor was but one more form of capital. Moreover, downsizing and divestiture did not foster the kind of innovation that industry-specific investments once did. Finally, Goldstein concluded, without a significant working-class reform movement, investors would likely continue such slash-and-burn strategies.[99] If so, other communities like those of Hancock County would continue to be treated like entries on a ledger sheet rather than as communities of human beings built on a foundation of wage work.

Conclusion

Regardless of the desires of local workers and voters, global forces ultimately overwhelmed their ability to control their employment. Steelworkers in Weirton attempted to cement their control by creating an employee stock ownership plan to take over the steel company, but the worker-owned company, suffering from massive debts, mismanagement, fickle capital investment, and global overcapacity in the steel industry, went bankrupt. Foreign competition drove several local pottery companies out of business, contributing to rising levels of unemployment. By the century's end, few of the county's industrial jobs remained.

All the while, rural-industrial workers in Hancock County had to negotiate changing gender and racial divisions. Women and African Americans demanded access to better jobs at Weirton Steel, now aided by the Civil Rights Act of 1964, and Weirton Steel responded by opening up new departments and jobs to them. Women in the potteries demanded an end to discriminatory practices as well, especially separate pay scales for men and women. For women and African Americans, these were important steps toward equality, but true economic equality was never realized because just as women and African Americans gained access to better jobs, the jobs began disappearing by the thousands. Capital mobility, which had once brought jobs to this rural-industrial place, had undone it by the 1990s.

CONCLUSION

Country People and Capital Mobility

Richard Cameron worked at Weirton Steel most of his adult life, as did many of his family members. In 2007, the mill was nearly gone. Fewer than a thousand people worked in some of the finishing departments, but basic steel production there had come to a halt. Workers in Hancock County had struggled for decades to achieve modest, dependable incomes and decent lives. During those decades, they continually adapted to new technologies, shifting markets, and changes within the working class. The wrenching economic changes of the last quarter of the twentieth century left many working families wondering what it was all about. Cameron summarized these feelings when he said:

> Both my brothers worked at Weirton. My brother-in-law worked at Weirton. Dad worked at Weirton. I'm telling you, Weirton was good to us. And right today, I don't know what I'd be if it wasn't for Weirton Steel, because they were really good to me. And it's a shame to see it go this way. It hurts. And even after I retired—and it's been twenty years now—I'd like to see it come back. But I don't know if it will or not. Because, you know, Lou, you take 14,500 employees, that's a lot of people. And when I was a welder, I built—we built—Number 5 Tandem, Number 5 electrolytic line, Number 4 electrolytic line. And it's done.[1]

For Cameron and many others—who created a world based on job stability and family security through many years of hard work, self-reliance, and local control, and who lived comfortable lives during those decades of prosperity—the arbitrariness of industrial restructuring was deeply unsettling.

The construction of new factories transformed Hancock County, West Virginia, into a rural-industrial place at the start of the twentieth century, and as the companies installed new technologies, country people came to play increasingly important roles in the production processes of those factories. Industrialists' ideas about the country and country people figured prominently into their relocations to "undeveloped" places. The 1880s and 1890s witnessed the rise of the American city but also concerns about urban disorder and corruption. The rapid, unplanned growth of cities coincided with a myriad of ever-worsening problems such as fires, epidemics, crime, and violence, and the countryside, in contrast, appeared tranquil and healthy. In an era when the American elite believed that one's environment could have a salutary or degrading effect on the individual, relocating to the countryside, so the logic went, would also result in a more orderly and efficient workforce.[2] Not only could they relocate skilled workers from the city to the country, they could employ the virtuous sons and daughters of farmers.[3] Ironically, many manufacturers envisioned farm boys and farm girls making ideal employees at the same time that some "local color" writers promulgated ideas about rural people being hopelessly backwards, untouched by the modernizing influences shaping the rest of the nation.[4]

The realities of country life and country people were never so simple. The portrait that emerges from this study of working people in northern West Virginia during the twentieth century is one of continual adaptation and search for stability.[5] These rural people—whether they came to Hancock County from central Appalachia, the American South, or Europe—formed new communities in and around these small factory towns and adjusted their lifestyles to the continually changing production processes, to evolving political and legal climates, to the success and failure of unionization drives, and to improving and declining paychecks. A collection of strangers grafted their notions of community onto the rural places and factory towns they found when they arrived looking for factory jobs. They had a desire for local control and worked to protect their small measure of stability in the chaotic world of industrial restructuring. For as long as these goals lined up with local industrialists' goals of maintaining local variations, such as low wages, company loyalty, or a lack of militancy, workers and managers made good allies, whether it was testifying to Congress about the dangers of foreign competition or negotiating wages and benefits without strikes.[6] When their goals clashed, rural-industrial workers and their employers clashed as well, but neither labor nor management looked to overturn an essentially local system of negotiation.

The politics of the working families of Hancock County emanated from a desire for local control as well, and the workers viewed the issues of welfare, unionism, and international trade through that lens. It is instructive to compare them to the workers of Chicago during the 1920s and 1930s. Workers in Chicago and Hancock County shared the same long-term goals, but their strategies differed. Lizabeth Cohen found that industrial workers in Chicago developed survival strategies to cope with the uncertainties of life under industrial capitalism that included the development of ethnic mutual benefit networks and participation in the welfare capitalism programs of their employers. But as workers' needs during the Great Depression overwhelmed those networks and programs, they turned to the Democratic Party to extend the obligations of the federal welfare state and to provide federal protections for stronger industrial unions. She concludes:

> During the 1930s, American industrial workers sought to overcome the miseries and frustrations that long had plagued their lives neither through anticapitalist and extragovernmental revolutionary uprisings nor through perpetuation of the status quo of welfare capitalism but rather through their growing investment in two institutions they felt would make capitalism moral and fair—an activist welfare state concerned with equalizing wealth and privilege and a national union movement of factory workers committed to keeping a check on self-interested employers.[7]

As frontline shop stewards preached a culture of unity and as workers enjoyed improved wages and benefits as a result of national collective action, their commitment to national unions and national politics deepened.

While Chicago's industrial workers were driven to "look beyond their ethnic networks and bosses for help," workers in Hancock County were not. The Great Depression neither devastated local industries nor these rural-industrial workers' survival strategies, which relied heavily on "making do." They built their own homes, gardened, raised livestock, preserved much of the harvest, and hunted for local game. In doing so, their identification with the land, their place, their family, and their community grew stronger, strengthening the preexisting localism of their rural culture. They also did not—or could not—join the national labor movement and did not experience the disciplined collective actions that welded together a great New Deal coalition of diverse and far-flung working communities.

Yet, workers in Hancock County lived in a political economy that was greatly influenced by urban workers, national union leaders, and New Deal Democrats. While Hancock County's industrial workers benefited from the unionization movement of the 1930s and 1940s and the extension of the welfare state, it was not truly a world of their making, and these steel and pottery workers came to prefer local control of unions and companies and did not agitate for either greater federal intervention in the workplace or greater union authority to combat management. They tasked politicians, especially in the 1950s and 1960s, with protecting their communities from powerful outside forces—the powerful bureaucratic administrations in Washington, the powerful union bosses in Pittsburgh, and the powerful forces of global trade.

Working-class agency is a pivotal issue for labor historians looking at twentieth-century history, and the postwar reversal of labor's political fortunes has led historians to question how much control the American working class truly possessed. Cohen found agency among Chicago's working class in the 1930s to a remarkable degree. Through collective action, they shaped welfare capitalism, CIO organizing strategies, New Deal programs, and Democratic Party platforms. Then, in a brief paragraph at the end of her marvelous study, Cohen outlines the sad fate of working-class agency after 1940, noting that the Democratic Party, the federal government, and the CIO became less responsive to working-class influences and more controlling. She summarizes, "The Democratic Party came out of the war committed to using the powers of government to ensure economic growth and no longer as concerned about balancing that goal with efforts to tame capitalism's excesses." When President Truman intervened on behalf of employers during the 1945–1946 strike wave and Congress passed the Taft-Hartley amendments, it became clear that the federal government was no longer strengthening the power of unions. "Government intervention in industrial relations that in the 1930s had protected workers' rights," Cohen wrote, "now presided over their restriction. It became harder for workers and their unions to strike, to establish the closed shop, to influence employers' hiring and firing, to take sides in federal elections, and to tolerate political diversity within their own ranks. During the war years, moreover, the CIO itself became increasingly entrenched in bureaucratic politics that served to reinforce the power of the leadership over the grassroots and the power of political centrists over progressives."[8]

It is not uncommon for labor historians to portray the CIO and the Democratic Party as forces that turned against industrial workers during and after World War II, but examining more and more groups like the rural-industrial workers of northern West Virginia may complicate that narrative. Certainly many working-class militants and progressives in Chicago and other cities found themselves at odds with the institutions they had so effectively shaped during the 1930s, but the rural-industrial workers of Hancock County saw their values increasingly reflected in those governmental restrictions of union power. Steel and pottery workers and their families sent explicit orders to their politicians to limit the authority of unions and union officials, to limit the welfare state, and to protect their industries from foreign competition above all other concerns. In other words, they joined with other segments of society to thwart the efforts of workers in cities like Chicago to continue on a path toward social democracy. Instead, Hancock County's industrial workers envisioned a world where local people still controlled their own fate, and for decades they accomplished that very thing.

The divergent paths of the rural-industrial workers of Hancock County and the urban-industrial workers of places like Chicago suggests that place and local culture must be examined to fully understand national changes. Studies of workers in a handful of major cities across the country are not necessarily representative of the experiences of the American working class as a whole. Many scholars have treated workers' places as nothing more than settings where events occur, but place figured into workers' identities, enabled them to retain some cultural practices but not others, and resulted in a great diversity of beliefs and behaviors among the working class. Finally, workers' attachments to their places became a liability of sorts in the age of capital mobility.[9]

The communities that these rural-industrial workers formed must have seemed as though they were built upon a stable and solid foundation: the industrial economy. In the center of one of the leading industrial nations in the world, it must have seemed to working people that their communities would last as long as any of history's great empires. Sadly, those communities, once formed, struggled to last beyond three generations of workers. In 1999, Weirton mayor and steelworker Dean Harris said that the American Dream was being "taken" from the people of Weirton. He said, "We thought that if we worked hard, we'd attain that dream, and now we're losing it."[10] One journalist observed that there was a "pervasive sense here that 'our fate is out of our hands.'" The people of Weirton, he continued, would commonly say, "We did everything we were asked to do." They would say, "We downsized, we modernized, we made sacrifices. But none of that matters. It's still not good enough. What do we do now? Who can tell us?" As the future of the American steel industry waits to be decided, he wrote, "Weirton is trembling."[11]

In his book *Striking Steel, Solidarity Remembered*, Jack Metzgar writes that the working class in mid-twentieth-century America valued belonging to a community much more than career achievements. In fact, when his father insisted he get on the "college track" in high school, most of Jack's friends felt sorry for him. Furthermore, aspiring to a middle-class job seemed inextricably linked to relocating away from home, away from his community. Metzgar writes, "Though many eventually would, hardly anybody *wanted* to 'leave the valley' then. I didn't."[12] In his book *Steelworker Alley*, Robert Bruno also presents a portrait of a place where people are defined by their relationship to others. They lived in a community of steelworkers that had its own values and its own culture, a world unto itself that they had created, a world where they belonged.[13] Through their desire for local control, the rural-industrial workers of Hancock County similarly declared their membership in a community that, in turn, defined their place in the world.

But those values and those understandings of the world clashed with the goals of industrial capitalism's power brokers. Viewing working-class communities within the broader context of global industrial restructuring brings up the question of whether any community built on industrial jobs can hope for anything approaching permanence. If the working class constructs a world largely defined by family, community, and place, their efforts to build such a world will be continually frustrated when capital relocates, and the result will in essence be one identity crisis after another. The people of Hancock County are once again grappling with their place in the world, new forms of work, and new identities, and they are relocating in search of new jobs, new communities, and new ways of living.

The rural-industrial working-class culture that emerged in Hancock County—based on adapting rural habits to life in factory towns—gradually disappeared in the late twentieth century. First, the ethic of making do traveled well from the farm to the factory town, but it began its decline in the late 1960s and 1970s as buying power increased and industrial workers focused more on vacations or socializing and less on making do. While many people in Hancock County still tend gardens, work on their houses, hunt, and fish, these activities no longer supplement family income the way they did in the 1950s. The localism of their culture may have persisted in some ways to the present, but a localized system of negotiation that local manufacturers helped create disappeared along with many of those companies. Between 1980 and 2010, one-quarter of the residents left the county as its population dropped from an all-time high of 40,418 to 30,676.[14] The largest employer in the county is now Mountaineer Casino Racetrack & Resort, directly employing 1,300 people in addition to 2,300 "licensed nonemployees" at the racetrack, such as jockeys and trainers.[15] As the workers who remain find themselves increasingly employed at the casino or commuting an hour or more to cities in the region, the rural-industrial culture that was once so pervasive is being replaced by a new way of life. Undoubtedly in potteries and steel mills on the latest frontiers of industrial capitalism, a new generation of country people is being introduced to factory systems with new business organizations, various sexual divisions of labor, and evolving production processes. Where their rural culture meets the latest industrial schemes, a new rural-industrial culture will emerge.

NOTES

INTRODUCTION

1. Louis Truax, "The 200th Anniversary of the City of Weirton, West Va., and My Life Story as I Have Seen Weirton Grow" (manuscript in author's possession [Weirton, 1971]), i, 8–9, 36–37, 46.

2. These small towns are subjects in the recent labor histories and are important exceptions: G. C. Waldrep III, *Southern Workers and the Search for Community: Spartanburg, South Carolina* (Urbana: University of Illinois Press, 2000); Wilson J. Warren, *Struggling with "Iowa's Pride": Labor Relations, Unionism, and Politics in the Rural Midwest Since 1877* (Iowa City: University of Iowa Press, 2000); Laurie Mercier, *Anaconda: Labor, Community, and Culture in Montana's Smelter City* (Urbana: University of Illinois Press, 2001); and William P. Jones, *The Tribe of Black Ulysses: African American Lumber Workers in the Jim Crow South* (Urbana: University of Illinois Press, 2005).

3. Robert Bruno, Steelworker Alley: How Class Works in Youngstown (Ithaca, N.Y.: ILR Press, 1999).

4. Thomas Edsall and Mary Edsall, *Chain Reaction* (New York: Norton, 1991); Jonathan Reider, "The Rise of the 'Silent Majority'" in *The Rise and Fall of the New Deal Order, 1930–1980.* ed. Steve Fraser and Gary Gerstle (Princeton, N.J.: Princeton University Press, 1990).

5. Art Preis, *Labor's Giant Step: Twenty Years of the CIO* (New York: Pioneer Press, 1964).

6. Staughton Lynd, "The Possibility of Radicalism in the Early 1930s: The Case of

Steel," *Radical America* 6 (1972); Nelson Lichtenstein, *Labor's War at Home: The CIO in World War II* (New York: Cambridge University Press, 1982).

7. Becky Nicolaides, *My Blue Heaven: Life and Politics in the Working-Class Suburbs of Los Angeles, 1920–1965* (Chicago: University of Chicago Press, 2002); Kenneth Durr, *Behind the Backlash: White Working-Class Politics in Baltimore, 1940–1980* (Chapel Hill: University of North Carolina Press, 2003); Thomas Sugrue, *The Origins of the Urban Crisis: Race and Inequality in Postwar Detroit* (Princeton, N.J.: Princeton University Press, 1996).

8. In the introduction to his history of rural America, for example, David B. Danbom writes that what his book actually delivers is "mainly a study of farm people in America" partly because the "vast bulk of the rural social, economic, and political history produced in the past generation has focused on farm people." *Born in the Country: A History of Rural America* (Baltimore: Johns Hopkins University Press, 1995), xi.

9. For example, Alan Brinkley writes, "The industrialization and commercialization of America changed the face of society in countless ways. Nowhere were these changes more profound than in the growth of cities and the creation of an urban society and culture." *American History: A Survey*, 9th ed. (New York: McGraw-Hill, 1995), 507.

10. Richard Simon, "The Development of Underdevelopment: The Coal Industry and Its Effect on the West Virginia Economy" (PhD diss., University of Pittsburgh, 1978), 290.

11. Ronald L. Lewis, *Transforming the Appalachian Countryside: Railroads, Deforestation, and Social Change in West Virginia, 1880–1920* (Chapel Hill: University of North Carolina Press, 1998); Larry Lankton, *Cradle to Grave: Life, Work, and Death at the Superior Copper Mines* (New York: Oxford University Press, 1991); Carl Smith, *Urban Disorder and the Shape of Belief: The Great Chicago Fire, the Haymarket Bomb, and the Model Town of Pullman* (Chicago: University of Chicago Press, 1994); Anne E. Mosher, *Capital's Utopia: Vandergrift, Pennsylvania, 1855–1916* (Baltimore: Johns Hopkins University Press, 2004); Margaret Crawford, *Building the Workingman's Paradise: The Design of American Company Towns* (New York: Verso, 1995).

12. David L. Carlton, "The American South and the American Manufacturing Belt," in *The South, the Nation, and the World: Perspectives on Southern Economic Development*, ed. David L. Carlton and Peter Coclanis (Charlottesville: University of Virginia Press, 2003), 175–76.

13. There were 2,692,187 wage earners outside of towns and cities with populations of ten thousand or more; 975,896 in towns between ten thousand and twenty-five thousand; 1,638,971 in towns between twenty-five thousand and one hundred thousand; and 3,789,918 in cities of one hundred thousand or more. U.S. Department of Commerce, *Statistical Abstract of the United States, 1921* (Washington, D.C.: Government Printing Office, 1922), 223.

14. Ronald L. Lewis, "Appalachian Restructuring in Historical Perspective: Coal, Culture and Social Change in West Virginia," *Urban Studies* 30 (1993): 299, 301. He writes that in 1930, 72 percent lived in rural areas.

15. Doreen Massey, *Spatial Divisions of Labor: Social Structures and the Geography of Production*, 2nd ed. (New York: Routledge, 1995), 31–34, 53–56, 65–120.

16. For one example, see Bill Jones and Ronald L. Lewis, "Gender and Transnationality Among Welsh Tinplate Workers in Pittsburgh: The Hattie Williams Affair, 1895," *Labor History* 48 (May 2007): 175–94.

17. Alice Galenson provides an overview of the shift in *The Migration of the Cotton Textile Industry from New England to the South: 1880–1930* (New York: Garland, 1985).

18. James C. Cobb, *Industrialization and Southern Society, 1877–1984* (Lexington: University Press of Kentucky, 1984); Bruce J. Schulman, *From Cotton Belt to Sunbelt: Federal Policy, Economic Development, and the Transformation of the South, 1939–1980* (New York: Oxford University Press, 1991).

19. Sugrue, *The Origins of the Urban Crisis*, 125–27.

20. Jefferson Cowie, *Capital Moves: RCA's Seventy-Year Quest for Cheap Labor* (New York: New Press, 2001), 2.

21. Mosher, *Capital's Utopia*.

22. Ken Fones-Wolf, *Glass Towns: Industry, Labor, and Political Economy in Appalachia, 1890–1930s* (Urbana: University of Illinois Press, 2007).

23. The best histories of the pottery industry are Marc J. Stern, *The Pottery Industry of Trenton: A Skilled Trade in Transition, 1850–1929* (New Brunswick, N.J.: Rutgers University Press, 1994); and William C. Gates, *The City of Hills and Kilns: Life and Work in East Liverpool, Ohio* (East Liverpool, Ohio: East Liverpool Historical Society, 1984).

24. For studies of the tinplate industry, see Donald E. Dunbar, *The Tin-Plate Industry: A Comparative Study of Its Growth in the United States and in Wales* (Boston: Houghton Mifflin, 1915); and Louis C. Martin, "Tin Plate Towns, 1890–1910: Local Labor Movements and Workers' Response to the Crisis in the Steelworkers' Union," *Pennsylvania History* 74 (Autumn 2007): 492–528.

25. Massey, *Spatial Divisions of Labor*, 31–34, 39–43. Massey also makes the point that the social status of the person employed in a certain job—rather than the tasks of the job—may in fact determine whether that job is skilled or not.

26. Lewis, "Appalachian Restructuring in Historical Perspective," 299, 301.

27. Classic labor histories often discussed "preindustrial" culture. See Sidney Pollard, "Factory Discipline in the Industrial Revolution," *Economic History Review* 16 (1963): 254–71; Herbert G. Gutman, "Work, Culture, and Society in Industrializing America, 1815–1919," *American Historical Review* 78, no. 3 (June 1973): 531–88. There are several histories that examine rural-industrial workers without explicitly searching for a rural-industrial culture. See the studies in note 2 above as well as David Alan Corbin, *Life, Work, and Rebellion in the Coal Fields: The Southern West Virginia Miners, 1880–1922* (Urbana: University of Illinois Press, 1981).

28. For descriptions of this trend in labor history, see Leon Fink, *In Search of the Working Class: Essays in American Labor History and Political Culture* (Urbana: University of Illinois Press, 1994), 186; and Cowie, *Capital Moves*, 7.

29. Lizbeth Cohen, *Making a New Deal: Industrial Workers in Chicago, 1919–1939* (New York: Cambridge University Press, 1990), 157–58.

30. For one study of such exaggerations, see J. W. Williamson, *Hillbillyland: What the Movies Did to the Mountains and What the Mountains Did to the Movies* (Chapel Hill: University of North Carolina Press, 1995).

31. Thomas E. Williams, "Rural America in an Urban Age, 1945–1960," in *Reshaping America: Society and Institutions, 1945–1960*, ed. Robert H. Bremmer and Gary W. Reichard (Columbus: Ohio State University Press, 1982), 149.

32. Susan Carol Rogers, *Shaping Modern Times in Rural France: Transformation and Reproduction of an Aveyronnais Community* (Princeton, N.J.: Princeton University Press, 1991), 12.

33. Rogers, *Shaping Modern Times*, 73.

34. For the phrase "self-reliant independence," see Hal S. Barron, *Mixed Harvest: The Second Great Transformation in the Rural North, 1870–1930* (Chapel Hill: University of North Carolina Press, 1997), 21–22. Also see Jeanette Keith, *Country People in the New South: Tennessee's Upper Cumberland* (Chapel Hill: University of North Carolina Press, 1995).

35. Anthony Cohen, "Belonging: The Experience of Culture," in *Belonging: Identity and Social Organisation in British Rural Cultures*, ed. Anthony Cohen (Manchester, UK: Manchester University Press, 1982), 6–7.

36. Cohen, *Making a New Deal*, 253.

37. Labor studies scholar Jack Metzgar uses the phrase "disciplined collective action" in his study of steelworkers' solidarity *Striking Steel: Solidarity Remembered* (Philadelphia: Temple University Press, 2000), 29–30.

38. Jeremy Brecher, *Strike!*, rev. and updated (Cambridge, Mass.: South End Press, 1997), 283–84. For more on the CIO "culture of unity," see Cohen, *Making a New Deal*, chap. 8.

39. U.S. Department of Labor, Bureau of Labor Statistics, "Employment and Earnings Statistics for the United States, 1909–1960," Bulletin No. 1312, 1961, pp. 87–99.

40. Metzgar, *Striking Steel*, 30. For Metzgar's broader discussion of the 1945–1946 strike wave see "The 1945–1946 Strike Wave," in *The Encyclopedia of Strikes in American History*, ed. Aaron Brenner, Benjamin Day, and Immanuel Ness (Armonk, N.Y.: M. E. Sharpe, 2009), 216–24.

41. Rick Halpern, *Down on the Killing Floor: Black and White Workers in Chicago's Packinghouses, 1904–54* (Urbana: University of Illinois Press, 1997), 190–91.

42. Lisa M. Fine, *The Story of Reo Joe: Work, Kin, and Community in Autotown, U.S.A.* (Philadelphia: Temple University Press, 2004), 6.

43. See Janet Irons, *Testing the New Deal: The General Textile Strike of 1934 in the American South* (Urbana: University of Illinois Press, 2000), 73–76. Also see Waldrep's comparison of the mill villages of Clifton and Judson in *Southern Workers and the Search for Community*, 64.

44. Deborah Fink, *Cutting into the Meatpacking Line: Workers and Change in the Rural Midwest* (Chapel Hill: University of North Carolina Press, 1998), 165–66.

45. Doreen Massey argues that distance has been "a great divider of the working class." *Spatial Divisions of Labor*, 53.

46. Melissa Walker, "'All We Knew to Do Was Farm': Gender, Class, Race, and Change Among East Tennessee Farm Women, 1920–1941" (PhD diss., Clark University, 1996), chap. 2. See page 52 for this definition of "making do."

47. Gerald Zahavi, "Negotiated Loyalty: Welfare Capitalism and the Shoeworkers of Endicott Johnson, 1920–1940," *Journal of American History* 70 (December 1983): 602–20.

48. For coverage of Weirton Steel's pension problems, see Vicki Smith, "Weirton Steel Reorganization Plan Calls for Job Cuts, Elimination of Pension, Health Care for Retirees," *Pittsburgh Post Gazette*, October 8, 2003; Smith, "Weirton Steel Retirees Outraged Over Plan that Wipes Out Pensions," *Pittsburgh Post Gazette*, October 9, 2003; Len Boselovic, "Weirton Steel Pension Plan Terminated," *Pittsburgh Post Gazette*, October 22, 2004, all articles accessed online at post-gazette.com August 7, 2012.

49. For a story about workers trying to adapt to the factories of Apple in China, see Charles Duhigg and David Barboza, "In China, Human Costs Are Built Into an iPad," *New York Times*, January 25, 2012.

CHAPTER 1.
A RURAL PLACE AND A RURAL PEOPLE

1. Lyman Stedman, Farmer and Politician, Diary, 1880–1885, A&M 2042, West Virginia and Regional History Collection, Morgantown, West Virginia (hereafter cited as Stedman diary); U.S. Bureau of the Census, 1870 United States Federal Census Population Schedules, West Virginia, Hancock County, Butler Division, Roll M593, accessed online at www.ancestry.com on August 8, 2012; 1880 United States Federal Census Population Schedules, West Virginia, Butler Division, Roll 1403, accessed online at www.ancestry.com on August 8, 2012. Note that by 1880, Audubon Stedman lived next door to Lyman with his own wife and child and is listed in the census as A. J. Stedman. Also, it is not surprising that Blanche was seldom mentioned as she had moved out of the house by the 1880s, but for simplicity I wanted to list the entire family as it was in 1870, which is discussed later in the chapter.

2. J. H. Newton, G. G. Nichols, and A. G. Sprankle, *History of the Pan-Handle; being Historical Collections of the Counties of Ohio, Brooke, Marshall, and Hancock, West Virginia* (Wheeling, W.V.: J. A. Caldwell, 1879), 421.

3. Thomas P. Slaughter, *The Whiskey Rebellion: Frontier Epilogue to the American Revolution* (New York: Oxford University Press, 1986), 66; Donald Edward Davis, *Where There Are Mountains: An Environmental History of the Southern Appalachians* (Athens: University of Georgia Press, 2000), chap. 5.

4. Joseph Doddridge, *Notes on the Settlement and Indian Wars of the Western Parts of Virginia and Pennsylvania from 1763 to 1783*, reprint of 3rd ed. (Parsons, W.V.: McClain Publishing, 1996), quote on 87; biographical sketch on 243–60.

5. Doddridge, *Notes on the Settlement*, 19.

6. Otis K. Rice, *The Allegheny Frontier: West Virginia Beginnings, 1730–1830* (Lexington: University Press of Kentucky, 1970), 321–22.

7. John Richard Beach, "The Sheep Industry in Upper Ohio Area, 1770–1973: A Geographical Analysis" (PhD diss., University of Pittsburgh, 1975), 63–64, 102.

8. Ibid., 69, 170–71.

9. Ibid., 116.

10. For the 1860 average of northern farms, see Dwight B. Billings and Kathleen M. Blee, *The Road to Poverty: The Making of Wealth and Hardship in Appalachia* (New York: Cambridge University Press, 2000), 180. I surveyed every tenth farm in the 1850 agricultural census in Hancock, Brooke, and Ohio counties in what was then Virginia. U.S. Bureau of the Census, Schedule 2—Productions of Agriculture, Brooke, Hancock, Ohio Counties, State of Virginia, 1850, microfilm, West Virginia and Regional History Collection, Morgantown, West Virginia.

11. Nancy Lee Caldwell, *A History of Brooke County* (Wellsburg, W.V.: Brooke County Historical Society, 1975), 117; Rice, *The Allegheny Frontier*, 322. The mill in Steubenville was known as the Wells and Dickinson Mill. Beach, "The Sheep Industry in Upper Ohio Area," 71, 82.

12. Charles Franklin Conklin, "A Study of the Economic Development of the Northern Panhandle of West Virginia" (PhD diss., University of Pittsburgh, 1959), 208.

13. James Morton Callahan, *History of West Virginia Old and New* (Chicago: American Historical Society, 1923), 527–28; Conklin, "A Study of the Economic Development," 115–16; Jack Welch, *History of Hancock County, Virginia and West Virginia*, rev. ed. (1963; repr. Abilene, Tex.: WriteRight Publishing, 1992), 18–20.

14. Barbara Rasmussen, National Register of Historic Places Form, "Hellings, Nathan, Apple Barn," http://www.wvculture.org/shpo/nr/pdf/hancock/02001529.pdf, accessed on February 9, 2015. See also Frank Chapman, "History of the Grimes Golden Apple" (typescript at West Virginia and Regional History Collection, Wellsburg, W.V., 1929).

15. For a discussion of "subsistence-surplus," see Christopher Clark, *Roots of Rural Capitalism: Western Massachusetts, 1780–1860* (Ithaca, N.Y.: Cornell University Press, 1990), 28–38. Clark's book was the culmination of a multidecade debate over whether an entrepreneurial spirit existed among northern farmers. That topic is well beyond the scope of this study, but the fact that the county's agriculture was so diversified in the age of railroads suggests that farmers still prized subsistence above profit.

16. U.S. Bureau of the Census, Schedule 2—Productions of Agriculture in Butler District of the County of Hancock, State of West Virginia, 1880, microfilm, West Virginia and Regional History Collection, Morgantown, West Virginia.

17. Ibid. On helper girls, see Laurel Thatcher Ulrich, "Martha Ballard and Her Girls: Women's Work in Eighteenth-Century Maine," in *Work and Labor in Early America*, ed. Stephen Innes (Chapel Hill: University of North Carolina Press, 1988) 70–105.

18. James R. Dietz, *Memoir of James R. Dietz* (Weirton, W.V.: James R. Dietz, 1979), 17. His family's farm was near Mount Lookout in Nicholas County.

19. Melissa Walker, *All We Knew Was to Farm: Rural Women in the Upcountry South, 1919–1941* (Baltimore: Johns Hopkins University Press, 2000), chap. 2. I rely heavily on Walker's discussion of making do.

20. Newton, Nichols, and Sprankle, *History of the Pan-Handle*, 421.

21. Erma Huff, *Up High and Down Main in Pughtown, W. Va.* (New Cumberland, W.V.: Hancock County Courier Printing Company, 1981); David T. Javersak, *History of Weirton, West Virginia* (Virginia Beach, Va.: Donning, 1999), 17–32; Welch, *History of Hancock County*, 78.

22. Welch, *History of Hancock County*, 43–44.

23. Stephanie McCurry, *Masters of Small Worlds: Yeoman Households, Gender Relations, & the Political Culture of the Antebellum South Carolina Low Country* (New York: Oxford University Press, 1995); Joan M. Jensen, *Loosening the Bonds: Mid-Atlantic Farm Women, 1750–1850* (Princeton, N.J.: Yale University Press, 1986); Walker, *All We Knew Was to Farm*; Jeannette Keith, *Country People in the New South: Tennessee's Upper Cumberland* (Chapel Hill: University of North Carolina Press, 1995), chap. 2.

24. Robert Richardson, *Memoirs of Alexander Campbell* (Philadelphia: J. B. Lippincott & Co., 1868), 465–66. Also see Thomas Jefferson, *Notes on the States of Virginia*, wherein he writes, "Those who labour in the earth are the chosen people of God, if ever he had a chosen people, whose breasts he has made his peculiar deposit for substantial and genuine virtue." *Notes on the State of Virginia*, ed. Merrill D. Patterson (orig. 1781–1782; New York: Library of America, 1984), accessed at http://etext.lib.virginia.edu/toc/modeng/public/JefVirg.html on March 3, 2011.

25. McCurry, *Masters of Small Worlds*, 56. For a study of the political and economic division between western Virginia and the Tidewater, see Charles H. Ambler, *Sectionalism in Virginia from 1776 to 1861*, 2nd ed. (1910; repr. Morgantown: West Virginia University Press, 2008).

26. *New Cumberland Independent*, April 18, 1907.

27. Newton, Nichols, and Sprankle, *History of the Pan-Handle*, 440, 443, 446.

28. Beach, "The Sheep Industry in Upper Ohio Area," 82, 162, 170–71.

29. Stedman diary, August 1880 through October 1880, pages 1–12.

30. Ibid., November 1880 through April 1881, pages 12–28.

31. Ibid., April 1881 through May 1881, pages 28–35.

32. Ibid., June 1881 through August 188, pages 35–48.

33. Doddridge, *Notes on the Settlement*, 98–101; also see Kim M. Gruenwald, *River of Enterprise: The Commercial Origins of Regional Identity in the Ohio Valley, 1790–1850* (Bloomington: Indiana University Press, 2002), 31, on pelt business in the region.

34. Louis Truax, "The 200th Anniversary of the City of Weirton, West Va., and My Life Story as I Have Seen Weirton Grow" (manuscript in author's possession [Weirton, 1971]), 41. Also see Durwood Dunn, *Cades Cove: The Life and Death of a Southern Appalachian Community, 1818–1937* (Knoxville: University of Tennessee Press, 1988), 27–30, for a brief discussion of the hunting practices of pioneers and farmers.

35. According to Mary Beth Pudup, historians have also tended to ignore the role women played in the nineteenth-century economic history of West Virginia, first by viewing the agricultural period (during which a woman's contribution to the cash income of the household often equaled that of her husband) as merely a transitory stage to industrial capitalism, and second by discussing the market activities of male farmers almost exclusively. "Women's Work in the West Virginia Economy," *West Virginia History* 49 (1990): 7–20. Accessed online at http://www.wvculture.org/history/journal_wvh/wvh49-2.html.

36. McCurry, *Masters of Small Worlds*, 58. Faragher also makes the point that women's work was essential. *Sugar Creek*, 100–101.

37. For discussions of reproductive work see Faragher, *Sugar Creek*, chap. 12; Jensen, *Loosening the Bonds*, chap. 3; and Pudup, "Women's Work," 7–20.

38. For a thorough and authoritative discussion of women's farm work including butter production, see Jensen, *Loosening the Bonds*, chaps. 2, 3, 5, and 6. For Stedman and Truax butter production, see U.S. Bureau of the Census, Schedule 2—Productions of Agriculture in Butler District of the County of Hancock, State of West Virginia, 1880.

39. McCurry, *Masters of Small Worlds*, chap. 3.

40. Quoted in Pudup, "Women's Work."

41. Stephanie McCurry makes this point very well. *Masters of Small Worlds*, 75.

42. Dietz, *Memoir of James R. Dietz*, 22–23.

43. John Walker Dinsmore, *Scotch-Irish in America* (Chicago, 1906), 186–93, quoted in Peter E. Gilmore, "Rebels and Revivals: Ulster Immigrants, Western Pennsylvania Presbyterianism and the Formation of Scotch-Irish Identity, 1780–1830" (PhD diss., Carnegie Mellon University, 2009), 674. On corn husks, see Keith, *Country People*, 16–17.

44. On letting hogs roam free, see Altina Waller, *Feud: Hatfields, McCoys, and Social Change in Appalachia, 1860–1900* (Chapel Hill: University of North Carolina Press, 1988), 63–65; Jack Temple Kirby, *Poquosin: A Study in Rural Landscape and Society* (Chapel Hill: University of North Carolina Press, 1995), 98–103. For a more general discussion of the interdependency of farming families in the northern United States in the nineteenth century, see Clark, *Roots of Rural Capitalism*.

45. Gilmore, "Rebels and Revivals," 673–76.

46. Faragher, *Sugar Creek*, 133–34.

47. Keith, *Country People*, 20.

48. Keith, *Country People*, 26. Faragher also discusses kinship in *Sugar Creek*.

49. Chad Montrie, *Making a Living: Work and Environment in the United States* (Chapel Hill: University of North Carolina Press, 2008), chap. 1.

50. Mary Meek Atkeson, *The Woman on the Farm* (New York: The Century Co., 1924), 11.

51. Hal S. Barron, *Mixed Harvest: The Second Great Transformation in the Rural North, 1870–1930* (Chapel Hill: University of North Carolina Press, 1997), 14, 21–22.

52. "Unfortunate Poor People," *New York Times*, March 30, 1881.

53. *New Cumberland Independent*, February 14, 1907.

54. On tariffs and industry in West Virginia, see Ken Fones-Wolf, *Glass Towns: Industry, Labor, and Political Economy in Appalachia, 1890–1930s* (Urbana: University of Illinois Press, 2007), 66–67; also see Ken Fones-Wolf, "'Caught Between Revolutions': Wheeling Germans in the Civil War Era," in *Transnational West Virginia: Ethnic Communities and Economic Change, 1840–1940*, ed. Ken Fones-Wolf and Ronald L. Lewis (Morgantown, W.V.: West Virginia University Press, 2002), 19–47, on the rise of the Republican Party in Wheeling, West Virginia. See also "Mr. Hubbard Talks on New Tariff Bill," *New Cumberland Independent*, August 12, 1909.

55. For a thorough discussion of the "development faith," see Fones-Wolf, *Glass Towns*, chap. 3. For farmers' opposition to railroads, see Ronald L. Lewis, *Transforming the Appalachian Countryside: Railroads, Deforestation, and Social Change in West Virginia, 1880–1920* (Chapel Hill: University of North Carolina Press, 1998), chap. 9; William D. Barnes, "The Grange and Populist Movements in West Virginia, 1873–1914" (PhD diss., West Virginia University, 1946).

56. Michael J. Dubin, *United States Gubernatorial Elections, 1861–1911: The Official Results by State and County* (Jefferson, N.C.: MacFarland & Co., 2010).

57. George W. Atkinson and Alvaro F. Gibbens, *Prominent Men of West Virginia* (Wheeling, W.V.: W. L. Callin, 1890), 812–14.

58. George W. Atkinson, "Inaugural Address, Delivered March 4, 1897." At http://www.wvculture.org/history/atkinsonia.html, accessed March 18, 2012.

59. Barron, *Mixed Harvest*, 21–22.

60. *New Cumberland Independent*, March 4, 1909.

61. *New Cumberland Independent*, March 11, 1909.

62. *New Cumberland Independent*, March 18, 1909.

63. *New Cumberland Independent*, April 29, 1909.

64. West Virginia Department of Highways, "Yesterday and Today . . . : A Highway History of West Virginia from Colonial Time to the Present" (West Virginia Department of Highways, Advanced Planning Division, December 1973), 14.

65. Callahan, *History of West Virginia Old and New*, 527.

66. For a thorough discussion of the harmful effects of railroads and competition on West Virginia farmers, see Ronald L. Lewis, *Transforming the Appalachian Countryside: Railroads, Deforestation, and Social Change in West Virginia, 1880–1920*

(Chapel Hill: University of North Carolina Press, 1998), chap. 9. For a discussion of the failing agriculture of the region and the choices farmers faced, see Paul Salstrom, *Appalachia's Path to Dependency: Rethinking a Region's Economic History, 1730–1940* (Lexington: University Press of Kentucky, 1994) esp. 11, 20–26, 38–40.

67. Conklin, "A Study of the Economic Development," 211.

68. Frank Crim McCuskey, "The Decline of the Sheep Industry in West Virginia" (master's thesis, West Virginia University, 1915), 4, 6, 9.

69. Conklin, "A Study of the Economic Development," 209–10.

70. McCuskey, "The Decline of the Sheep Industry in West Virginia," 9.

71. Historical Census Browser, University of Virginia, Geospatial and Statistical Data Center: http://mapserver.lib.virginia.edu, accessed on February 9, 2015.

72. For the use of "old settler," see Inez Orler, *Frontiersmen ESOP* (Parsons, W.V.: McClain Printing Company, 1984), 29.

73. Truax, "The 200th Anniversary of the City of Weirton," 11.

74. Welch, *History of Hancock County*, 83; Orler, *Frontiersmen ESOP*, 9.

75. Truax, "The 200th Anniversary of the City of Weirton," 22.

CHAPTER 2.
BUILDING FACTORIES IN THE COUNTRY

1. On surveying the ground, see *Weirton Steel Employees Bulletin*, June 1949; quoted in Louis Truax, "The 200th Anniversary of the City of Weirton, West Va., and My Life Story as I Have Seen Weirton Grow" (manuscript in author's possession [Weirton, 1971]), 14.

2. David Brody, *Steelworkers in America: The Non-Union Era* (1960; repr., Urbana: University of Illinois Press, 1998), 2. For a statistical study of the steelmaking elite and their paths to power, see John N. Ingham, *The Iron Barons: A Social Analysis of an American Urban Elite, 1874–1965* (Westport, Conn.: Greenwood Press, 1978).

3. Margaret Berry Downs, "Industrial Structure and Pattern of the Wheeling District: Its Evolution and Development, 1840–1950" (PhD diss., University of Maryland, 1956), table 7.

4. Allen J. Dieterich-Ward, "Mines, Mills, and Malls: Regional Development in the Steel Valley" (PhD diss., University of Michigan, 2006), chap. 2.

5. William C. Gates, *The City of Hills and Kilns: Life and Work in East Liverpool, Ohio* (East Liverpool, Ohio: East Liverpool Historical Society, 1984), 31–38, 88–91, 163–68.

6. Marc J. Stern, *The Pottery Industry of Trenton: A Skilled Trade in Transition, 1850–1929* (New Brunswick, N.J.: Rutgers University Press, 1994), 8–9.

7. Gates, *City of Hills and Kilns*, 157, 166–69; Regina Lee Blaszczyk, "'Reign of the Robots': The Homer Laughlin China Company and Flexible Mass Production," *Technology and Culture* 36, no. 4: 869.

8. Don Shotliff, "The History of the Labor Movement in the American Pottery In-

dustry: The National Brotherhood of Operative Potters–International Brotherhood of Operative Potters, 1890–1970" (PhD diss., Kent State University, 1977), 20–22.

9. U.S. Industrial Commission, *Report on the Relations and Conditions of Capital and Labor Employed in Manufactures and General Business*, 19 vols. (Washington, D.C.: Government Printing Office, 1901), 14:651, 656.

10. Gates, *City of Hills and Kilns*, 167, 363.

11. Ibid., 31–38, 88–91, 163–68.

12. Bart Richards, interview with Joe Uehlein, February 21, 1974, Pittsburgh, Pennsylvania, transcript, United Steelworkers of America Archive and Oral History Collection, Historical Collections and Labor Archives, Pennsylvania State University, 6.

13. Donald E. Dunbar, *The Tin-Plate Industry: A Comparative Study of Its Growth in the United States and in Wales* (Boston: Houghton Mifflin, 1915), 11.

14. W. C. Cronemeyer, "The Development of the Tin-Plate Industry," *Western Pennsylvania Historical Magazine* 13 (January 1930): 28, 31.

15. Bill Jones and Ronald L. Lewis, "Gender and Transnationality Among Welsh Tinplate Workers in Pittsburgh: The Hattie Williams Affair, 1895," *Labor History* 48 (May 2007): 186. The tariff's impact on the growth of the tinplate industry in the United States is still debated by economists. See Douglas A. Irwin, "Did Late Nineteenth-Century U.S. Tariffs Promote Infant Industries?: Evidence from the Tinplate Industry," Working Paper Series, Working Paper No. 6835 (Cambridge, Mass.: National Bureau of Economic Research, 1998).

16. On the cost of the mills, see Brody, *Steelworkers in America*, 16–17. For examples of the partnerships, see Louis C. Martin, "Causes and Consequences of the 1909–1910 Steel Strike in the Wheeling District" (MA thesis, West Virginia University, 1999), 9–11.

17. For biographical information on Ernest Weir, see John D. Ubinger, "Ernest Tener Weir: Last of the Great Steelmasters," *Western Pennsylvania Historical Magazine* 58 (July 1975).

18. David Montgomery, *Workers' Control in America: Studies in the History of Work, Technology, and Labor Struggles* (New York: Cambridge University Press, 1979); Stern, *The Pottery Industry of Trenton*.

19. Descriptions of nineteenth-century production techniques are from Stern, *Pottery Industry of Trenton*, 29–36, unless otherwise noted. For descriptions of more modern techniques see David A. McCabe, *National Collective Bargaining in the Pottery Industry* (Baltimore: Johns Hopkins University Press, 1932), 4–12; and Blaszczyk, "Reign of the Robots," 863–911.

20. Bill Pomeroy, interview with the author, digital recording, April 15, 2005, Newell, West Virginia.

21. When I worked at Moderne Glass in East Liverpool in the 1990s, they still employed skilled women to hand paint gold around the rims of glassware.

22. U.S. Industrial Commission, *Report of the Industrial Commission*, 14:644.

23. Regina Lee Blaszczyk, "Imagining Consumers: Manufacturers and Markets in Ceramics and Glass, 1865–1960" (PhD diss., University of Delaware, 1995), 68; Stern, *Pottery Industry of Trenton*, 47; Carroll D. Wright, *Regulation and Restriction of Output: Eleventh Special Report of the Commissioner of Labor* (Washington, D.C.: Government Printing Office, 1904), 668. For a discussion of autonomous craftsmen, see Brent Soffer, "A Theory of Trade Union Development: The Role of the 'Autonomous' Workman," *Labor History* 1 (Spring 1960): 141–63.

24. U.S. Industrial Commission, *Report*, 14:651.

25. Paul Krause, *The Battle For Homestead, 1880–1892: Politics, Culture, and Steel* (Pittsburgh: University of Pittsburgh Press, 1992), 51–56; Brody, *Steelworkers in America*, chap. 1.

26. David Montgomery, *The Fall of the House of Labor* (Cambridge: Cambridge University Press, 1987), chap. 1.

27. The descriptions of the process of tinplate production come from Dunbar, *The Tin-Plate Industry*; Martin, "Causes and Consequences of the 1909–1910 Steel Strike," 5–8; and William R. Stewart, "Great Industries of the United States: Part IV, Tin Terne Plate," *Cosmopolitan* 37 (October 1904): 639–50.

28. Elizabeth Beardsley Butler, *Women and the Trades: Pittsburgh, 1907–1908*, the Pittsburgh Survey, ed. Paul Kellogg (New York: Russell Sage Foundation, 1909), 227–28.

29. Ibid.

30. Jeanne Boydston, *Home and Work: Housework, Wages, and the Ideology of Labor in the Early Republic* (New York: Oxford University Press, 1993); Wally Seccombe, "Patriarchy Stabilized: The Construction of the Male Breadwinner Wage Norm in Nineteenth-Century Britain," *Journal of Social History* 2 (January 1986): 53–76.

31. Stern, *Pottery Industry of Trenton*, 41–45.

32. U.S. Industrial Commission, *Report*, 14:646.

33. U.S. Census Bureau, *Twelfth Census of the United States: Volume 9, Manufactures, Part 3* (Washington, D.C.: Government Printing Office, 1902), 913.

34. Jones and Lewis, "Gender and Transnationality," 178.

35. Regina Lee Blaszczyk, "The Aesthetic Moment: China Decorators, Consumer Demand, and Technological Change in the American Pottery Industry," *Winterthur Portfolio* 29, no. 2/3: 147–50; Blaszczyk, "Imagining Consumers," 111–13.

36. Pomeroy, interview; Blaszczyk, "The Aesthetic Moment," 147–50. Decals only had one chance on porous bisque ware, but later, decorations added to glazed ware could be applied and wiped off.

37. Stern, *Pottery Industry of Trenton*, 110–13.

38. Ibid., 47, 112–13.

39. Blaszczyk, "Reign of the Robots," 875–78 and note 25; Jo Cunningham, *Homer Laughlin: A Giant Among Dishes, 1873–1939* (Atglen, Pa.: Shiffer Publishing, 1988), 96. Quaker Oats continued to buy premiums from Homer Laughlin until 1929.

40. U.S. Census Bureau, *Twelfth Census of the United States: Volume 9, Manufactures, Part 3*, 913.

41. U.S Industrial Commission, *Report*, 7:471.

42. Pomeroy, interview.

43. Jones and Lewis, "Gender and Transnationality."

44. The American Sheet & Tin Plate Company mill in Chester employed 450 men and nine women, and the Weirton Steel Company employed 7,973 men and 60 women. Peter Boyd, *History of Northern West Virginia Panhandle, Embracing Ohio, Marshall, Brooke, and Hancock Counties* (Topeka, Kan.: Historical Publishing, 1927), 290–91.

45. Edward W. Bemis, "The Homestead Strike," *Journal of Political Economy* 11 (June 1894): 375, quoted in Brody, *Steelworkers in America*, 51.

46. U.S. Congress, Senate, *Report on the Conditions of Employment in the Iron and Steel Industry*, 62d Cong., 1st sess. (Washington, D.C.: Government Printing Office, 1913), 3:516–22.

47. W. C. Cronemeyer, "The Development of the Tin-Plate Industry," *Western Pennsylvania Historical Magazine* 13 (January 1930): 119; John Fitch, *The Steel Workers* (Pittsburgh: Russell Sage Foundation, 1910), 56.

48. U.S. Congress, *Report on the Conditions*, 3:181.

49. Ibid., 3:184.

50. U.S. Industrial Commission, *Report*, 1:879.

51. Ubinger, "Ernest Tener Weir," 299.

52. Shotliff, "History of the Labor Movement," 42–45; T. J. Duffy, *An Early History of the National Brotherhood of Operative Potters* (East Liverpool, Ohio: Potters Herald Print, 1901), 10–11; Stern, *Pottery Industry of Trenton*, chaps. 4 and 5.

53. Shotliff, "History of the Labor Movement," 50–51.

54. Ibid., 87. On the AFGWU see Ken Fones-Wolf, *Glass Towns: Industry, Labor, and Political Economy in Appalachia, 1890–1930s* (Urbana: University of Illinois Press, 2007), 8–11. Historian Colin Gordon discusses "regulatory unionism" in *New Deals: Business, Labor, and Politics in America, 1920–1935* (New York: Cambridge University Press, 1994), chap. 3.

55. Shotliff, "History of the Labor Movement," 53; Duffy, *Early History*, 17–19.

56. Shotliff, "History of the Labor Movement," 55–64.

57. Duffy, *Early History*, 31.

58. Shotliff, "National Brotherhood of Operative Potters," 55–75; Duffy, *Early History*, 29–38.

59. Duffy, *Early History*, 36–68.

60. McCabe, *National Collective Bargaining in the Pottery Industry*, 320–27.

61. Wright, *Regulation and Restriction of Output*, 667.

62. Ibid., 668.

63. Duffy, *Early History*, 41; Shotliff, "History of the Labor Movement," 76.

64. On the membership gains in the 1890s, see Fitch, *The Steel Workers*, 133. For the history of the slow death of the Amalgamated Association, see Brody, *Steelworkers in America*, chaps. 1, 2, and 3; Martin, "Causes and Consequences of the 1909–1910 Steel Strike." One of the best histories of the early years of the Amalgamated Association remains Jesse S. Robinson, *The Amalgamated Association of Iron, Steel, and Tin Workers* (Baltimore: Johns Hopkins University Press, 1920).

65. Dunbar, *Tin-Plate Industry*, 75.

66. Wright, *Regulation and Restriction of Output*, 256–62.

67. Ibid., 259.

68. U.S. Industrial Commission, *Report*, 1: 855.

69. Naomi R. Lamoreaux, *The Great Merger Movement in American Business, 1895–1904* (Cambridge: Cambridge University Press, 1985), 38–41.

70. The annual capacity of the American Tin Plate Company in 1900 was almost as much as all the manufacturers in Wales had produced in 1890, when that country produced 9.5 million boxes, or about one billion pounds. U.S. Census Bureau, *Twelfth Census of the United States: Volume 10, Manufactures, Part 4* (Washington, D.C.: Government Printing Office, 1902), 118; U.S. Commissioner of Corporations, *Report on the Steel Industry* (Washington, D.C.: Government Printing Office, 1911–1913), 1:3; U.S. Industrial Commission, *Report*, 1:858. On the companies that consolidated, see Cronemeyer, "Development of the Tin-Plate Industry," 133, and Dunbar, *Tin-Plate Industry*, 79.

71. Brody, *Steelworkers in America*, 60–61.

72. John Garraty, "The U.S. Steel Corporation versus Labor: The Early Years," *Labor History* 1 (1960): 3–38.

73. Ibid., 6.

74. Brody, *Steelworkers in America*, 64; Fitch, *The Steel Workers*, 133.

75. "Ovations at Wheeling," *National Labor Tribune*, August 22, 1901.

76. Robinson, *Amalgamated Association*, 162; Brody, *Steelworkers in America*, 67. Also see John Benjamin Moore, "Collective Bargaining in the Iron and Steel Industry, 1876–1910" (MA thesis, University of Missouri, 1939), 124–25.

77. *National Labor Tribune*, September 19, 26, 1901.

78. *National Labor Tribune*, July 22, 1904.

79. U.S. Industrial Commission, *Report*, 1:904–6.

80. Brody, *Steelworkers in America*, 69.

81. William Z. Foster, *The Great Steel Strike and Its Lessons* (New York: B. W. Huebsch, 1920), 12; Horace B. Davis, *Labor and Steel* (New York: International Publishers, 1933), 230.

82. Martin, "Causes and Consequences of the 1909–1910 Steel Strike."

83. Jack Welch, *History of Hancock County, Virginia and West Virginia*, rev. ed. (1963; Abilene, Tex.: WriteRight Publishing, 1992), 48–50.

84. Historical Census Browser, University of Virginia, Geospatial and Statisti-

cal Data Center: http://mapserver.lib.virginia.edu/, accessed February 9, 2015. On floods, fires, and the brick companies see Welch, *History of Hancock County*, 123–25.

85. J. Russell Smith, *Element of Industrial Management* (Philadelphia: J. B. Lippincott Company, 1915), 98–110.

86. Ibid., 111–13.

87. Roy C. Cashdollar, *A History of Chester: The Gateway to the West* (Newell, W.V.: Tri-State Genealogical & Historical Society, 2000), 10–11.

88. C. A. Smith, *Chester on the Ohio* (n.p., 1905?), quoted in Cashdollar, *History of Chester*, 21.

89. Ibid., 23.

90. Ibid., 28, 29–31.

91. Cashdollar, *History of Chester*, 67–69.

92. Ruth Henthorne, Ann Cawthon, Ronald Smith, Lola Barber, Richard Brenneman, Albert Logston, and Leah Rae Smith, *The History of Newell and Vicinity*, 2nd ed. (Newell, W.V.: Tri-State Genealogical & Historical Society, 1982), 13. Bisque kilns hardened the soft clay ware while glost kilns (pronounced "gloss kills") fused glazes onto the ware and decorating or muffle kilns fused on any decorations.

93. Blaszczyk, "Reign of the Robots," 876–77.

94. Arthur Wells, interview with Thomas Hess, transcript, Youngstown State University Oral History Program, October 21, 1976.

95. Newell's history has been obscured by the fact that it remains to this day unincorporated and therefore unlisted in the published census records. Furthermore, there have been no published studies of the town other than one book by a team of local historians, Henthorne et al., *The History of Newell and Vicinity*, 13–16.

96. Sanborn Map Company, *Newell, West Virginia, 1923*. Map Division of the Library of Congress.

97. On Phillips' death see "J. R. Phillips Victim," *The Connellsville Courier*, May 12, 1905. On National Biscuit Company, see Charles Morrell Watson, *Ernest Tener Weir: Weir of Weirton* (1949), excerpted in Inez Orler, *Frontiersmen ESOP* (Parsons, W.V.: McClain Printing Company, 1984), 46.

98. Fones-Wolf, *Glass Towns*, 135–36.

99. *Iron Age*, October 21, 1909.

100. Welch, *History of Hancock County*, 83; Orler, *Frontiersmen ESOP*, 9.

101. *Wheeling Intelligencer*, April 9, 1910; *National Labor Tribune*, August 12, 1909.

102. Ubinger, "Ernest Tener Weir," 298. Also see Theresa Ankney, "Pendulum of Control: The Evolution of the Weirton Steel Company, 1909–1951" (PhD. diss., Catholic University, 1993), 41; Richard Lizza, "Some Dimensions of the Immigrant Experience: Italians in Steubenville, Ohio and Weirton, West Virginia" (PhD diss., West Virginia University, 1984), 53; John Hennen, "E. T. Weir, Employee Representation, and the Dimensions of Social Control: Weirton Steel, 1933–1937," *Labor Studies Journal* 26, no. 3 (Fall 2001): 28.

103. Anne Elaine Mosher, "Capital Transformation and the Restructuring of Place: The Creation of a Model Industrial Town" (PhD diss., Pennsylvania State University, 1989), 160–92; also see Anne Mosher, *Capital's Utopia: The Steel Industry's Search for Urban Order at Vandergrift, 1855–1916* (Johns Hopkins University Press, 2004).

104. Thanks to Weirton historian Dennis Jones for the information about the town name. *Wheeling Intelligencer*, April 9, 1910; *National Labor Tribune*, August 12, 1909.

105. Truax, "The 200th Anniversary of the City of Weirton," 10.

106. *Weirton Steel Employees Bulletin*, June 1949, quoted in Truax, "The 200th Anniversary of the City of Weirton," 15.

107. John N. Grajciar, interview with Arthur S. Weinburg, July 2, 1968, transcript, United Steelworkers of America Archive and Oral History Collection, Historical Collections and Labor Archives, Pennsylvania State University.

108. *Weirton Steel Employees Bulletin*, June, 1949 quoted in Truax, "The 200th Anniversary of the City of Weirton," 15; M. Roinila, "From Monessen to Clarksburg and Beyond: The Finnish Ethnicity in Central Appalachia," *Journal of Appalachian Studies* (2003). On recruiting in Clarksburg see Ankney, "Pendulum of Control," 43–44.

109. Truax, "The 200th Anniversary of the City of Weirton," 10.

110. Frank A. Pietranton, *History of Weirton and Holliday's Cove and Life of J. C. Williams* (Pittsburgh: Pittsburgh Printing Company, 1936), 116–17.

111. Lizza, "Some Dimensions of the Immigrant Experience," 165.

112. Orler, *Frontiersmen ESOP*, 17.

113. U.S. Industrial Commission, *Report*, 1:880.

114. Truax, "The 200th Anniversary of the City of Weirton," 37.

115. Ibid., 43–44.

116. John L. Lewis to Frank Morrison, June 30, 1913, AFL National and International Union Correspondence and Jurisdictional Dispute Records, Amalgamated Association of Iron, Steel, and Tin Workers File, Reel 38–6.

117. Frederick Allan Barkey, "The Socialist Party in West Virginia From 1898 to 1920: Study in Working Class Radicalism" (PhD diss., University of Pittsburgh, 1971), 156–58; Martin, "Causes and Consequences of the 1909–1910 Steel Strike," 83–86.

118. "The Second Largest Dinner-Ware Factory in the United States," *West Virginia Review* (September 1930): 438.

119. Don Shotliff, "History of the Labor Movement," 159–63. For information on the chairmanship of the Labor Committee, see Shotliff, "History of the Labor Movement," 359–61 and note 26.

120. Labor Committee of the United States Potters' Association to the Executive Board of the National Brotherhood of Operative Potters, June 7, 1921, International Brotherhood of Pottery and Allied Workers, Records, 1889–1971, Kent State University, Kent, Ohio (hereafter IBOP Papers), Box 1, Folder 33.

121. Stern, *Pottery Industry of Trenton*, 196–208; Shotliff, "History of the Labor Movement," 164, 177–81, 189, 195–96, 199–200.

122. Stern, *Pottery Industry of Trenton*, 196–208; Shotliff, "History of the Labor Movement," 164, 177–81, 189, 195–96, 199–200.

123. Blaszczyk, "Reign of the Robots," 875–78 and note 25.

124. Ibid., 884–86 and see figure 4.

125. "Friday evening January 16–1925, Mr. W. E. Wells Statements," IBOP Papers, Box 19, Folder 33.

126. Standing Committee Minutes, April 5, 1932, p. 26, IBOP papers, Box 198, Folder 1.

127. Blaszczyk, "Reign of the Robots," 879–82, 890, quote on 896.

128. Walter Howard Emerson, "A Pottery Plant on a Conveyor," *Ceramic Industry* 24 (June 1935): 342–47, quoted in Blaszczyk, "Reign of the Robots," 901.

129. "Kilnmen Iron Horse Conference," July 31, 1935, IBOP papers, Box 19, Folder 35. Also see, "Record of Protest on the Conveyors," September 14, 1935, IBOP papers, Box 19, Folder 35.

130. Blaszczyk, "Reign of the Robots," 896–97.

131. Ibid., 902–6.

132. *Potters Herald*, November 26, 1953.

133. *Potters Herald*, December 24, 1953.

134. *Potters Herald*, January 6, 1955.

135. On employment of finishers, see "In the Matter of the Arbitration between the United States Potters' Association and the National Brotherhood of Operative Potters," December 26, 1950. File No. 50A/542. Opinion and Decision of the Arbitrator. IBOP Papers, Box 71, Folder 28. In the second paragraph it says, "Prior to installation of the automatics in 1941, finishers were employed by jiggermen rather than by the Company."

136. *Weirton Steel Employee Bulletin*, June 1949, quoted in Truax, "The 200th Anniversary of the City of Weirton," 14.

137. Orler, *Frontiersman ESOP*, 67, 104–9; and F. A. Hanlin, "Weirton Steel Company—the Mushroom of the Steel Industry," *West Virginia Review* 3 (June 1926): 346–47.

138. *Iron Age*, May 19 and June 16, 1927.

139. Richards, interview, 4.

140. *Iron Age*, May 19, 1927, 1435.

141. *Iron Age*, May 19, 1927, 1438.

142. *Iron Age*, June 16, 1927 1731–32.

143. William T. Hogan, *Economic History of the Iron and Steel Industry in the United States*, vol. 3, parts IV and V (Lexington, Mass.: Lexington Books, 1971), 954. Inez Orler reports that construction began in 1925. *Frontiersmen ESOP*, 106. Note that according to Orler, Weirton Steel began construction on the world's first forty-eight-inch continuous hot strip in 1926 but probably did not perfect its operation before Columbia Steel or the American Rolling Mill Company.

144. "Weirton Steel to Use Rolling Mill Patents," *Wall Street Journal*, December 30, 1927.

145. Truax, "The 200th Anniversary of the City of Weirton," 44.

146. Historical Census Browser, University of Virginia, Geospatial and Statistical Data Center: http://mapserver.lib.virginia.edu/, accessed February 9, 2015.

CHAPTER 3.
RISE OF THE RURAL-INDUSTRIAL WORKERS

1. Margaret Heaton, interview with the author, digital recording, July 28, 2005, Weirton, West Virginia.

2. Historical Census Browser, University of Virginia, Geospatial and Statistical Data Center: http://mapserver.lib.virginia.edu/, accessed February 9, 2015.

3. Paul Salstrom, *Appalachia's Path to Dependency: Rethinking a Region's Economic History, 1730–1940* (Lexington: University Press of Kentucky, 1994), chap. 1; Ronald L. Lewis, *Transforming the Appalachian Countryside: Railroads, Deforestation, and Social Change in West Virginia, 1880–1920* (Chapel Hill: University of North Carolina Press, 1998), chap. 9.

4. Between 1900 and 1930, the populations in the counties of Doddridge (–3,201), Jackson (–6,863), Pleasants (–2,800), Ritchie (–3,307), Tyler (–5,467), Wetzel (–546), and Wirt (–3,926) decreased by a total of 26,110 from their 1900 total of 116,338 while Wirt (+7,587) and Wood (+22,069) increased by a total of 29,656 over their 1900 total of 58,071. Historical Census Browser, University of Virginia, Geospatial and Statistical Data Center: http://mapserver.lib.virginia.edu, accessed February 9, 2015.

5. This impression comes from obituaries in the *Potters Herald*, January through December 1951, a time when many of the in-migrants were dying. Out of a sample of twenty-three obituaries that appeared January 18, February 1 and 8, March 22 and 29, April 5, 12, and 26, May 3, July 12, November 8 and 29, and December 13, eight of the individuals, more than one-third, were born in one of those counties.

6. Susan Weaver, "Hoopies," *Goldenseal* 12 (Summer 1986): 65. There is an extensive literature on Appalachian migration. Some of the best works include Chad Berry, *Southern Migrants, Northern Exiles* (Urbana: University of Illinois Press, 2000); Phillip J. Obermiller, Thomas E. Wagner, and E. Bruce Tucker, eds., *Appalachian Odyssey: Historical Perspectives on the Great Migration* (Westport, Conn.: Praeger, 2000); Susan Johnson, "West Virginia Rubber Workers in Akron," in Ken Fones-Wolf and Ronald L. Lewis, *Transnational West Virginia: Ethnic Communities and Economic Changes, 1840–1940* (Morgantown: West Virginia University Press, 2002); J. Trent Alexander, "'They're Never Here More Than a Year': Return Migration in the Southern Exodus, 1940–1970," *Journal of Social History* 38 (Spring 2005): 653–71. For a discussion of nineteenth-century migration as well, see Dwight B. Billings and Kathleen M. Blee, *The Road to Poverty: The Making of Wealth and Hardship in Appalachia* (New York: Cambridge University Press, 2000).

7. Ruth Henthorne, Ann Cawthon, Ronald Smith, Lola Barber, Richard Brenneman, Albert Logston, and Leah Rae Smith, *The History of Newell and Vicinity*, 2nd ed. (Newell, W.V.: Tri-State Genealogical & Historical Society, 1982), 13–16.

8. Allison Glock, *Beauty Before Comfort: A Memoir* (New York: Alfred A. Knopf, 2003), 23.

9. "An Old Art in the Modern Manner," *West Virginia Review* (November, 1936): 79.

10. For nativist activity among the potters, see William C. Gates, *The City of Hills and Kilns: Life and Work in East Liverpool, Ohio* (East Liverpool, Ohio: East Liverpool Historical Society, 1984), 276. Also see Marc J. Stern, *The Pottery Industry of Trenton: A Skilled Trade in Transition, 1850–1929* (New Brunswick, N.J.: Rutgers University Press, 1994), 121. On Klan activity, see Gates, *City of Hills and Kilns*, 276–77, 316; and Roy Cashdollar, *A History of Chester: The Gateway to the West*, 2nd ed. (Newell, W.V.: Tri-State Genealogical & Historical Society, 2000), 250.

11. Gates, *City of Hills and Kilns*, 276–77, 316.

12. U.S. Census Bureau, *Fifteenth Census of the United States, 1930, Population Schedule, West Virginia, Hancock County, Grant District*, microfilm, West Virginia and Regional History Center, West Virginia University Libraries, Morgantown, West Virginia.

13. Arthur Wells, interview with Thomas Hess, transcript, October 21, 1976, Newell, West Virginia, Youngstown State University Oral History Program: http://www.maag.ysu.edu/oralhistory/cd1/OH380.pdf, accessed on February 9, 2015.

14. John Hinshaw, *Steel and Steelworkers: Race and Class Struggle in Twentieth-Century Pittsburgh* (Albany: State University of New York Press, 2002), 42–43; Kenneth R. Bailey, "A Judicious Mixture: Negroes and Immigrants in the West Virginia Mines, 1880–1917," *West Virginia History* 34 (July 1973).

15. Historical Census Browser, University of Virginia, Geospatial and Statistical Data Center: http://mapserver.lib.virginia.edu/, accessed February 9, 2015. Richard Lizza's dissertation remains the most detailed historical analysis of immigrants in Weirton. "Some Dimensions of the Immigrant Experience: Italians in Steubenville, Ohio and Weirton, West Virginia" (PhD diss, West Virginia University, 1984).

16. David T. Javersak, "Weirton," in *The West Virginia Encyclopedia*, ed. Ken Sullivan (Charleston: West Virginia Humanities Council, 2006), 754.

17. Heaton, interview.

18. Quoted in Teresa Lynn Ankney, "The Pendulum of Control: The Evolution of the Weirton Steel Company, 1909–1951" (PhD diss., Catholic University of America, 1993), 53–54.

19. Alice C. Boomsliter, "A Selection of General Science Textbook Material to Meet the Needs of Junior High School Children in an Industrial Community" (master's thesis, West Virginia University, 1936), 2.

20. Lizza, "Some Dimensions of the Immigrant Experience," 167, 174, 260.

21. Theodore Saloutos, *The Greeks in the United States* (Cambridge, Mass.: Harvard University Press, 1964), 45–47. Also see Gunther Peck, *Reinventing Free Labor:*

Padrones and Immigrant Workers in the North American West, 1880–1930 (New York: Cambridge University Press, 2000), for an excellent study of the dynamics of working-class Greek migration to the West.

22. Horace B. Davis, *Labor and Steel* (New York: International Publishers, 1933), 30. On the number of Hancock County residents born in Greece, Historical Census Browser, University of Virginia, Geospatial and Statistical Data Center: http://mapserver.lib.virginia.edu/, accessed February 9, 2015.

23. Pamela Makricosta, "A Bundle of Treasures: Greeks in West Virginia," *Goldenseal Magazine* (Winter 1997): 33–34. See also, George B. Hines III and Lou Martin, *Images of America: Hancock County* (Charleston, S.C.: Arcadia Publishing, 2006), 103.

24. Makricosta, "A Bundle of Treasures," 39–42.

25. U.S. Census Bureau, *Fifteenth Census of the United States 1930, Population Schedules, Butler District, Hancock County, West Virginia*, microfilm, West Virginia and Regional History Center, West Virginia University Libraries, Morgantown, West Virginia.

26. U.S. Census Bureau, *Twelfth Census of the United States: Volume 1, Population, Part 1* (Washington, D.C.: Government Printing Office, 1901); *Fifteenth Census of the United States: Volume 3: Population, Part 2* (Washington, D.C.: Government Printing Office, 1932).

27. Ankney, "Pendulum of Control," 42–43. For a more exploitative version of this practice in the southern coalfields, see Kenneth R. Bailey, "A Temptation to Lawlessness: Peonage in West Virginia, 1903–1908," *West Virginia History* 50 (1991): 25–45.

28. Kimberley L. Phillips, *AlabamaNorth: African-American Migrants, Community, and Working-Class Activism in Cleveland, 1915–1945* (Urbana: University of Illinois Press, 1999), chap. 1.

29. Dennis C. Dickerson, *Out of the Crucible: Black Steelworkers in Western Pennsylvania, 1875–1980* (Albany: State University of New York Press, 1986), chap. 2. This same concept is thoroughly explored in Joe W. Trotter Jr., *Coal, Class, and Color: Blacks in Southern West Virginia, 1915–1932* (Urbana: University of Illinois Press, 1990).

30. U.S. Census Bureau, *Fifteenth Census of the United States: Volume 3, Population, Part 2* (Washington, D.C: Government Printing Office, 1932), 1289.

31. Frank A. Pietranton, *History of Weirton and Holliday's Cove and Life of J. C. Williams* (Pittsburgh: Pittsburgh Printing Company, 1936), 132–33.

32. Frank Gregory, interview with the author, digital recording, February 3, 2012, Weirton, West Virginia.

33. U.S. Census Bureau, *Fifteenth Census of the United States, 1930, Population Schedules, Clay District, Hancock County, West Virginia*, microfilm, West Virginia and Regional History Center, West Virginia University Libraries, Morgantown, West Virginia.

34. Cashdollar, *A History of Chester*, 81–87.

35. Ibid., 88–91.

36. Pietranton, *History of Weirton and Holliday's Cove*, 18–21.

37. For a stereotypical view of Appalachian religion, see Berthold E. Schwarz, "Ordeal by Serpents, Fire, and Strychnine: A Study of Some Provocative Psychosomatic Phenomenon (1960)," in *Appalachian Folk Images and Popular Culture*, ed. W. K. McNeil, 2nd ed. (Knoxville: University of Tennessee Press, 1995), 285–306. For an overview of the 1960 election in West Virginia, see Otis Rice and Stephen Brown, *West Virginia: A History* (Lexington: University Press of Kentucky, 1993), 281–83. For an excellent study of stereotypes of Appalachia, see Dwight Billings, Gurney Norman, and Katherine Ledford, eds., *Back Talk from Appalachia: Confronting Stereotypes* (Lexington: University Press of Kentucky, 2000).

38. Ronald L. Lewis, "Appalachian Restructuring in Historical Perspective: Coal, Culture and Social Change in West Virginia," *Urban Studies* 30, no. 2 (1993). For further discussion of household production by industrial workers in West Virginia, see Chad Montrie, "Continuity in the Midst of Change: Work and Environment for West Virginia Mountaineers," *West Virginia History* (Spring 2007): 1–22; Janet Greene, "Strategies for Survival: Women's Work in the Southern West Virginia Coal Camps," *West Virginia History* 49 (1990): 37–54; and Mary Beth Pudup, "Women's Work in the West Virginia Economy," *West Virginia History* 49 (1990): 7–20.

39. Salstrom, *Appalachia's Path to Dependency*, 60–67.

40. Jane Addams, *Twenty Years at Hull House* (New York: MacMillan Company, 1911), 294.

41. David Brody, *Steelworkers in America: The Non-Union Era* (1960; repr., Urbana: University of Illinois Press, 1998), 103.

42. Joel A. Tarr, *The Search for the Ultimate Sink: Urban Pollution in Historical Perspective* (Akron, Ohio: University of Akron Press, 1996), 90–92.

43. Henry "Tex" Burns, interview with the author, digital recording, April 9, 2005, Trinity Hospital, Steubenville, Ohio.

44. Henry Burns made this point in his interview as does Becky Nicolaides in her book about the Los Angeles suburb of South Gate. My thinking on this subject and self-help activities was significantly shaped by Nicolaides, *My Blue Heaven: Life and Politics in the Working-Class Suburbs of Los Angeles, 1920–1965* (Chicago: University of Chicago Press, 2002), esp. 13–29.

45. John Bodnar, *The Transplanted: A History of Immigrants in Urban America*, First Midland Book Edition (Bloomington: Indiana University Press, 1987), 71–83.

46. For 1926 factory employment statistics, see Peter Boyd, *History of Northern West Virginia Panhandle, Embracing Ohio, Marshall, Brooke, and Hancock Counties* (Topeka, Kan.: Historical Publishing Company, 1927), 290–91. For families in the North End, I completed the survey using microfilm copies of the 1930 manuscript census, recording information for every tenth "family," which often included boarders who were not actual relatives of the head of household. U.S. Census Bureau, *Fifteenth Census of the United States, 1930, Population Schedules, Butler District, Hancock County, West Virginia*, microfilm, West Virginia and Regional History Center, West Virginia University Libraries, Morgantown, West Virginia.

47. U.S. Census Bureau, *Fifteenth Census of the United States: Volume 3, Population, Part 2* (Washington, D.C.: Government Print Office, 1932), 1289; *Sixteenth Census of the United States: Volume 2, Population, Part 7* (Washington, D.C.: Government Printing Office, 1943), 488.

48. Heaton, interview.

49. Robert H. Zeiger, *The CIO, 1935–1955* (Chapel Hill: University of North Carolina Press, 1995). For the surge in rank-and-file unionism, see Staughton Lynd, ed., *"We Are All Leaders": The Alternative Unionism of the Early 1930s* (Urbana: University of Illinois Press, 1996), esp. "Introduction," 1–26.

50. "The Second Largest Dinner-Ware Factory in the United States," *West Virginia Review* (September 1930): 439.

51. Stern, *Pottery Industry of Trenton*, 47–49.

52. Ibid., 47–48. Also see Lizabeth Cohen, *Making a New Deal: Industrial Workers in Chicago, 1919–1939* (New York: Cambridge University Press, 1990), 191–211.

53. C. L. Sebring to James Duffy, June 8, 1945, International Brotherhood of Pottery and Allied Workers, Records, 1889–1971, Kent State University, Kent, Ohio (hereafter IBOP Papers), Box 64.

54. James Duffy, NBOP President, to Arthur Hollins, Secretary, National Society Workers, Stoke-on-Trent, January 23, 1930, IBOP Papers, Box 4, Folder 46.

55. Don Shotliff, "The History of the Labor Movement in the American Pottery Industry: The National Brotherhood of Operative Potters-International Brotherhood of Operative Potters, 1890–1970" (PhD diss., Kent State University, 1977), 225.

56. Ibid., 161–62.

57. NBOP Executive Board, minutes, April 16, 1934, IBOP Papers, Box 2, Folder 25; Shotliff, "The History of the Labor Movement," 222–23, 235–36.

58. Shotliff, "The History of the Labor Movement," 255.

59. *Potters Herald*, June 30, 1938.

60. *Potters Herald*, September 29, 1938.

61. Shotliff, "The History of the Labor Movement," 255–57, 263–64, quote on 257.

62. Ibid., 261.

63. Ankney, "Pendulum of Control," 54.

64. For a discussion of the new role of foremen and managers in the steel industry from 1890 to 1920, see Katherine Stone, "The Origins of Job Structures in the Steel Industry" in *Labor Market Segmentation*, ed. Richard C. Edwards, Michael Reich, and David M. Gordon (Lexington, Mass.: D.C. Heath and Company, 1973), 27–84.

65. Davis, *Labor and Steel*, 84.

66. Ibid., 54.

67. Quoted in Ankney, "Pendulum of Control," 54.

68. Ibid., 65.

69. John Fitch, *The Steel Workers* (1910; repr., Pittsburgh: University of Pittsburgh Press, 1989), 183–87, 201, 214–20.

70. Davis, *Labor and Steel*, 142.

71. Ankney, "Pendulum of Control," 76.

72. Weirton Steel modeled their ERP on one created by Tom Girdler, a dictatorial steel executive who led Jones & Laughlin Steel and later Republic Steel. Thomas Edward Posey, "The Labor Movement in West Virginia, 1900–1948" (PhD diss., University of Wisconsin, 1948).

73. Staughton Lynd, "The Possibility of Radicalism in the Early 1930s: The Case of Steel," *Radical America* 6 (1972): 36–65; John Hennen, "E. T. Weir, Employee Representation, and the Dimensions of Social Control: Weirton Steel, 1933–1937," *Labor Studies Journal* 26, no. 3 (Fall 2001).

74. Hennen, "E. T. Weir," 34.

75. *New York Times*, October 16, 1934.

76. Hennen, "E. T. Weir," 33–35.

77. Davis, *Labor and Steel*, 270–71.

78. Hennen, "E. T. Weir," 35–36.

79. John Alatis, interview with the author, tape recording, February 3, 2005, Weirton, West Virginia.

80. Paul Barkhurst, interview with the author, tape recording, Summer 2002, Frankfort Springs, Pennsylvania.

81. Zeiger, *The CIO*, chaps. 2, 3, and 4; Irving Bernstein, *The Turbulent Years: A History of the American Worker, 1933–1941* (1969) (Chicago: Haymarket Books, 2010), chaps. 10 and 13. Also see Louis Martin, "The 1936 Portsmouth Steel Strike: 'As Portsmouth Goes So Goes the Steel Industry,'" Parts 1 and 2, *Portsmouth Free Press*, vol. 2, no. 2 (Summer 2006) and no. 3 (Fall 2006).

82. Elizabeth Fones-Wolf and Ken Fones-Wolf, "Cold War Americanism: Business, Pageantry, and Antiunionism in Weirton, West Virginia," *Business History Review* 77 (Spring 2003): 65–66.

83. Alatis, interview.

84. National Labor Relations Board, "In the Matter of Weirton Steel Company and Steel Workers Organizing Committee," Case No. C-1184, Case No. R-1229.

85. Hennen, "E. T. Weir," 42.

86. National Labor Relations Board, "In the Matter of Weirton Steel."

87. *New York Times*, April 17, 1937.

88. *New York Times*, August 23, 1937.

89. *New York Times*, August 17, 1937, and August 18, 1937. On Conway's weight, see *New York Times*, July 12, 1937.

90. *New York Times*, June 28, 1941. Also see "In the Matter of Weirton Steel Company and Steel Workers Organizing Committee," Case No. C-1184, Case No. R-1229. National Labor Relations Board 32 N.L.R.B. 1145; 1941 NLRB LEXIS 2327; 8 L.R.R.M. 247; 32 NLRB No. 179 June 25, 1941. On the new union's creation and its first contract, see Posey, "The Labor Movement in West Virginia, 275. Weirton Steel's lawyers appealed the 1941 decision until 1943 and even then refused to comply with parts of the ruling. See *National Labor Relations Board v. Weirton Steel Company Et Al.* No. 8041

United States Court Of Appeals Third Circuit, 183 F.2d 584; 1950 U.S. App. LEXIS 3491; 26 L.R.R.M. 2443; 18 Lab. Cas. (CCH) P65,915. June 12, 1950, Heard; July 28, 1950, Decided. Hennen, "E. T. Weir," 44–45.

91. Posey, "The Labor Movement in West Virginia," 293–94.

92. *New York Times*, April 4, 1944.

93. Susan Carnahan Lindsey, "Hancock County in World War II" (master's thesis, West Virginia University, 1949), 42; and *National Labor Relations Board v. Weirton Steel Company et al.* No. 8041 (3rd Cir. Appeals, 1950).

94. Mark Esposito, "The UAW, American Trade Policy, and the Transformation of the Global Automobile Industry, 1945–1973" (PhD diss., West Virginia University, 2004), 7, 20, 24.

95. Ibid., quoted on 19 and 20.

96. Ibid., 9, 29.

97. Gates, *City of Hills and Kilns*, 320–23.

98. Esposito, "UAW, American Trade Policy," 29. On AFL attitudes toward Asian and Asian American workers, see Alexander Saxton, *The Indispensable Enemy: Labor and the Anti-Chinese Movement in California* (Berkeley: University of California Press, 1971); Gwendolyn Mink, *Old Labor and New Immigrants in American Political Development: Union, Party, and State, 1875–1920* (Ithaca, N.Y.: Cornell University Press, 1986).

99. Gates, *City of Hills and Kilns*, 320–23.

100. *Weirton Daily Times*, November, 2, 1936.

101. *New York Times*, August 24, 1937.

102. Alatis, interview. Election results from Hancock County Elections Office, New Cumberland, West Virginia.

103. Hancock County Elections Office, New Cumberland, West Virginia.

104. Alatis, interview.

105. According to the 1930 census, his son Francis was born in Pennsylvania in 1918 and his daughter Mary was born in West Virginia in 1920. U.S. Bureau of the Census, *Fifteenth Census of the United States, 1930, Population Schedules, Butler District, Hancock County, West Virginia*, microfilm, West Virginia and Regional History Center, West Virginia University Libraries, Morgantown, West Virginia.

106. Ibid.; West Virginia State Senate, *West Virginia Blue Book* (Charleston, W.V.: Jarrett Printing, 1937); and Hennen, "E. T. Weir." Also see, James B. Lieber, *Friendly Takeover: How an Employee Buyout Saved a Steel Town* (New York: Viking, 1995), 29.

107. Hancock County Elections Office, New Cumberland, West Virginia.

108. *Weirton Daily Times*, October 28, 1936.

109. *Weirton Daily Times*, November 2, 1936.

110. *Weirton Daily Times*, November 2, 1936.

111. *Weirton Daily Times*, November 2, 1936.

112. Hancock County Elections Office, New Cumberland, West Virginia; *Weirton Daily Times*, November 4, 1936.

113. *Journal of the House of Delegates, Forty-Third Legislature of West Virginia Regular*

Session, 1938 and Second Extraordinary Session (December 14–16, 1936), 74, 198, 1230, 1397, 1419. Quotes on 1230 and 1419. For a discussion of yellow dog contracts in West Virginia, see Richard D. Lunt, *Law and Order vs. the Miners, West Virginia, 1907–1933* (Hamden, Conn.: Archon Books, 1979).

114. Hancock County Elections Office, New Cumberland, West Virginia.

115. Alatis, interview.

116. Hancock County Elections Office, New Cumberland, West Virginia.

CHAPTER 4.
PROSPEROUS, INDEPENDENT RURAL-INDUSTRIAL WORKERS

1. R. H. Markham, "Steelmaking: The 'American Way' Shines Bright Amid Smoke and Toil," *Christian Science Monitor*, May 26, 1945, p. 11.

2. Alex Zucosky, interview with the author, digital recording, November 14, 2005, Weirton, West Virginia.

3. Ibid. For descriptions of near death accidents, see *Weirton Steel Employees Bulletin*, October 1956.

4. Walter Danna, interview with the author, digital recording, May 10, 2005, near Burgettstown, Pennsylvania.

5. Ibid.

6. Ibid. Also see Richard Cameron, interview with the author, digital recording, March 28, 2007, New Manchester, West Virginia.

7. Regina Lee Blaszczyk, "'Reign of the Robots': The Homer Laughlin China Company and Flexible Mass Production," *Technology and Culture* 36, no. 4.

8. For some job descriptions, see Don Shotliff, "The History of the Labor Movement in the American Pottery Industry: The National Brotherhood of Operative Potters—International Brotherhood of Operative Potters, 1890–1970," (PhD diss., Kent State University, 1977), 431–34; George Hines III and Lou Martin, *Images of America: Hancock County* (Charleston, S.C.: Arcadia Publishing, 2006), 83–92; and thanks to Homer Laughlin engineers Sean Adkins and the late Bill Pomeroy for explaining a lot about modern pottery work.

9. Lula "Pug" Rigdon, interview with the author, digital recording, March 20, 2007, East Liverpool, Ohio.

10. Linda Dickey, interview with the author, digital recording, June 8, 2006, East Liverpool, Ohio.

11. Fay Haught, interview with the author, digital recording, September 19, 2005, Chester, West Virginia.

12. Dickey, interview.

13. "In the Matter of the Arbitration between the United States Potters Association and the National Brotherhood of Operative Potters," December 26, 1950. File No. 50A/542. Opinion and Decision of the Arbitrator. International Brotherhood of

Pottery and Allied Workers, Records, 1889–1971, Kent State University, Kent, Ohio (hereafter IBOP Papers), Box 71, Folder 28.

14. "Hearing Before the Discharge Committee of The United States Potters Association and the National Brotherhood of Operative Potters," at the Offices of the United States Potters Association, East Liverpool, Ohio, December 22, 1950. IBOP Papers, Box 71, Folder 28.

15. "In the Matter of the Arbitration between the United States Potters Association and the National Brotherhood of Operative Potters," December 26, 1950. File No. 50A/542. Opinion and Decision of the Arbitrator. IBOP Papers, Box 71, Folder 28.

16. Lizabeth Cohen, *Making a New Deal: Industrial Workers in Chicago, 1919–1939* (New York: Cambridge University Press, 1990), 253.

17. Ibid., esp. chap. 8; and Jack Metzgar, *Striking Steel: Solidarity Remembered* (Philadelphia: Temple University Press, 2000), 29–30.

18. Jeremy Brecher, *Strike!*, rev. and updated ed. (Cambridge, Mass.: South End Press, 1997), 283–84.

19. U.S. Department of Labor, Bureau of Labor Statistics, "Employment and Earnings Statistics for the United States, 1909–1960," Bulletin No. 1312, 1961, pp. 87–99; Alan Derickson, "The United Steelworkers of America and Health Insurance, 1937–1962," in *American Labor in the Era of World War II*, ed. Sally M. Miller and Daniel A. Cornford (Westport, Conn.: Greenwood Publishing Group, 1995), 69–85; William T. Hogan, *Economic History of the Iron and Steel Industry in the United States*, vol. 4, part VI (Lexington, Mass.: Lexington Books, 1971), 1620–41; Metzgar, *Striking Steel*, 165. Note that this simple narrative of the USWA health insurance program conceals a complex series of negotiations and disagreements and is still a subject for debate.

20. Metzgar, *Striking Steel*, 38–40.

21. Thomas J. Sugrue, "Crabgrass-Roots Politics: Race, Rights, and the Reaction against Liberalism in the Urban North, 1940–1964," *Journal of American History* 82 (Sept. 1995): 551–78; Arnold Hirsch, "Massive Resistance in the Urban North: Trumbull Park, Chicago, 1953–1966," *Journal of American History* 82 (Sept. 1995): 522–550; Becky Nicolaides, *My Blue Heaven: Life and Politics in the Working-Class Suburbs of Los Angeles, 1920–1965* (Chicago: University of Chicago Press, 2002); Kenneth Durr, *Behind the Backlash: White Working-Class Politics in Baltimore, 1940–1980* (Chapel Hill: University of North Carolina Press, 2003).

22. Regarding the local economy during the Great Depression, see Louis C. Martin, "Working for Independence: The Failure of New Deal Politics in a Rural-Industrial Place" (PhD diss., West Virginia University, 2008)," 101–103. For Weirton (National) Steel, see Hogan, *Economic History of the Iron and Steel Industry*, vol. 3, parts IV and V, 957–58, 1056–60, 1243–46, 1383–86. On Homer Laughlin China, see Peter Boyd, *History of Northern West Virginia Panhandle, Embracing Ohio, Marshall, Brooke, and Hancock Counties* (Topeka, Kan.: Historical Publishing Company, 1927), 290–91; "An Old Art in the Modern Manner," *West Virginia Review*, November 1936, 79; and Jack Welch, "The Homer Laughlin China Company," *Goldenseal* 11 (1985): 10–11.

23. For a great example of a study faced with this challenge, see Rachel Ann Batch, "Finding Stability in a Company Town: A Community Study of Slickville, Pennsylvania, 1916–1943" (PhD diss., University of Pennsylvania, 2000).

24. Teresa Ankney, "The Pendulum of Control: The Evolution of the Weirton Steel Company, 1909–1951" (PhD diss., Catholic University of America, 1993); Elizabeth Fones-Wolf and Ken Fones-Wolf, "Cold War Americanism: Business, Pageantry, and Antiunionism in Weirton, West Virginia," *Business History Review* 77 (Spring 2003): 61–91; and John Hennen, "E. T. Weir, Employee Representation, and the Dimensions of Social Control: Weirton Steel, 1933–1937," *Labor Studies Journal* 26, no. 3 (Fall 2001). For a Little Steel example, see James Green, "Democracy Comes to 'Little Siberia': Steel Workers Organize in Aliquippa, Pennsylvania, 1933–1937," *Labor's Heritage* 5 (1993): 4–27.

25. Green, "Democracy Comes to 'Little Siberia.'"

26. Fones-Wolf and Fones-Wolf, "Cold War Americanism," 82, 87. Also see the description of Weirton by Paul Rusen Jr. in Ankney, "Pendulum of Control," 184. He was the USWA district 23 director from 1977 to 1986, and his father had been the district director from 1942 to 1969, during which time the USWA tried repeatedly to organize Weirton Steel. Ankney, "Pendulum of Control," 183.

27. *Pittsburgh Post-Gazette*, October 23, 1958.

28. *ISU Independent News*, December 1, 1958. This letter to the editor was anonymous.

29. John Bodnar makes this point effectively in *Workers' World: Kinship, Community, and Protest in an Industrial Society, 1900–1940* (Baltimore: Johns Hopkins University Press, 1982), 184. Also see Lizabeth Cohen's discussion of workers' desire for "moral capitalism" in *Making a New Deal*, esp. 355–56.

30. Ankney, "Pendulum of Control"; Fones-Wolf and Ken Fones-Wolf, "Cold War Americanism"; and Hennen, "E. T. Weir."

31. These concepts come from Gerald Zahavi, "Negotiated Loyalty: Welfare Capitalism and the Shoeworkers of Endicott Johnson, 1920–1940," *Journal of American History* 70 (December 1983): 602–20.

32. It is not entirely clear that Weirton steelworkers had the same level of "workplace contractualism" that David Brody describes in "Workplace Contractualism: A Historical/Comparative Analysis," in *In Labor's Cause: Main Themes on the History of the American Worker* (New York: Oxford University Press, 1993), 221–51.

33. Thomas Edward Posey, "The Labor Movement in West Virginia, 1900–1948" (PhD diss., University of Wisconsin, 1948), 287. The Little Steel formula for wages applied to "independent" companies like the National Steel Corporation that were not subsidiaries of the U.S. Steel Corporation.

34. For national averages, see Bureau of Labor Statistics, "Employment and Earnings Statistics for the United States, 1909–1960," Bulletin No. 1312, 1961, pp. 87–99. For West Virginia wages see U.S. Department of Labor, Bureau of Labor Statistics, "Employment and Earnings, States and Areas, 1939–78," Bulletin 1370-13, p. 679. For the years 1958 and 1959, for example, the difference is one penny.

35. Quoted in Posey, "The Labor Movement in West Virginia," 289.

36. Case No. R-1229-Weirton Steel Company-Steel Workers Organizing Committee-1939, p. 69, 70, 71, quoted in Posey, "The Labor Movement in West Virginia," 265–66. Also see Posey, "The Labor Movement in West Virginia," 280–82. It is important to note that Teresa Lynn Ankney searched but could not find evidence that such a grievance ever reached arbitration, which suggests that Weirton Steel workers did not have the same protections that USWA members enjoyed. Ankney, "Pendulum of Control," 188–89. For an enlightening discussion of arbitration and the American Arbitration Association, see Daniel Clark, *Like Night and Day: Unionization in a Southern Mill Town* (Chapel Hill: University of North Carolina Press, 1997), 125–28.

37. Alex Fiedorczyk, interview with the author, digital recording, March 28, 2007, Weirton, West Virginia.

38. Fiedorczyk, interview; John Alatis, interview with the author, tape recording, February 3, 2005, Weirton, West Virginia. Other interviewees, such as Hugh Snider, Henry Burns, and Walter Danna, all mentioned that foremen had authority over them in the 1950s and 1960s but that that authority had its limits.

39. Posey, "The Labor Movement in West Virginia," 296.

40. Ibid., 263; Ankney, "Pendulum of Control," 55–57. WEIR first began broadcasting in 1950. Jack Welch, *History of Hancock County, Virginia and West Virginia*, rev. ed. (1963; Abilene, Tex.: WriteRight Publishing, 1992), 99.

41. Elizabeth Fones-Wolf, *Selling Free Enterprise: The Business Assault on Labor and Liberalism, 1945–60* (Urbana University of Illinois Press, 1994), chap. 3, phrase "noneconomic needs" appears on page 79.

42. Posey, "The Labor Movement in West Virginia," 296–97.

43. *NLRB v. Weirton Steel Co.* No. 8041 (3rd Cir. Appeals, 1950). Also see Fones-Wolf and Fones-Wolf, "Cold War Americanism."

44. Fones-Wolf and Fones-Wolf, "Cold War Americanism."

45. James B. Lieber, *Friendly Takeover: How an Employee Buyout Saved a Steel Town* (New York: Viking, 1995), 35–37; Fones-Wolf and Fones-Wolf, "Cold War Americanism," 82–85.

46. Derickson, "The United Steelworkers of America and Health Insurance," 69–73, quote on 72–73.

47. *ISU Independent News*, October 1950.

48. Fones-Wolf and Fones-Wolf, "Cold War Americanism," 89.

49. On the vote tally, see Fones-Wolf and Fones-Wolf, "Cold War Americanism," 89.

50. *ISU Independent News*, October 23, 1950.

51. *ISU Independent News*, April 23, 1954.

52. *ISU Independent News*, January 28, 1959. For other examples, see Posey, "The Labor Movement in West Virginia," 296–97.

53. *ISU Independent News*, October 1950.

54. Welch, *History of Hancock County*, 98–99. For a flattering biography of Millsop, see William Gill, "Up from the Open Hearth," *Pittsburgh Post*, October 25, 1958.

55. *Weirton Steel Employees Bulletin,* October 1955.

56. *Weirton Daily Times,* May 21, 1954; Alatis, interview; Ankney, "Pendulum of Control," 56–57.

57. *Pittsburgh Post-Gazette,* October 23, 1958.

58. Metzgar, *Striking Steel,* 165; Hogan, *Economic History of the Iron and Steel Industry,* vol. 4, part VI, 1622–41.

59. *ISU Independent News,* August 24, 1956.

60. See comments of USWA officials in *Wall Street Journal,* August 5, 1959, reprinted in *Weirton Steel Employees Bulletin,* September 1959.

61. Ibid.

62. Louis Truax, "The 200th Anniversary of the City of Weirton, West Va., and My Life Story as I Have Seen Weirton Grow" (manuscript in author's possession [Weirton, 1971]), ii.

63. Several Weirton steelworkers expressed this to me in interviews, including Richard Cameron, interview with the author, New Manchester, West Virginia, March 28, 2007 (digital recording); Alatis, interview; Henry Burns, interview; and Mike Garan, interview with the author, tape recording, July 6, 2002, Weirton, West Virginia.

64. Shotliff, "The History of the Labor Movement," 307 note 25.

65. "Statement made by Edna Brereton, member of Shop Committee at Homer Laughlin's No. 5, and representing Local Union No. 132. (Statement made to Frank Dales.)" April 29, 1955. IBOP Papers, Box 80, Folder 1.

66. Shotliff, "The History of the Labor Movement," 329–30.

67. *Potters Herald,* June 14, 1956.

68. Shotliff, "The History of the Labor Movement," 368, 331, 356.

69. Ibid., 353, 369–70.

70. E. L. Wheatley to John N. Siddall, August 7, 1961, IBOP Papers, Box 64.

71. *Potters Herald,* September 13, 1956.

72. E. L. Wheatley to Iona Shroades, May 3, 1956, IBOP Papers, Box 71, Folder 21.

73. E. L. Wheatley to Willis Van Dyne, November 21, 1956, IBOP Papers, Box 79, Folder 50.

74. Quoted in Marc Jeffrey Stern, *The Pottery Industry of Trenton: A Skilled Trade in Transition, 1850–1929* (New Brunswick, N.J.: Rutgers University Press, 1994), 44.

75. U.S. Treasury Department, Public Health Services, Public Health Bulletin No. 244, February 1939, *Silicosis and Lead Poisoning Among Pottery Workers* (Washington, D.C.: Government Printing Office, 1939), 128–29.

76. *Silicosis and Lead Poisoning Among Pottery Workers,* 71–73, 119–23.

77. A Clarksburg, West Virginia, pottery met with the union to outline their plan to combat silicosis in 1954. *Potters Herald,* September 2, 1954.

78. Frank Hull to State Office Building, Health Department of Factories, November 16, 1953, IBOP Papers, Box 71, Folder 20.

79. George L. Wilson to Frank Hull, December 15, 1953, IBOP Papers Box 71, Folder 20.

80. J. M. Wells to Frank Hull, December 22, 1953, IBOP Papers Box 71, Folder 20; *Potters Herald*, December 10, 1953.

81. Vesta Hickman to President Hull, January 15, 1954, IBOP Papers, Box 71, Folder 21; Frank Hull to State Office Building, Health Department of Factories, February 19, 1954, IBOP Papers, Box 71, Folder 21; George L. Wilson to Frank Hull, July 15, 1954, IBOP Papers, Box 71, Folder 21.

82. Vesta Phillips to Sir, May 15, 1954, IBOP Papers, Box 71, Folder 21.

83. Arthur A. Wells to Frank Hull, January 24, 1955, IBOP Papers, Box 71, Folder 21.

84. E. L. Wheatley to Vesta Phillips, October 8, 1956, IBOP Papers, Box 71, Folder 21. Jobs in the mill, it should be remembered, did base compensation on the level of hazards workers faced.

85. Vesta Phillips to Sir, December 14, 1957, IBOP Papers, Box 71, Folder 21; James T. Slaven to West Virginia Department of Labor, Safety & Welfare, February 12, 1958, IBOP Papers, Box 71, Folder 21.

86. Harvey J. Roberts to C. Frank Dales, January 22, 1960, IBOP Papers, Box 71, Folder 22.

87. Sean Adkins, Homer Laughlin China engineer, phone conversation, April 24, 2008.

88. Shotliff, "The History of the Labor Movement," 377–78.

89. Ibid., 373. Some mergers include 4, 11, 12, 22, and 29 into LU 320; 53, 121, and 1932 into LU 321; 155 transferred to 123; 17, 18, and 130 into LU 9; and LU 138 merged with 141.

90. Frank Dales to President Wheatley, September 5, 1959, IBOP Papers, Box 71, Folder 22.

91. Corrine Richard, Helen Enoch, and Betty Goppert to E. Wheatley, May 26, 1961, IBOP Papers, Box 71, Folder 22; E. L. Wheatley to Corrine Richard, Helen Enoch, and Betty Goppert, May 29, 1961, IBOP Papers, Box 71, Folder 22.

92. U. S. Department of Labor, Bureau of Labor Statistics, "Employment and Earnings Statistics for the United States, 1909–1960," Bulletin No. 1312, 1961, pp. 87–99.

93. Shotliff, "The History of the Labor Movement," 306. For the Homer Laughlin payroll numbers, see William C. Gates Jr., *The City of Hills and Kilns: Life and Work in East Liverpool, Ohio* (East Liverpool, Ohio: East Liverpool Historical Society, 1984), 356–58.

94. Shotliff, "The History of the Labor Movement," 302.

95. U. S. Department of Labor, Bureau of Labor Statistics, "Employment and Earnings Statistics for the United States, 1909–1960," Bulletin No. 1312, 1961, pp. 87–99.

96. James H. Thompson, *The Manufacturing Industries of West Virginia* (Morgantown: Bureau of Business Research, West Virginia University, 1952), 25.

97. Tom Rector, interview with the author, digital recording, September 19, 2005, Newell, West Virginia.

98. Fay Haught and her husband were one example of this, but it was a long-standing tradition in the pottery industry dating back to the early nineteenth century

in Staffordshire, England. See Haught, interview; Bill Pomeroy, interview with the author, digital recording, April 15, 2005, Newell, West Virginia; and Richard Whipp, *Patterns of Labour: Work and Social Change in the Pottery Industry* (London: Routledge, 1990).

99. U.S. Census Bureau, *Seventeenth Census of the United States: Volume 2, Population, Part 48* (Washington, D.C.: Government Printing Office, 1952), 51.

100. *Potters Herald*, June 17, 1948; Shotliff, "The History of the Labor Movement," 320–21, 352–53.

101. Shotliff, "The History of the Labor Movement," 333, 322, 356, 357, 361–63.

102. U.S. Department of Labor, Bureau of Labor Statistics, "Employment and Earnings, States and Areas, 1939–78," Bulletin 1370–13, p. 679.

103. *Potters Herald*, May 14, 1959; Gates, *City of Hills and Kilns*, 361; Shotliff, "The History of the Labor Movement," 359–60.

104. Rigdon, interview.

105. Dickey, interview.

106. Jack Metzgar, "The 1945–1946 Strike Wave," in *The Encyclopedia of Strikes in American History*, ed. Aaron Brenner, Benjamin Day, and Immanuel Ness (Armonk, N.Y.: M. E. Sharpe, 2009): 216–25; Melvyn Dubofsky, *The State and Labor in Modern America* (Chapel Hill: University of North Carolina Press, 1994), chap. 8.

107. Todd H. Bullard, *Labor and the Legislature: The West Virginia Labor Federation and the West Virginia Legislature, 1957–1961*, Publication No. 43 (Morgantown, W.V.: Bureau for Government Research, 1965), 15–66, 62.

108. Ibid., 61–72.

109. Ibid., quoted in 50–55.

110. Ibid., 119–20, quote on 133.

111. Sugrue, "Crabgrass-Roots Politics"; Hirsch, "Massive Resistance in the Urban North."

112. On union structure see Shotliff, "The History of the Labor Movement," 50–51. For a detailed analysis of the flint glass workers of Moundsville, see Ken Fones-Wolf, *Glass Towns: Industry, Labor, and Political Economy in Appalachia, 1890–1930s* (Urbana: University of Illinois Press, 2007), chap. 4.

113. The ISU did not endorse political candidates in the pages of the *ISU Independent News* and there is no evidence that they attempted to influence members through mailings.

114. Information on affiliated locals and officers of the West Virginia State Federation of Labor found in Evelyn Harris and Frank Krebs, *From Humble Beginnings: West Virginia State Federation of Labor, 1903–1957* (Charleston, W.V.: West Virginia Labor History Pub. Fund, 1960), 522–42.

115. Shotliff, "The History of the Labor Movement," 371–72, 378.

116. James Duffy to "Dear Sir and Brother," February 23, 1948, IBOP Papers, Box 71, Folder 19; James Duffy and Chas. F. Jordan to Iona Shroades, May 8, 1948, IBOP Papers, Box 71, Folder 19.

117. On the Democratic statehouse machine, see Gerald W. Johnson, "West Virginia Politics: A Socio-Cultural Analysis of Voter Participation" (PhD diss., University of Tennessee, 1970).

118. Brad Crouser, *Arch: The Life of Governor Arch A. Moore, Jr.* (Chapmanville, W.V.: Woodland Press, LLC, 2006), 52–65; Larry A. Sayre, "Arch Moore: Man on the Move" (master's thesis, West Virginia University, 1966), 10–21.

119. Sayre, "Arch Moore," 15, 20, 26, 30, 36, 41.

120. Sayre, "Arch Moore," 35–37. Both men were incumbents in this 1962 election because they had represented two districts that were being combined because of population loss.

121. Crouser, *Arch*, 9–47, 59; Sayre, "Arch Moore," 16.

122. Sayre, "Arch Moore," 57. Bullard goes so far as to say that COPE alienated some voters by refusing to endorse Arch Moore. Bullard, *Labor and the Legislature*, 73.

123. Sayre, "Arch Moore," quote on 44, 53–57, 69–70, 74, 85.

124. For example, see *Wall Street Journal*, August 5, 1959; reprinted in *Weirton Steel Employees Bulletin*, September 1959.

125. See for example, E. L. Wheatley to Shirley Yoakum (Local Union No. 132), February 3, 1961, IBOP Papers, Box 80, Folder 2.

126. Ralph Powell of New Cumberland to Arch Moore, July 23, 1959, Arch A. Moore Papers, West Virginia and Regional History Collection, Morgantown, W.V. (hereafter cited as AAM Papers), Box GM11, Folder "Anti-Landrum-Griffin." For a similar position, see Karl F. Walker to Arch Moore, July 22, 1959, AAM Papers, Box GM11, Folder "Anti-Landrum-Griffin."

127. Mr. and Mrs. John A. Crow to Arch Moore, July 28, 1959, AAM Papers, Box GM11, Folder "Letters on Labor Inspired by Bob Kennedy."

128. Mrs. Robert L. Doughty to Arch Moore, July 23, 1959, AAM Papers, Box GM11, Folder "Letters on Labor Inspired by Bob Kennedy." Also see Mr. and Mrs. Carl D. Crow (Weirton) to Arch Moore, August 8, 1959, AAM Papers, Box GM11, Folder "Pro-Landrum-Griffin."

129. Sayre, "Arch Moore," 28.

130. The "traitor" accusation comes from Miles Barrett, Milner Hotel, Wheeling, to Arch Moore, August 17, 1959, AAM Papers, Box GM11, Folder "Letters on Labor Inspired by Bob Kennedy"; letters of support and disappointment are in AAM Papers, Box GM11, Folders "Anti-Landrum-Griffin" and "Pro-Landrum-Griffin."

131. Dorothy B. Mayles to Arch Moore, May 26, 1965, AAM Papers, Box GM34, Folder "Taft-Hartley (for repeal 14b)."

132. John R. Major (Sixth St, Chester) to Arch Moore, May 16, 1965, AAM Papers, Box GM34, Folder "Taft-Hartley (for repeal 14b)."

133. Mrs. William J. McConnell to Arch Moore, May 26, 1965, AAM Papers, Box GM34, Folder "Taft-Hartley (for repeal 14b)." For another example of this approach, see Thomas E. Ridge Jr. to Arch Moore, July 18, 1965, AAM Papers, Box GM34, Folder "Taft-Hartley (for repeal 14b)."

134. Arch Moore to Violet Gayle Miller, June 4, 1965, AAM Papers, Box GM34, Folder "Taft-Hartley-Section 14 (b)."

135. Arch Moore to Francis M. Rich, May 24, 1965, and Francis M. Rich to Arch Moore, May 19, 1965, AAM Papers, Box GM34, Folder "Taft-Hartley-Section 14 (b)."

136. See "'Right to Work' Repeal Again Loses in Senate," *CQ Almanac 1966*, 22nd ed., 837–40. Washington, DC: Congressional Quarterly, 1967. http://library.cqpress.com/cqalmanac/cqal66-1300523, accessed on February 9, 2015. Moore's vote is recorded in *CQ Almanac 1965*, 21st ed., 982–83. For articles regarding the repeal of 14 (b) as it worked its way through Congress, see the *New York Times*, May 2, 1965; July 29, 1965; October 1, 1965; and October 25, 1965.

137. Jack Metzgar's *Striking Steel* thoroughly analyzes the strike and presents it as the culmination of organizing efforts that began in the 1930s. Ironically, this well-concerted national strike was an effort to preserve the local conditions clause of the industry-wide contact, even though Weirton steelworkers often saw—and sometimes with good reason—the USWA as a dictatorial organization that lacked sensitivity to local conditions.

CHAPTER 5.
WORK AND IDENTITY IN THE FACTORY AND AT HOME

1. Lula "Pug" Rigdon, interview with the author, digital recording, March 20, 2007, East Liverpool, Ohio; Fay Haught, interview with the author, digital recording, September 19, 2005, Chester, West Virginia.

2. On employment of finishers, see "In the Matter of the Arbitration between the United States Potters Association and the National Brotherhood of Operative Potters," December 26, 1950, File No. 50A/542, Opinion and Decision of the Arbitrator. International Brotherhood of Operative Potters Collection, Kent State University (hereafter IBOP Papers), Box 71, Folder 28. In the second paragraph it says, "Prior to installation of the automatics in 1941, finishers were employed by jiggermen rather than by the Company."

3. "A Member NBOP" to Mr. Duffy, September 15, 1941. IBOP Papers, Box 71, Folder 18.

4. Bill Pomeroy, interview with the author, digital recording, April 15, 2005, Newell, West Virginia.

5. Susan Carnahan Lindsey, "Hancock County in World War II" (master's thesis, West Virginia University, 1949), 43. Also see, U.S. Bureau of Labor Statistics, "Wages in Pottery Manufacture in East Liverpool (Ohio) Area, October 1944," *Monthly Labor Review* 61 (July 1945): 105. Obviously Homer Laughlin no longer uses uranium in any of its products.

6. *Weirton Daily Times*, October 23, 1941.

7. On servicemen, see Lindsey, "Hancock County," 4. On the male population of the county age fourteen and older, see U.S. Census Bureau, *Sixteenth Census of the*

United States: Volume 2, Population, Part 48 (Washington, D.C.: Government Printing Office, 1943), 488.

8. Don Shotliff, "The History of the Labor Movement in the American Pottery Industry: The National Brotherhood of Operative Potters-International Brotherhood of Operative Potters, 1890–1970," (PhD diss., Kent State University, 1977), 297.

9. Haught, interview.

10. U.S. Treasury Department, Public Health Services, Public Health Bulletin No. 244, February 1939, *Silicosis and Lead Poisoning Among Pottery Workers* (Washington, D.C.: Government Printing Office, 1939), 7–8; U.S. Bureau of Labor Statistics, "Wages in Pottery Manufacture," 108.

11. Gladys Hartzell to James Duffy, April 26, 1941, IBOP Papers, Box 71, Folder 18.

12. Gladys Hartzell to James Duffy, October 19, 1942, IBOP Papers, Box 71, Folder 18.

13. Shotliff, "The History of the Labor Movement," 289, 296.

14. There were 459 women in Local 94 Warehousewomen and 337 women in Local 195 Warehousewomen. See table 5.

15. The local union membership numbers come from IBOP Papers, Box 62, Folder 3 (lists trades and district locals) and Folder 5 (lists of local memberships, 1953, 1959).

16. U.S. Census Bureau, *Seventeenth Census of the United States: Volume 2, Population, Part 48* (Washington, D.C.: Government Printing Office, 1952), 159; *Eighteenth Census of the United States: Volume I, Characteristics of the Population, Part 50* (Washington, D.C.: Government Printing Office, 1961), 285–87.

17. Richard Whipp, *Patterns of Labour: Work and Social Change in the Pottery Industry* (London: Routledge, 1990), 58–63.

18. U.S. Bureau of Labor Statistics, "Wages in Pottery Manufacture," 107. For a thorough discussion of gender inequality in the potteries of northern West Virginia, see Virginia C. Young, "'We Do the Same Work as the Men Did': The Development of Working-Class Feminism in the Glass and Pottery Industries of West Virginia, 1930–1970" (PhD diss., West Virginia University, 2013).

19. Ibid., 108.

20. Rigdon, interview.

21. Shotliff, "The History of the Labor Movement," 364.

22. William C. Gates Jr., *The City of Hills and Kilns: Life and Work in East Liverpool, Ohio* (East Liverpool, Ohio: East Liverpool Historical Society, 1984), 361.

23. Whipp, *Patterns of Labour*, 76.

24. Shotliff, "The History of the Labor Movement," 364. Note that the National Brotherhood of Operative Potters changed its name to the International Brotherhood of Operative Potters in 1951.

25. See this example from the meatpacking industry: Bruce Fehn, "'Chickens Come Home to Roost': Industrial Reorganization, Seniority, and Gender Conflict in the United Packinghouse Workers of America, 1956–1966," *Labor History* (March 1993): 324–41.

26. *Potters Herald*, November 19, 1953.

27. *Potters Herald*, June 23, 1955.

28. *Potters Herald*, February 1972.

29. Haught, interview.

30. Rigdon, interview.

31. Linda Dickey, interview with the author, digital recording, June 8, 2006, East Liverpool, Ohio.

32. U.S. Census Bureau, *Seventeenth Census of the United States: Volume 2, Population, Part 48* (Washington, D.C.: Government Printing Office, 1952), calculated from figures on pages 48, 51, and 75.

33. U.S. Census Bureau, *Seventeenth Census of the United States: Volume 2, Population, Part 48* (Washington, D.C.: Government Printing Office, 1952), 159; *Eighteenth Census of the United States: Volume 1, Characteristics of the Population, Part 50* (Washington, D.C.: Government Printing Office, 1961), 285–87.

34. U.S. Census Bureau, *Seventeenth Census of the United States: Volume 2, Population, Part 48* (Washington, D.C.: Government Printing Office, 1952), 196.

35. U.S. Census Bureau, *Sixteenth Census of the United States: Volume 2, Population, Part 7* (Washington, D.C.: Government Printing Office, 1943), 488.

36. Lindsey, "Hancock County," 41–42.

37. Jim Rose, "'The Problem Every Supervisor Dreads': Women Workers at the U.S. Steel Duquesne Works during World War II," *Labor History* 36 (Winter 1995): 38–39.

38. Mary Margaret Fonow, *Union Women: Forging Feminism in the United Steelworkers of America*, vol. 17 in Social Movements, Protest, and Contention series (Minneapolis: University of Minnesota Press, 2003), 83; Rose, "The Problem Every Supervisor Dreads," 38–39.

39. Fonow, *Union Women*, 26–33.

40. R. H. Markham, "Steelmaking: The 'American Way' Shines Bright Amid Smoke and Toil," *Christian Science Monitor*, May 26, 1945, p. 11. On sex-typing jobs, see Ruth Milkman, *Gender at Work: The Dynamics of Job Segregation by Sex During World War II* (Urbana: University of Illinois Press, 1987).

41. Fonow, *Union Women*, 28.

42. Ibid., 83; Milkman, *Gender at Work*, chap. 7; Rose, "The Problem Every Supervisor Dreads."

43. *Weirton Steel Employees Bulletin*, April 1957.

44. Ramona "Boots" Hines, interview with the author, digital recording, March 20, 2007, New Cumberland, West Virginia.

45. Margaret Heaton, interview with the author, digital recording, July 28, 2005, Weirton, West Virginia.

46. Hines, interview.

47. U.S. Census Bureau, *Seventeenth Census of the United States: Volume 2, Population, Part 48* (Washington, D.C.; Government Printing Office, 1952), 51.

48. Alma Haning (Cleveland Ave Weirton) to Arch Moore, May 16, 1957, Arch

Moore Papers, West Virginia and Regional History Collection, Morgantown, W.V. (hereafter cited as AAM Papers), Box GM214a, Folder "Questionnaire April 1957—Correspondence."

49. See Fonow, *Union Women*, 80–81, for a description of a female steelworkers' experience with the service sector.

50. *Weirton Steel Employee Bulletin*, April–May 1959.

51. *Weirton Steel Employee Bulletin*, March 1960.

52. *Weirton Steel Employee Bulletin*, July 1958.

53. Mark McColloch, "Modest But Adequate: The Standard of Living for Mon Valley Steelworkers in the Union Era," in *U.S. Labor in the Twentieth Century: Studies in Working-Class Struggles and Insurgency*, ed. John Hinshaw and Paul LeBlanc (Amherst, N.Y.: Humanity Books, 2000), 248–55. Also see Jack Metzgar, *Striking Steel: Solidarity Remembered* (Philadelphia: Temple University Press, 2000), 40.

54. The 1959 modest but adequate household income was $5,180, which would have been $42,432 in 2014 according to www.usinflationcalculator.com, which is based on Consumer Price Index data. Accessed February 8, 2015.

55. David Dempsey, "Steelworkers: 'Not Today's Wage, Tomorrow's Security,'" *New York Times Magazine*, August 7, 1949, in *American Labor Since the New Deal*, ed. Melvyn Dubofsky (Chicago: Quadrangle Books, 1971), 192–201, quotes on 194 and 196.

56. Metzgar, *Striking Steel*, 24, 40–41, 67–68.

57. Becky Nicolaides, *My Blue Heaven: Life and Politics in the Working-Class Suburbs of Los Angeles, 1920–1965* (Chicago: University of Chicago Press, 2002), quotes on 13 and 205.

58. Metzgar, *Striking Steel*, 24, 40–41, 67–68.

59. Carlos Beagle was one of the few people I interviewed who did not remember his family ever having a garden, livestock, a self-built house, or other aspects of this self-help lifestyle. Instead, his family focused on living as simply as possible. Similarly, if people migrated from large cities, like Francis Asfour, who came from Haifa, they often did not have rural folkways to transplant. See Carlos Beagle, interview with the author, digital recording, July 2, 2008, New Cumberland, West Virginia; Francis Asfour, interview with the author, digital recording, March 28, 2007, Weirton, West Virginia.

60. U.S. Census Bureau, *1960 Census of Population: Volume 1, Characteristics of the Population, Part 50* (Washington, D.C.: Government Printing Office, 1961), 50-16. Note that about 24,000 of Weirton's 28,000 inhabitants lived in Hancock County while about 4,000 lived in Brooke County.

61. Henry "Tex" Burns, interview with the author, digital recording, April 9, 2005, Trinity Hospital, Steubenville, Ohio.

62. Frank Gregory, interview with the author, digital recording, February 3, 2012, Weirton, West Virginia.

63. Burns, interview; Alex Fiedorczyk, interview with the author, digital recording, March 28, 2007, Weirton, West Virginia.

64. *The Code of the City of Weirton, West Virginia, 1956* (Charlottesville, Va.: Michie City Publications Company, 1957), 74–75. Both Henry Burns and Frank Gregory recalled that the livestock restrictions began when the city incorporated in 1947 because of the smells and nuisances.

65. Frank Maslowski, interview with the author, digital recording, April 6, 2007, Weirton, West Virginia.

66. Fiedorczyk, interview.

67. *Weirton Daily Times*, May 23, 1955, June 27, 1955. For other examples in the summer of 1955, see April 11, June 20, June 27, July 11, and August 15. All included ads for farms, all under $8,000.

68. *The Daily Herald* (Chicago), June 23, 1955, p. 35.

69. Hugh and Garnet Snider, interview with the author, digital recording, February 8, 2006, Weirton, West Virginia. For more about West Virginia outmigration, see Susan Johnson, "West Virginia Rubber Workers in Akron," in *Transnational West Virginia: Ethnic Communities and Economic Changes, 1840–1940*, ed. Ken Fones-Wolf and Ronald L. Lewis (Morgantown: West Virginia University Press, 2002).

70. Walter Danna, interview with the author, digital recording, May 10, 2005, near Burgettstown, Pennsylvania.

71. "Wildlife Survey of Hancock, Brooke, and Ohio Counties, West Virginia, Pittman-Robertson Project 8-R 1943" (manuscript held at West Virginia and Regional History Collection, n.p., 1943), 6, 18, and table V. According to the 1940 census, there were 307 farms of full owners, 9 farms of part owners, and 67 tenant farms. Historical Census Browser, University of Virginia, Geospatial and Statistical Data Center: http://mapserver.lib.virginia.edu, accessed January 12, 2014.

72. *Weirton Steel Employees Bulletin*, January 17, 1936.

73. *Potters Herald*, August 4, 1949.

74. Hugh and Garnet Snider, interview.

75. *Weirton Steel Employees Bulletin*, September 1958.

76. George D. Strayer, *A Report of a Survey of Public Education in the State of West Virginia* (Legislative Interim Committee, State of West Virginia, 1945), 467.

77. See the essays in Sarah Stage and Virginia B. Vincenti, *Rethinking Home Economics: Women and the History of a Profession* (Ithaca, N.Y.: Cornell University Press, 1997), esp. Ronald R. Kline, "Agents of Modernity: Home Economics and Rural Electrification, 1925–1950," pp. 237–52.

78. Gertrude Humphreys, *Adventures in Good Living*, West Virginia Extension Homemakers Council (Parsons, W.V.: McClain Printing Company, 1972), 244–45.

79. Haught, interview.

80. John Alatis, interview with the author, tape recording, February 3, 2005, Weirton, West Virginia.

81. For examples, see *Recipes from the Kitchens of West Virginia* (Glenville: West Virginia Folk Fest, 1969), 68–74.

82. Heaton, interview.

83. Theresa V. DeCaria, *The Table My Mother Set: A Collection of Traditional Family Recipes From My Mother's Italian Kitchen* (Weirton, W.V.: Theresa V. DeCaria, 2007), 1, 27, 61, 73, 96.

84. Gregory, interview.

85. Nicolaides, *My Blue Heaven*, 27.

86. Markham, "Steelmaking," 11.

87. *Weirton Daily Times*, November 13, 1941.

88. *ISU Independent News*, April 1954.

89. U.S. Census Bureau, *Sixteenth Census of the United States: Volume 1, Housing, Part 2* (Washington, D.C.: Government Printing Office, 1943), 723; *Eighteenth Census of the United States: Volume 1, States and Small Areas, Part 8* (Washington, D.C.: Government Printing Office, 1963), 50-15.

90. Bob Rossell, interview with the author, digital recording, March 10, 2005, Weirton, West Virginia.

91. Haught, interview. For more on self-building homes, see Nicolaides, *My Blue Heaven*; and Richard Harris, "Self-Building in the Urban Market," *Economic Geography* 67 (January 1991): 1–21.

92. Maslowski, interview.

93. Fiedorczyk, interview.

94. Paul Barkhurst, interview with the author, digital recording, 2004, Frankfort Springs, Pennsylvania.

95. Lisa Fine, *The Story of REO Joe: Work, Kin, and Community in Autotown, U.S.A.* (Philadelphia: Temple University Press, 2004), 141.

96. Gordon L. Palmer, "It's Good for What Ails You!," *West Virginia Conservation* (September 1960): 18–20.

97. *Weirton Daily Times*, November 11, 1941. There were 12,357 males ages fourteen and older according to the 1940 census. Historical Census Browser, University of Virginia, Geospatial and Statistical Data Center: http://mapserver.lib.virginia.edu/, accessed December 14, 2011.

98. "Wildlife Survey of Hancock, Brooke, and Ohio Counties, West Virginia," 6, 18, and table V.

99. Kenneth Dale McIntosh, "Privately-Owned Hunting Lands in West Virginia: Supply, Quality, and Access Arrangements" (PhD diss., University of Wisconsin, 1966), 109.

100. Haught, interview.

101. Danna, interview.

102. Dan Cantner, "Mr. Whistle Pig," *West Virginia Conservation* (August 1960): 1, 30–32.

103. Maslowski, interview.

104. On residents traveling outside of Hancock County to hunt, see "Wildlife Survey of Hancock, Brooke, and Ohio Counties, West Virginia," 6, 18, and table V. As for "down hoopie," people still say this in Hancock County.

105. Maslowski, interview. Also see the "Indoorsman" column in *Weirton Daily Times*, June 10, 1954, for an example of an outing hosted by the Hancock County Sportsmen's Association.

106. Hal S. Barron, *Mixed Harvest: The Second Great Transformation in the Rural North, 1870–1930* (Chapel Hill: University of North Carolina Press, 1997), 21–22.

107. H. Clay Tate, *Building a Better Home Town: A Program of Community Self-Analysis and Self-Help* (New York: Harper & Brothers, 1954), 6.

108. Todd H. Bullard, *Labor and the Legislature: The West Virginia Labor Federation and the West Virginia Legislature, 1957–1961*, Publication No. 43 (Morgantown, W.V.: Bureau for Government Research, 1965), 15–16, 62.

109. *ISU Independent News*, October 22, 1958. For another article about the Community Chest in Weirton, see *Weirton Steel Employees Bulletin*, May 1, 1936.

110. Hancock County Elections Office, New Cumberland, West Virginia.

111. "1964 Hancock County Results," in AAM Papers, Box GM11, Folder "Hancock Elections."

112. Lawrence Savors to Arch Moore, May 7, 1958, AAM Papers, Box GM214a, Folder "Questionnaire 1958." When letter writers did not list their occupation in the letter, I used the city directory to find them. *Weirton (Hancock County, W.V.) Directory* (Richmond, Va.: R. L. Polk & Co., 1962).

113. Myron O. Batson questionnaire, AAM Papers, Box GM214a, Folder "April 1957—Correspondence."

114. *Your Washington Report* (April 1957), in AAM Papers, Box GM214a, Folder "Newsletter, April 1957."

115. Hancock County Elections Office, New Cumberland, West Virginia.

116. Carl M. Frasure and Leonard M. Davis, eds., *Eight Years: Official Statements & Papers, The Honorable Arch A. Moore, Jr., Governor of West Virginia, 1969–1977*, vol. III (Beckley, W.V.: BJW Printers), 29, 32, 38.

117. Ibid., 32, 38.

118. An example of this use of "welfare mothers" appeared in a *Time* magazine article titled "The American Underclass" that reported that the "underclass" was "made up mostly of impoverished urban blacks" and as a group produced a "highly disproportionate number of the nation's juvenile delinquents, school dropouts, drug addicts and *welfare mothers* [my emphasis]." *Time*, August 29, 1977, accessed online at http://www.time.com/time/magazine/article/0,9171,915331,00.html. Also see Michael B. Katz, *Improving Poor People: The Welfare State, the "Underclass," and Urban Schools as History* (Princeton, N.J.: Princeton University Press, 1995).

119. Thomas J. Sugrue, "Crabgrass-Roots Politics: Race, Rights, and the Reaction against Liberalism in the Urban North, 1940–1964," *Journal of American History* 82 (September 1995): 551–78; Thomas J. Sugrue, *The Origins of the Urban Crisis: Race*

and Inequality in Postwar Detroit (Princeton, N.J.: Princeton University Press, 1996); Nicolaides, *My Blue Heaven*; and Kenneth Durr, *Behind the Backlash: White Working-Class Politics in Baltimore, 1940–1980* (Chapel Hill: University of North Carolina Press, 2003).

120. Metzgar, *Striking Steel*, esp. 80–92.

121. Nelson Lichtenstein, *Walter Reuther: The Most Dangerous Man in Detroit* (Urbana: University of Illinois Press, 1995), quoted on page 368.

CHAPTER 6.
MOVEMENTS FOR EQUALITY IN A TIME
OF INDUSTRIAL RESTRUCTURING

1. This chapter explores the struggles of these two industries locally, but for an overview of broader economic changes in the 1970s and 1980s, see Barry Bluestone and Bennett Harrison, *The Deindustrialization of America: Plant Closings, Community Abandonment, and the Dismantling of Basic Industry* (New York: Basic Books, 1982).

2. *Weirton Daily Times*, October 23, 1941.

3. William C. Gates, *The City of Hills and Kilns: Life and Work in East Liverpool, Ohio* (East Liverpool, Ohio: East Liverpool Historical Society, 1984), 327.

4. Mark Esposito, "The UAW, American Trade Policy, and the Transformation of the Global Automobile Industry, 1945–1973" (PhD diss., West Virginia University, 2004), 8, 37–46.

5. Address in New York on May 15, quoted in Department of State *Bulletin* 38, no. 988, pub. 6649, June 2, 1958, page 899.

6. Quoted in Esposito, "UAW, American Trade Policy," 98.

7. Esposito, "UAW, American Trade Policy," chapter 4 and 185–86.

8. *Hearings Before the Committee on Ways and Means, House of Representatives, Eighty-Fourth Congress, First Session on H.R. 1, a Bill to Extend the Authority of the President to Enter Into Trade Agreements under Section 350 of the Tariff Act of 1930, as Amended, and for Other Purposes* (Washington, D.C.: Government Printing Office, 1955), 767.

9. Ibid., 774.

10. Don Shotliff, "The History of the Labor Movement in the American Pottery Industry: The National Brotherhood of Operative Potters-International Brotherhood of Operative Potters, 1890–1970" (PhD diss., Kent State University, 1977), 306.

11. Gates, *City of Hills and Kilns*, 356–58.

12. *Potters Herald*, March 22, 1962.

13. Gates, *City of Hills and Kilns*, 356–58.

14. Ibid., 327.

15. *Hearings Before the Committee on Ways and Means*, 1029.

16. Ibid., 1029.

17. Ibid., 1036–37.

18. *Life*, June 23, 1958, 96.

19. Ibid., 101.

20. Ibid., 102.

21. Ruth DeLong to Arch Moore, Arch A. Moore Papers, West Virginia and Regional History Collection, Morgantown, W.V. (hereafter cited as AAM Papers), Box GM214a, Folder "Questionnaire 1958."

22. Dale E. Highfield to Arch Moore, May 8, 1958. AAM Papers, Box GM210a, Envelope G.

23. Frank Blaskovich to Arch Moore, July 29, 1959, AAM Papers, GM214a, Folder "Questionnaire June 1959—Correspondence."

24. Arch Moore, *Your Washington Report* (June 1957). AAM Papers, Box GM214a.

25. Arch Moore, *Your Washington Report* (April 1957), AAM Papers, GM214a, Folder Newsletter April 1957.

26. David T. Javersak, *History of Weirton, West Virginia* (Virginia Beach, Va.: Donning, 1999), 102–3, 111.

27. Cecelia Arnett (pseudonym), interview with the author, digital recording, May 7, 2007, Morgantown, West Virginia.

28. Inez Orler, *Helping Children Learn Their Rich Ethnic Culture: A Story of Weirton* (New York: Carlton Press, 1979), 19–21.

29. Henry "Tex" Burns, interview with the author, digital recording, April 9, 2005, Trinity Hospital, Steubenville, Ohio.

30. Javersak, *History of Weirton*, 102.

31. Burns, interview.

32. Arnett, interview.

33. Javersak, *History of Weirton*, 102–7.

34. Burns, interview.

35. Walter Danna, interview with the author, May 10, 2005, Washington County, Pennsylvania.

36. Ibid.; Dennis C. Dickerson, *Out of the Crucible: Black Steelworkers in Western Pennsylvania, 1875–1980* (Albany: State University of New York Press, 1986); Bruce Nelson, *Divided We Stand: American Workers and the Struggle for Black Equality* (Princeton, N.J.: Princeton University Press, 2001).

37. U.S. Census Bureau, *Census of the United States: Volume 2, Characteristics of the Population, Part 48* (Washington, D.C.: Government Printing Office, 1952), 51–53; *Census of the United States: Volume 1, Characteristics of the Population, Part 50* (Washington, D.C.: Government Printing Office, 1961), 135, 143.

38. There were 59 household servants and 17 professionals, which included schoolteachers, out of 165 nonwhite females employed in Weirton. U.S. Census Bureau, *Census of Population: 1960, Volume 1, Characteristics of the Population, Part 50* (Washington, D.C.: Government Printing Office, 1961), 143.

39. Arnett, interview.

40. There were 165 nonwhite women employed in Weirton out of 485 that were

over the age of fourteen. U.S. Census Bureau, *Census of the United States: Volume 1, Characteristics of the Population, Part 50* (Washington, D.C.: Government Printing Office, 1961), 43, 143.

41. U.S. Census Bureau, *Census of Population: 1950, Volume 2, Characteristics of the Population, Part 48* (Washington, D.C.: Government Printing Office, 1952), 54–55.

42. Burns, interview.

43. Karen Williams Harris, interview with the author, digital recording, April 9, 2005, Weirton, West Virginia.

44. Burns, interview.

45. Thomas Sugrue, *The Origins of the Urban Crisis: Race and Inequality in Postwar Detroit* (Princeton, N.J.: Princeton University Press, 1996), 164–77.

46. Nelson, *Divided We Stand*, chap. 7. Also see John Hinshaw, *Steel and Steelworkers: Race and Class Struggle in Twentieth-Century Pittsburgh* (Albany: State University of New York Press, 2002).

47. Burns, interview.

48. Danna, interview.

49. Frank Gregory, interview with the author, digital recording, February 3, 2012, Weirton, West Virginia.

50. Arnett, interview.

51. Nonwhite men in Weirton made $4,384 compared to $2,458 in Fairmont. U.S. Census Bureau, *Census of Population: 1960, Volume 1, Characteristics of the Population, Part 50* (Washington, D.C.: Government Printing Office, 1961), 143.

52. Burns, interview.

53. Ibid.

54. Danna, interview.

55. Javersak, *History of Weirton*, 163.

56. U.S. Census Bureau, *Census of the United States: Volume 2, Characteristics of the Population, Part 48* (Washington, D.C.: Government Printing Office, 1952), 51–53; *Census of the United States: Volume 1, Characteristics of the Population, Part 50* (Washington, D.C.: Government Printing Office, 1961), 135, 143; *Census of the United States: Volume 1, Characteristics of the Population, Part 50* (Washington, D.C.: Government Printing Office, 1973), 266, 273.

57. American Inns of Court, Professionalism Award recipients, http://staging.innsofcourt.org/Content/Default.aspx?Id=345, accessed February 9, 2015.

58. For biographical information on Hayden, see Rudy Abramson, "A Judge in Coal Country," *APF* (Alicia Patterson Foundation) *Reporter* 20, no. 3. Accessed online at http://www.aliciapatterson.org/APF2003/APF2003.html.

59. James B. Lieber, *Friendly Takeover: How an Employee Buyout Saved a Steel Town* (New York: Viking, 1995), 141.

60. *Weirton Daily Times*, March 1, 1983.

61. *Weirton Daily Times*, March 1, 1983.

62. *Williams v. Weirton Steel Division of National Steel Corporation and Independent*

Steelworkers Union; Allen, et al.; Equal Employment Opportunity Commission, Plaintiff-Intervenor v. Same; McKenzie v. Same. Nos. 69-30-W, 72-50-W, and 80-75-W. United States District Court for the Northern District of West Virginia. 1983 U.S. Dist. LEXIS 18961; 31 Fair Empl. Prac. Cas. (BNA) 1415. February 28, 1983.

63. *Ibid.*

64. For an overview of this period, see Alice Kessler-Harris, *Out to Work: A History of Wage-Earning Women in the United States* (1982; repr. New York: Oxford University Press, 2003), chap. 11. Statistics on page 301.

65. *Weirton Daily Times*, September 15, 1955.

66. The phrase "second shift" comes from Arlie Hochschild with Anne Machung, *The Second Shift: Working Families and the Revolution at Home* (1989) (New York: Penguin Books, 2003).

67. Ramona "Boots" Hines, interview with the author, digital recording, March 20, 2007, New Cumberland, West Virginia.

68. Ibid.

69. Margaret Fonow, *Union Women: Forging Feminism in the United Steelworkers of America*, vol. 17 in Social Movements, Protest, and Contention series (Minneapolis: University of Minnesota Press, 2003), 56–57.

70. Ibid., 71. The increases were calculated between 1975 and 1998 by the U.S. Equal Opportunity Commission.

71. Hines, interview.

72. Fonow, *Union Women*, 82.

73. Hines, interview.

74. Fonow, *Union Women*, chap. 4.

75. Virginia C. Young, "'We Do the Same Work as the Men Did': The Development of Working-Class Feminism in the Glass and Pottery Industries of West Virginia, 1930–1970" (PhD diss., West Virginia University, 2013), 180–89.

76. Ibid., chaps. 7 and 8, esp. 210–14.

77. Regina Lee Blaszczyk, "'Reign of the Robots': The Homer Laughlin China Company and Flexible Mass Production," *Technology and Culture* 36 (October 1995): 863–911.

78. Jack Welch, *History of Hancock County: Virginia and West Virginia*, rev. ed. (Abilene, Tex.: WriteRight Publishing, 1992), 136D–136E.

79. Shotliff, "The History of the Labor Movement," 346–47 note 7.

80. Gates, *City of Hill and Kilns*, 358–59.

81. J. M. Wells III, "Doing the Right Thing," *Industry Week* (August 16, 1993): 37.

82. William T. Hogan, *Economic History of the Iron and Steel Industry in the United States*, vol. 3, part VI (Lexington, Mass.: Lexington Books, 1971), 1731. For the $400 million figure, see Lieber, *Friendly Takeover*, 42.

83. Christopher L. G. Hall, *Steel Phoenix: The Rise and Fall of the U.S. Steel Industry* (New York: St. Martin's Press, 1997), 65.

84. The debate over the causes of the industry's decline continue. Early participants

include Paul Tiffany, who took an all-of-the-above approach in his book *The Decline of the American Steel Industry: How Management, Labor, and Government Went Wrong* (New York: Oxford University Press, 1988); and Hoerr, *And the Wolf Finally Came*. The classic example of shifting capital was U.S. Steel's buyout of Marathon Oil and its name change to USX.

85. Lieber, 15, *Friendly Takeover*, 44–45.

86. William T. Hogan, *Steel in the United States: Restructuring to Compete* (Lexington, Mass.: Lexington Books, 1984), 51–54.

87. Lieber, *Friendly Takeover*, 45.

88. Ibid., 14–17.

89. The back and forth between the JSC and the RFC takes up most of pages 42 to 223 in Lieber, *Friendly Takeover*.

90. Glenn Beamer, "Sustaining the Rust Belt: A Retrospective Analysis of the Employee Purchase of Weirton Steel," *Labor History* 48 (August 2007): 277–99, quote on page 282.

91. Lieber, *Friendly Takeover*, 125, 162, 168, 211, 217.

92. Phillip Hartley Smith, *Board Betrayal: Failed Governance and Management Hand in Hand with Arthur Andersen: An ESOP Fable* (Pittsburgh, Pa.: Ladlesheet Press, 2003).

93. Beamer, "Sustaining the Rust Belt," 288.

94. On steel import crisis in the late 1990s, see *New York Times*, November 6, 1996.

95. *New York Times*, March 6, 2002, August 23, 2002, December 5, 2003.

96. On the 1974 high being at 13,000 workers, see Beamer, "Sustaining the Rust Belt," 280. For the 2006 number, see Don Goldstein, "Weirton Revisited: Finance, the Working Class, and Restructuring in the Rust Belt," *Review of Radical Political Economics* 41 (2009): 355.

97. See esp. Beamer's conclusions, "Sustaining the Rust Belt," 292–94.

98. Judith Stein, *Running Steel, Running America: Race, Economic Policy, and the Decline of Liberalism* (Chapel Hill: University of North Carolina Press, 1998), 4–5.

99. Goldstein, "Weirton Revisited," 352–57, quotes on 356–57.

CONCLUSION:
COUNTRY PEOPLE AND CAPITAL MOBILITY

1. Richard Cameron, interview with the author, digital recording, March 28, 2007, New Manchester, West Virginia.

2. See Carl Smith, *Urban Disorder and the Shape of Belief: The Great Chicago Fire, the Haymarket Bomb, and the Model Town of Pullman* (Chicago: University of Chicago Press, 1994), esp. chap. 9.

3. As mentioned in chapter 2, the article titled "Labor Conditions in Country Towns" is a great example of this. *Iron Age*, October 21, 1909.

4. Darlene Wilson, "A Judicious Combination of Incident and Psychology: John Fox, Jr. and the Southern Mountaineer Motif," in *Back Talk from Appalachia: Confronting Stereotypes* (Lexington: University Press of Kentucky, 1999), 98–118.

5. John Bodnar stressed workers' concern for stability and regularity in *Workers' World: Kinship, Community, and Protest in an Industrial Society, 1900–1940* (Baltimore: Johns Hopkins University Press), esp. 184, as did Rachel Ann Batch, "Finding Stability In a Company Town: A Community Study of Slickville, Pennsylvania, 1916–1943" (PhD diss., University of Pennsylvania, 2000).

6. On local variations, see Doreen Massey, *Spatial Divisions of Labor: Social Structures and the Geography of Production*, 2nd ed. (1984; New York: Routledge, 1995), 53.

7. Lizabeth Cohen, *Making a New Deal: Industrial Workers in Chicago, 1919–1939* (New York: Cambridge University Press, 1990), 365.

8. Ibid., 367.

9. See Andrew Herrod, *Labor Geographies: Workers and Landscapes of Capitalism* (New York: The Guilford Press, 2001), esp. the introduction, for a reformulation of the role of place in capitalism and the lives of workers. Also, Jefferson Cowie began a re-examination of labor and place in his groundbreaking book *Capital Moves: RCA's Seventy-Year Quest for Cheap Labor* (New York: New Press, 2001).

10. Jay Nordlinger, "Anxiety in Steel Country," *National Review*, March 22, 1999, 44.

11. Ibid., 45–46.

12. Jack Metzgar, *Striking Steel: Solidarity Remembered* (Philadelphia: Temple University Press, 2000), 202–5. Quote on 205.

13. Robert Bruno, *Steelworker Alley: How Class Works in Youngstown* (Ithaca, N.Y.: Cornell University Press, 1999).

14. See U.S. Bureau of the Census, *West Virginia, Population of Counties by Decennial Census: 1900 to 1990*, comp. and ed. Richard L. Forstall (Washington, D.C.: Government Printing Office, 1995), http://www.census.gov/population/cencounts/wv190090.txt), accessed February 9, 2015; U.S. Bureau of the Census, "U.S. State and County Quickfacts," http://quickfacts.census.gov/qfd/states/54/54029.html, accessed February 9, 2015.

15. "Track-Casino Combo Sites Boost Jobs, Not Economy," *Springfield News Sun*, November 17, 2011. http://www.springfieldnewssun.com/news/news/local/track-casino-combo-sites-boost-jobs-not-economy-1/nMxHL/, accessed February 9, 2015.

INDEX

Aaron, Louis and Marcus, 31, 51
AFL-CIO, 116, 133, 153. *See also* American Federation of Labor (AFL); Congress of Industrial Organizations (CIO),
African Americans: and civil rights, 153–54, 155–56, 161–65, 166–68, 177; as migrants, 6, 70, 146, 150; in Newell, 68; in Weirton and Hancock County, 70, 106, 152, 165–66; women, 135, 164
Alabama, 70
Alatis, John, 83, 87, 90, 145
Aliquippa, 100 101
Amalgamated Association of Iron, Steel, and Tin Workers, 41, 44–46, 56, 81–82, 88, 91
American Cereal Company, 41
American Federation of Labor (AFL): John Lewis and, 56, 76; vs. local negotiations, 92; and majority rule, 79; and NBOP, 43, 79, 107; and politics, 116, 118; and trade agreements, 86, 87
American Flint Glass Workers Union (AFGWU), 43–44
American Rolling Mill Company, 61
American Sheet and Tin Plate Company, 51, 70–71
American Tin Plate Company, 33, 45–46, 55
America's Wage Earners' Protective Association, 87
Apollo, Pa., 54
Arango, Richard "Red," 174
Armstong, E. C., 118
Asfour, Francis, 140
Ashland, Ky., 61
assorters (steelworkers): and unionization efforts, 82; women as, 38, 41, 76, 126, 136, 137, 138; work environment for, 136, 169
Atkinson, George, 24–25
automatic jigger. *See under* pottery technology

Barkhurst, Paul, 83, 148
Barron, Hal, 25
batter-out. *See under* pottery workers
Beamer, Glenn, 174, 176
Bennett, James, 30
Bish, Walter, 175
Blair, Aneita Jean, 66

INDEX

Braddock Wire Company, 33
Brecher, Jeremy, 9
Bruno, Robert, 184
Burns, Rev. Henry "Tex," 74–75, 140, 161, 163–66
Bush, George W., 176
Butler, Elizabeth Beardsley, 38
Butler, Pa., 61

Cameron, Richard, 179
Carroll, J. C., 103
casters. *See under* pottery workers
ceramics industry. *See* pottery industry
Chadwick, Joshua, 129
Chelsea China Company, 48
Chester, W.Va., 140: churches in, 71–72; creation and growth of, 49–51, 66–67; employment goals in, 93; Ku Klux Klan in, 67; pottery industry in, 128, 172; and unions, 86–87, 118, 122; and Weirton, 55; women in workforce in, 41, 128, 131–32
Chicago, Ill., 3, 7, 9, 10–11, 97, 142, 144–45, 181–83
Christian Science Monitor, 93, 146
Civil Rights Act of 1964, 154–55, 166–67, 169, 176–77
Clarksburg, W.Va., 29, 52, 55, 60, 81, 118
Cohen, Lizabeth, 7–9, 181–82
Committee on Political Education (COPE), 116–19, 123,151
Congress of Industrial Organizations (CIO): and African Americans, 153, 165; creation of, 76–77, 83; culture of, 97, 99, 125, 182; vs. local negotiations, 92, 105, 123; and politics, 116; and pottery workers, 11, 79–80, 107; and steelworkers, 84–85, 88, 100–101, 103–4; and trade agreements, 86; and urban workers, 9
Cost of Living Adjustment (COLA), 98, 106
Cowie, Jefferson, 5
cup handlers/finishers. *See under* pottery workers

Danna, Walter, 94–95, 142, 149, 163, 165
Davis, Horace, 81–82
decalcomania (pottery), 39–41, 95
decal girls (pottery workers), 39–41, 95

Del Turco, Dominic, 100, 106
Democratic Party, 9, 10, 11, 24–25, 85–91, 97–99, 118–19, 123, 125, 152, 181–82
Dempsey, David, 139
Detroit, Mich., 2–3, 5, 7, 144, 154, 165
Dickey, Linda, 96, 115, 134
Dietz, James, 16, 21
Dinsmore, John Walker, 22
Doddridge, Joseph, 14–15, 20–21
dry finishing (pottery), 110–12
Duffy, James, 78–79, 86–87, 127, 129
Dunbar School, 161

East Liverpool, Ohio (town and district): and imports and trade agreements, 86–87, 113; and nationwide strike, 58; and NBOP, 43, 80; and Newell, 51–52; population growth in, 32; pottery industry in, 5, 30–31, 32, 40, 48–50, 172; and unions, 107–8, 112–13, 118; women in workforce in, 39, 41, 127, 129–32
Ebbert, Donald, 104
Edwin M. Knowles China Company, 51–52, 57, 77–78, 172
Eisenhower, Dwight, 140, 156–57, 160
Elish, Herb, 175
Ellis, Julia, 63–64, 68
Elwood, Ind., 55
Emerson, Walter, 59–60, 79
Evans, William, 31

family economy, 75–76, 91
family wage, 38–42, 126, 144, 170
farming, 1, 3–4, 6, 31, 62; of apples, 1, 13, 15–16, 19, 23, 26; before industries arrived, 13–28; of sheep, 13, 15–17, 19, 26–27, 74, 141; by rural-industrial workers, 64–66, 71, 75, 142–45. *See also* gardening
female workers. *See* gender division of labor
Ferguson, Cyrus, 27, 29
Fiedorczyk, Alex, 102, 141, 148
finishers (pottery), 39, 44, 60, 95, 110, 112–13, 127, 129–31, 170–71
Finnish immigrants, 55, 73
Fones-Wolf, Ken, 5
foremen: in pottery, 77, 107–8, 115; in steel, 72, 80–83, 102, 148, 163, 165–67

234

gardening, 19–20, 63, 74–76, 139–46, 150–51, 154, 181, 184–85. *See also* farming
gender division of labor, 13, 18–21, 27–28, 38–42, 126–38, 143–50, 155–56, 168–71, 177
General Agreement on Tariffs and Trade (GATT), 156, 172
Georgia, 64, 70–71, 74, 163
gilders and liners (pottery), 36, 130–31
Golden, Clinton, 88
Goldstein, Don, 176
Graham, Malcolm, 105
Great Depression, 9, 78, 85–86, 97, 99, 145, 181
Greek immigrants, 68–70, 74, 82–83, 87–88, 90, 106, 141
Green, William, 86
Gregory, Frank, 70, 141, 146, 165
grievance procedure, 9, 44, 77, 93, 101–2, 105, 107–9, 112–13, 115, 165, 170–71

Hancock County, W.Va.: early history, 13–17; early politics, 23–25; industrialists and, 5–6, 12, 29, 47–56, 180; population growth, 62–66, 140; Butler District, 66, 68, 70, 87, 89; Clay District, 66, 87; Grant District, 66, 87, 89; churches, 13, 17, 71–73, 81, 106, 161; labor force participation, 145; population decline, 184
Harker Pottery, 128, 158, 172
Harris, Dean, 183
Harris, Karen Williams, 164
Hartzell, Gladys, 129
Hatchet Gang (Weirton Steel Employees Security League), 81–85, 100
Haught, Fay, 96, 128, 134, 145, 147, 149
Hawley-Smoot Tariff of 1930, 86
heaters. *See under* steelworkers
Heaton, Margaret, 64, 68, 76, 137, 146
Hertnick, John, 88–89
Hines, Ramona "Boots," 136–37, 169–70
Hollidays Cove, 16–17, 27, 53–54
homebuilding, 147–48
home ownership, 54, 81, 141–42, 146–48
Homer Laughlin China Company, 31, 35, 40–41, 43, 51, 57–58; schemeware, 40–41; 1894 strike and, 43–44; expansion to Newell, 51; Plant No. 4, 51; Plant No. 5, 52, 59, 107, 111–12; Plant No. 6, 52, 58, 96, 110–11; Plant No. 7, 52, 129; Plant No. 8, 52, 112; Iron Horse, 59–60, 127; tunnel kilns, 58–60, 95, 127, 171; hiring rural migrants, 66–67; discontent among helpers, 79; Edwin Wheatley job at, 108; Epicure, 107–8; Fiestaware, 128, 171–72; employment decline, 113, 158, 172; union attitudes toward management, 115; World War II, 128–29; women potters, 132–34, 171; *See also* Edwin Wheatley, imports, pottery industry, pottery workers
Hoover, Herbert, 87
Hughes, Albert, 43–44
Hull, Frank, 108–10, 112
hunting: game trends in, 129 ; gender role of, 27, 150; in local culture, 10, 20, 148, 150, 181, 184; as self-help activity, 20, 141, 146, 148, 154; vs. unionism, 139
Huntington, W.Va., 65, 118

imports, 86, 113, 118, 123, 128, 156–61, 170; from England/UK, 31, 33, 87; from Japan, 86–87, 113, 157–59; from Italy, 113, 158
Independent News, 105, 147, 151
Independent Steelworkers Union (ISU), 104, 118, 147, 165, 167
industrial restructuring, 5, 12, 57–62, 155, 172–76, 180, 184
International Trade Organization (ITO), 156
Iron Age, 53, 61
Italian immigrants, 25, 68–69, 71, 74, 141–42, 146, 149

Jennings, Eddie Jim, 70
Jeter, Barth, Sr., 70
jigger, automatic. *See* pottery technology: automatic jigger
jiggermen (pottery workers), 6, 34; authority of, 33–34, 127; decline in number of, 129–31; in England, 39; as members of family crews, 41; and technological changes, 60, 127; and unions, 44, 57, 79, 108–9, 127
Johnstown, Pa., 98, 139, 151
Joint Study Committee (JSC), at Weirton Steel, 174

INDEX

Jones & Laughlin Steel (J&L), 100, 106
Jordan, Charles, 118

Kennedy, John F., 73, 119, 153
kiln types. *See under* pottery technology
kiln workers. *See* pottery workers
Koukoulis, Estratios (Charles), 70
Ku Klux Klan, 67, 163–64

labor gang. *See under* steelworkers
Labor's League of Political Education, 118
Landrum-Griffin Act, 121–22
Lansing, Mich., 10, 148
Laughlin, Homer and Shakespeare, 31
Lewis, John L., 56, 76–77, 79, 83, 99, 125, 153
Lewis, Ronald, 4, 7
"Little Steel" contract formula, 102, 129
localism, 3, 8–11, 23–25, 99–123, 150, 181, 184
lockouts. *See* strikes and lockouts
Long, William "Billy," 81–82, 88–90
Loucas, George, 90
Love, Howard "Pete," 174
Lynd, Staughton, 174–75

"making do," 10, 16, 91, 124–26, 143–51, 181, 184
Mannington Pottery Company, 114
Markham, R. H., 93, 135, 146–47
Maslowski, Frank, 141, 147, 150
McDonald, David J., 105, 157
McGown, Mollie, 134
McKenzie, Willie, 167–68, 174
McKinley, William, 32–33
McKinley Tariff of 1890, 33
McMurtry, George, 5, 54
Metzgar, Jack, 98, 183–84
Metzgar, Johnny, 98, 139, 151
migrants, rural, 1, 6, 64–65, 67, 72
Millsop, Thomas, 85, 104–5, 161, 167
mold runner. *See under* pottery workers
Monessen, Pa., 33, 46–47, 52, 54
Monongahela Tin Plate Company, 33, 41
Moore, Arch, 118–23, 151–53, 159–60
Moore, Mel, 81–82
Mosher, Anne, 5
Moundsville, W.Va., 119

National Association for the Advancement of Colored People (NAACP), 153, 165, 167

National Brotherhood of Operative Potters/International Brotherhood of Operative Potters (NBOP/IBOP): and AFL, 43, 107; and automation, 133; and benefits, 113–15; and CIO, 79–80; creation of, 43–44; declining power of, 58–59; grievance procedures of, 93, 107–8, 112–13; headquarters of, 107; and imports and trade agreements, 86, 113, 158; vs. local negotiations, 93; locals in, 131–32; and skilled vs. unskilled and semikilled workers, 65, 78–80, 91; strike by, in 1922, 57–53; and working conditions, 43, 59–60, 91, 93, 107, 109–10; and wages, 57–60, 114, 129; and women, 127, 129, 170–71
—Local Unions of: No. 9, 58, 131; No. 53, 111, 131; No. 94, 131; No. 130, 60, 109, 132; No. 131, 79, 132
National Industrial Recovery Act (NIRA), 76–79, 81–82, 88
National Labor Board (NLB), 79, 82
National Labor Relations Act (Wagner Act), 76, 83, 100, 129
National Steel Corporation (parent of Weirton Steel), 81, 169–70, 173–76
National War Labor Board (NWLB), 76, 84–85, 89, 93, 100–4
Neely, Matthew M., 85
New Castle, Pa., 54, 80
New Cumberland, W.Va.: early development of 17, 48; Masonic Lodge in, 105; and NLRB, 84; and politics, 24, 87, 89; population of, 66, 140; "Steel Men" in, 143
New Cumberland Independent, 18, 24
New Deal, 2–3, 10–11, 78, 80, 82–83, 85–91, 98–99, 126, 151, 153, 181–82
Newell, W.Va., 4, 49, 51–52, 58, 66–68, 71, 86, 93, 140, 172
New Manchester, W.Va., 17

Ohio River Valley, 6, 13–15, 29–30, 32, 51, 53, 62, 65–66, 100, 103, 117, 140, 159, 165
Oliver, Henry W., 33, 41
Olmsted, Frederick Law, 54
O'Neill, John, 31, 36

Phillips, J. R., 47, 52
Phillips, Vesta, 112

INDEX

Phillips Sheet and Tin Plate Company, 52, 54, 56, 60
Pittsburgh, Pa., 3–4, 7, 14, 29–31, 33, 51, 53, 74, 88, 104–5, 139, 144, 154, 182
Pittsburgh Post-Gazette, 100
Pomeroy, Bill, 39, 41, 127
Pope Sheet and Tin Plate Company, 60
Porter, Capt. John, 48
Potters Herald, 78, 109–10, 133, 143, 158
pottery industry: automation in, 58, 60, 95; craftsmen in, 33–34, 36, 57–58, 60; in Chester and Newell, 66–67; in East Liverpool, 30–31, 32; foreign competition in, 31–32, 43, 86–87, 113, 155–60, 170–72; gender in, 126–34, 170–71; and migrants and immigrants, 31, 66–67; monotony in, 95–96; silicosis in, 110–12; vs. steel industry, 113–16; speed in, 96–97; and tariffs, 31–32; towns established by, 49–52; transformations in, 5–6, 29–30, 38–41, 47–48, 57–59, 90–91; unions in, 43–44, 57,–58, 77, 107, 115. *See also* National Brotherhood of Operative Potters/International Brotherhood of Operative Potters (NBOP/IBOP)
pottery technology: automatic jigger, 60, 78, 96, 110, 113, 127, 171; kiln types, 35–36, 51, 58–60, 95, 127, 171; decalcomania, 39–41, 95; dry finishing, 110–12; Iron Horse, 59–60, 127
pottery workers: batter-out, 34, 41, 44, 60, 79, 127, 129–30, 132; casters, 34, 78, 95, 129, 131–32; cup handlers/finishers, 34, 71, 107–8, 113, 129, 171; decal girls, 39–41, 95; gilders and liners, 36, 130–31, kiln firemen, 36, 60, 109, 130–31; kilnmen, 33, 36, 57–58, 60, 130–31; kiln placers, 35–36, 59, 95; mold runner, 34, 41, 44, 60, 78–79, 127, 129–32; warehousemen and warehouse women, 35–36, 39, 41, 66, 95, 129–32. *See also* finishers; jiggermen

Quaker Oats, 41

Ramsay, Robert L., 88
Rank and File Committee (RFC), at Weirton Steel, 174–75
Reardon, William, 55, 88
reciprocal trade agreements, 86–87, 158–60
Rector, Tom, 114
Republican Party, 13, 24–25, 32–33, 85–90, 116, 118–20, 151–52, 160
Reuther, Walter, 153, 157
Rhead, Frederick Hurten, 171
Rigdon, Lula "Pug," 95, 115, 130, 134
Rock Springs Park, 50, 67
Rogers, Susan Carol, 8
rollers (steelworkers), 6: authority of, 36–37, 42, 56; and automation, 61; tinplate, 32–33, 37, 42, 47, 55, 61–62; and the two-roll system, 47; and unions, 44
Roosevelt, Franklin, 82, 87–90, 99, 125
Rossell, Bob, 147
rural migrants, 1, 6, 64–65, 67, 72

Sayre, Larry, 119–20
self-built housing, , 147–48
self-help activities. *See* "making do"
semiskilled workers, 63–64, 75–76, 78, 80, 91–93
Shaffer, T. J., 46
silicosis, 110–12
skilled workers: as core workers, 4, 33, 95; declining power of, 64–65; as driving location of plants, 29–30, 33, 48; and family wage, 38–42; house building by, 148; in pottery industry, 34–36, 43–44, 57–60, 95, 107, 127, 129–30; and race, 162–63, 167; relocated, 6, 180; in steel and tinplate industry, 33, 36–37, 46, 47; and unions, 44–45, 46, 60–62, 81, 88; vs. unskilled and semikilled workers, 65, 78–80, 91; in Weirton, 54–56; women as, 170
Smith, Charles A., 49–51
Smith, J. Russell, 48–49
Smith, W. L., 87–89
Snider, Hugh and Garnet, 142–43
South Gate, Calif., 139
Sperry, Harvey, 175
Staffordshire, England, 34, 40, 130
Stedman family (Lyman), 13, 16–17, 19–21, 26
steelworkers: heaters, 32–33, 36–37, 42, 44, 54–56, 60–61, 143; labor gang, 70, 80, 135, 162–63, 167; warehousemen, 38. *See also* assorters; rollers

INDEX

Steel Workers Organizing Committee (SWOC), 83–85, 100
Stein, Judith, 176
Sterling China Company, 127–28, 172
Steubenville, Ohio, 15, 30, 55–57, 60, 81, 140, 165
strikes and lockouts: 1894 pottery, 43–44; 1901 steel, 46–47, 54; 1909–10 steel, 47; 1913 Steubenville, 56–57; 1922 pottery, 57–58; 1933 mold runners and batter-outs, 79; 1933 Weirton Steel, 81–83, 88; 1946 steel, 102; 1949 steel, 98, 104; 1949, 1952, and 1955 steel, 98; 1956 steel, 98, 106; 1959 pottery, 92, 115; 1959 steel, 106, 123, 153
Supplemental Unemployment Benefit (SUB), 98, 101, 106

Taft-Hartley Amendments, 116, 118, 122–23, 182
tariffs, 5, 24, 29, 31–33, 86–87, 156, 158–60, 172; Hawley-Smoot Tariff of 1930, 86; McKinley Tariff of 1890, 33; Wilson Tariff of 1894, 43
Taylor, Smith, and Taylor (TS&T), 51, 113, 128, 171–72
Tingler, Emory, 55
tinplate industry, 6, 27, 29–30, 32–33, 37–39, 41–47, 51–57, 60–62, 136, 159; Welsh tinplate, 6, 32–33, 39, 41, 45, 61
Titus, Lewis, 163, 166
trade agreements, reciprocal, 86–87, 158–60
Trenton, N.J., 5, 31–32, 39–40, 58, 80, 108
Truax, Jane Adair, 16, 21
Truax, Louis, 1, 20, 27, 55, 106

Union, S.C., 70, 141
United Auto Workers of America (UAW), 77, 99, 153, 157
United Mine Workers of America (UMWA), 77, 117, 119, 121
United States Bureau of Labor Statistics model budget, 138, 147
United States Potters' Association (USPA): creation of, 31; headquarters of, 107; and NBOP, 44, 79, 114–15; and quality, 57; and women, 127, 171
United States Steel Corporation, 46–47, 54, 83, 98, 165

United States Supreme Court, 24, 76, 83, 100, 166
United Steel Workers of America (USWA): and African Americans, 165, 167; and CIO, 77; local unions vs., 11, 103, 105, 121; as model for nonmembers, 102, 104, 106, 114–15; and politics, 119; and seniority, 102; strikes by, 98, 104, 106, 123, 153; and trade agreements, 156–57, 160; and Weirton, 100–103, 104–6, 121
unskilled workers, 59, 63–64, 66, 68, 70, 75–80, 88, 91–92

Vandergrift, Pa., 5, 54

W. W. Woolworth and Company, 58
Wagner Act (National Labor Relations Act), 76, 83, 100, 129
warehousemen and warehouse women. *See under* pottery workers; steelworkers
Warwick China Company, 79
Watts, Cornelius, 24–25
Weir, Ernest T., 27, 29–30, 33, 41, 46–47, 52–57, 60–61, 84, 87–88; and welfare capitalism, 81–83, 101, 103–6
Weir-Cove Fire Department, 55
Weirton, W.Va.: African Americans in, 70, 161, 163, 164–67; and American Dream, 183; charity in, 151–52; churches in, 72; as company town, 56, 81, 88, 100, 105–6; employment alternatives in, 83; family security as goal in, 93, 101; foremen in, 80–81; founding and growth of, 53–55, 60, 66, 68, 140; home ownership in, 146–48, 152; immigrants to, 68–70, 71, 75, 140; as "Little Siberia," 100–101; in 1920s–1930s, 63, 65; in 1950s, 11, 140; outside labor organizers in, 11, 56, 81, 83–85, 95, 103–5; politics in, 87–91, 152; and the RFC, 174; rural residents and traditions in, 70–71, 75, 139–44; strike in, 81–83, 88; and workers' experiences, 99–101; women in, 114, 126, 134–38, 143–45, 164
—neighborhoods: Marland Heights, 147, 161, 164; North End, 63, 66, 68–71, 140–41; Weirton Heights, 141–42, 147, 152, 164
Weirton Boosters Club, 55
Weirton Daily Times, 87, 89, 128, 141, 168

Weirton Independent Union (WIU), 85, 101–4
Weirton Steel Corporation, 11, 60–61; coke ovens, 61, 70–71, 94, 135, 162, 163, 167; continuous rolling mill, 37, 46, 47, 61; Employee Stock Ownership Plan (ESOP), 174–76; ethnicity and race of workers at, 68–70, 80–81, 161–68; gender and hiring and promotions at, 41, 54–56, 80–82, 134–38, 168–71, 177; and the mill of the future, 172; Twenty-Five Year Club, 103, 162. *See also* Independent Steelworkers Union; Phillips Sheet and Tin Plate Company
Weirton Steel Employee Bulletin, 103, 138, 143
Weirton Steel Employees Security League (Hatchet Gang), 81–85, 100
welfare capitalism. *See under* Weir, Ernest T.
Wells, Arthur, 68, 112
Wells, Joe, Jr., 130
Wells, Joseph, III, 172
Wells, Joseph M., 68, 79, 87, 128, 156, 158–60
Wells, W. Edwin, 31, 49–51, 57–58
Wellsburg, W.Va., 15, 27
Wellsville, Ohio, 33, 127, 172

West Virginia Bureau of Industrial Hygiene, 112
West Virginia Labor Federation, 116
West Virginia State Department of Health, 110
West Virginia State Federation of Labor, 118
Wheatley, Edwin, 108–15, 133
Wheeling, W.Va., 30, 46, 54, 79, 118, 122
Wheeling Intelligencer, 175
Wheeling Steel Corporation, 83, 122, 165
Williams, Hattie, 41
Wilson Tariff of 1894, 43
women in labor force. *See* gender division of labor
World War II; and African Americans, 161, 166; and politics, 11, 98, 116, 123, 151, 182; and shifts in pottery industry, 68, 113; and trade, 113, 156, 158; and women's employment, 126–30, 135–37, 168–69

Youngstown, Ohio, 83, 85, 165, 174–75

Zahavi, Gerald, 11
Zon, Mary Goddard, 119
Zucosky, Alex, 94

LOU MARTIN is an assistant professor
of history at Chatham University.

THE WORKING CLASS IN AMERICAN HISTORY

Worker City, Company Town: Iron and Cotton-Worker Protest in Troy and
   Cohoes, New York, 1855–84   *Daniel J. Walkowitz*
Life, Work, and Rebellion in the Coal Fields: The Southern West Virginia Miners,
   1880–1922   *David Alan Corbin*
Women and American Socialism, 1870–1920   *Mari Jo Buhle*
Lives of Their Own: Blacks, Italians, and Poles in Pittsburgh, 1900–1960
   John Bodnar, Roger Simon, and Michael P. Weber
Working-Class America: Essays on Labor, Community, and American Society
   Edited by Michael H. Frisch and Daniel J. Walkowitz
Eugene V. Debs: Citizen and Socialist   *Nick Salvatore*
American Labor and Immigration History, 1877–1920s: Recent European Research
   Edited by Dirk Hoerder
Workingmen's Democracy: The Knights of Labor and American Politics
   Leon Fink
The Electrical Workers: A History of Labor at General Electric and Westinghouse,
   1923–60   *Ronald W. Schatz*
The Mechanics of Baltimore: Workers and Politics in the Age of Revolution,
   1763–1812   *Charles G. Steffen*
The Practice of Solidarity: American Hat Finishers in the Nineteenth Century
   David Bensman
The Labor History Reader   *Edited by Daniel J. Leab*
Solidarity and Fragmentation: Working People and Class Consciousness in
   Detroit, 1875–1900   *Richard Oestreicher*
Counter Cultures: Saleswomen, Managers, and Customers in American
   Department Stores, 1890–1940   *Susan Porter Benson*
The New England Working Class and the New Labor History
   Edited by Herbert G. Gutman and Donald H. Bell
Labor Leaders in America   *Edited by Melvyn Dubofsky and Warren Van Tine*
Barons of Labor: The San Francisco Building Trades and Union Power in
   the Progressive Era   *Michael Kazin*
Gender at Work: The Dynamics of Job Segregation by Sex during World War II
   Ruth Milkman
Once a Cigar Maker: Men, Women, and Work Culture in American Cigar
   Factories, 1900–1919   *Patricia A. Cooper*
A Generation of Boomers: The Pattern of Railroad Labor Conflict in
   Nineteenth-Century America   *Shelton Stromquist*
Work and Community in the Jungle: Chicago's Packinghouse Workers,
   1894–1922   *James R. Barrett*
Workers, Managers, and Welfare Capitalism: The Shoeworkers and Tanners
   of Endicott Johnson, 1890–1950   *Gerald Zahavi*

Men, Women, and Work: Class, Gender, and Protest in the New England Shoe Industry, 1780–1910   *Mary Blewett*

Workers on the Waterfront: Seamen, Longshoremen, and Unionism in the 1930s   *Bruce Nelson*

German Workers in Chicago: A Documentary History of Working-Class Culture from 1850 to World War I   *Edited by Hartmut Keil and John B. Jentz*

On the Line: Essays in the History of Auto Work   *Edited by Nelson Lichtenstein and Stephen Meyer III*

Labor's Flaming Youth: Telephone Operators and Worker Militancy, 1878–1923   *Stephen H. Norwood*

Another Civil War: Labor, Capital, and the State in the Anthracite Regions of Pennsylvania, 1840–68   *Grace Palladino*

Coal, Class, and Color: Blacks in Southern West Virginia, 1915–32   *Joe William Trotter Jr.*

For Democracy, Workers, and God: Labor Song-Poems and Labor Protest, 1865–95   *Clark D. Halker*

Dishing It Out: Waitresses and Their Unions in the Twentieth Century   *Dorothy Sue Cobble*

The Spirit of 1848: German Immigrants, Labor Conflict, and the Coming of the Civil War   *Bruce Levine*

Working Women of Collar City: Gender, Class, and Community in Troy, New York, 1864–86   *Carole Turbin*

Southern Labor and Black Civil Rights: Organizing Memphis Workers   *Michael K. Honey*

Radicals of the Worst Sort: Laboring Women in Lawrence, Massachusetts, 1860–1912   *Ardis Cameron*

Producers, Proletarians, and Politicians: Workers and Party Politics in Evansville and New Albany, Indiana, 1850–87   *Lawrence M. Lipin*

The New Left and Labor in the 1960s   *Peter B. Levy*

The Making of Western Labor Radicalism: Denver's Organized Workers, 1878–1905   *David Brundage*

In Search of the Working Class: Essays in American Labor History and Political Culture   *Leon Fink*

Lawyers against Labor: From Individual Rights to Corporate Liberalism   *Daniel R. Ernst*

"We Are All Leaders": The Alternative Unionism of the Early 1930s   *Edited by Staughton Lynd*

The Female Economy: The Millinery and Dressmaking Trades, 1860–1930   *Wendy Gamber*

"Negro and White, Unite and Fight!": A Social History of Industrial Unionism in Meatpacking, 1930–90   *Roger Horowitz*

Power at Odds: The 1922 National Railroad Shopmen's Strike   *Colin J. Davis*

The Common Ground of Womanhood: Class, Gender, and Working Girls' Clubs, 1884–1928   *Priscilla Murolo*
Marching Together: Women of the Brotherhood of Sleeping Car Porters   *Melinda Chateauvert*
Down on the Killing Floor: Black and White Workers in Chicago's Packinghouses, 1904–54   *Rick Halpern*
Labor and Urban Politics: Class Conflict and the Origins of Modern Liberalism in Chicago, 1864–97   *Richard Schneirov*
All That Glitters: Class, Conflict, and Community in Cripple Creek   *Elizabeth Jameson*
Waterfront Workers: New Perspectives on Race and Class   *Edited by Calvin Winslow*
Labor Histories: Class, Politics, and the Working-Class Experience   *Edited by Eric Arnesen, Julie Greene, and Bruce Laurie*
The Pullman Strike and the Crisis of the 1890s: Essays on Labor and Politics   *Edited by Richard Schneirov, Shelton Stromquist, and Nick Salvatore*
AlabamaNorth: African-American Migrants, Community, and Working-Class Activism in Cleveland, 1914–45   *Kimberley L. Phillips*
Imagining Internationalism in American and British Labor, 1939–49   *Victor Silverman*
William Z. Foster and the Tragedy of American Radicalism   *James R. Barrett*
Colliers across the Sea: A Comparative Study of Class Formation in Scotland and the American Midwest, 1830–1924   *John H. M. Laslett*
"Rights, Not Roses": Unions and the Rise of Working-Class Feminism, 1945–80   *Dennis A. Deslippe*
Testing the New Deal: The General Textile Strike of 1934 in the American South   *Janet Irons*
Hard Work: The Making of Labor History   *Melvyn Dubofsky*
Southern Workers and the Search for Community: Spartanburg County, South Carolina   *G. C. Waldrep III*
We Shall Be All: A History of the Industrial Workers of the World (abridged edition)   *Melvyn Dubofsky, ed. Joseph A. McCartin*
Race, Class, and Power in the Alabama Coalfields, 1908–21   *Brian Kelly*
Duquesne and the Rise of Steel Unionism   *James D. Rose*
Anaconda: Labor, Community, and Culture in Montana's Smelter City   *Laurie Mercier*
Bridgeport's Socialist New Deal, 1915–36   *Cecelia Bucki*
Indispensable Outcasts: Hobo Workers and Community in the American Midwest, 1880–1930   *Frank Tobias Higbie*
After the Strike: A Century of Labor Struggle at Pullman   *Susan Eleanor Hirsch*
Corruption and Reform in the Teamsters Union   *David Witwer*
Waterfront Revolts: New York and London Dockworkers, 1946–61   *Colin J. Davis*

Black Workers' Struggle for Equality in Birmingham   *Horace Huntley and David Montgomery*
The Tribe of Black Ulysses: African American Men in the Industrial South   *William P. Jones*
City of Clerks: Office and Sales Workers in Philadelphia, 1870–1920   *Jerome P. Bjelopera*
Reinventing "The People": The Progressive Movement, the Class Problem, and the Origins of Modern Liberalism   *Shelton Stromquist*
Radical Unionism in the Midwest, 1900–1950   *Rosemary Feurer*
Gendering Labor History   *Alice Kessler-Harris*
James P. Cannon and the Origins of the American Revolutionary Left, 1890–1928   *Bryan D. Palmer*
Glass Towns: Industry, Labor, and Political Economy in Appalachia, 1890–1930s   *Ken Fones-Wolf*
Workers and the Wild: Conservation, Consumerism, and Labor in Oregon, 1910–30   *Lawrence M. Lipin*
Wobblies on the Waterfront: Interracial Unionism in Progressive-Era Philadelphia   *Peter Cole*
Red Chicago: American Communism at Its Grassroots, 1928–35   *Randi Storch*
Labor's Cold War: Local Politics in a Global Context   *Edited by Shelton Stromquist*
Bessie Abramowitz Hillman and the Making of the Amalgamated Clothing Workers of America   *Karen Pastorello*
The Great Strikes of 1877   *Edited by David O. Stowell*
Union-Free America: Workers and Antiunion Culture   *Lawrence Richards*
Race against Liberalism: Black Workers and the UAW in Detroit   *David M. Lewis-Colman*
Teachers and Reform: Chicago Public Education, 1929–70   *John F. Lyons*
Upheaval in the Quiet Zone: 1199/SEIU and the Politics of Healthcare Unionism   *Leon Fink and Brian Greenberg*
Shadow of the Racketeer: Scandal in Organized Labor   *David Witwer*
Sweet Tyranny: Migrant Labor, Industrial Agriculture, and Imperial Politics   *Kathleen Mapes*
Staley: The Fight for a New American Labor Movement   *Steven K. Ashby and C. J. Hawking*
On the Ground: Labor Struggles in the American Airline Industry   *Liesl Miller Orenic*
NAFTA and Labor in North America   *Norman Caulfield*
Making Capitalism Safe: Work Safety and Health Regulation in America, 1880–1940   *Donald W. Rogers*
Good, Reliable, White Men: Railroad Brotherhoods, 1877–1917   *Paul Michel Taillon*

Spirit of Rebellion: Labor and Religion in the New Cotton South   *Jarod Roll*
The Labor Question in America: Economic Democracy in the Gilded Age
    Rosanne Currarino
Banded Together: Economic Democratization in the Brass Valley   *Jeremy Brecher*
The Gospel of the Working Class: Labor's Southern Prophets in
    New Deal America   *Erik Gellman and Jarod Roll*
Guest Workers and Resistance to U.S. Corporate Despotism   *Immanuel Ness*
Gleanings of Freedom: Free and Slave Labor along the Mason-Dixon Line,
    1790–1860   *Max Grivno*
Chicago in the Age of Capital: Class, Politics, and Democracy during the
    Civil War and Reconstruction   *John B. Jentz and Richard Schneirov*
Child Care in Black and White: Working Parents and the History
    of Orphanages   *Jessie B. Ramey*
The Haymarket Conspiracy: Transatlantic Anarchist Networks
    Timothy Messer-Kruse
Detroit's Cold War: The Origins of Postwar Conservatism   *Colleen Doody*
A Renegade Union: Interracial Organizing and Labor Radicalism   *Lisa Phillips*
Palomino: Clinton Jencks and Mexican-American Unionism in the
    American Southwest   *James J. Lorence*
Latin American Migrations to the U.S. Heartland: Changing Cultural Landscapes
    in Middle America   *Edited by Linda Allegro and Andrew Grant Wood*
Man of Fire: Selected Writings   *Ernesto Galarza, ed. Armando Ibarra
    and Rodolfo D. Torres*
A Contest of Ideas: Capital, Politics, and Labor   *Nelson Lichtenstein*
Making the World Safe for Workers: Labor, the Left, and Wilsonian
    Internationalism   *Elizabeth McKillen*
The Rise of the Chicago Police Department: Class and Conflict, 1850–1894
    Sam Mitrani
Workers in Hard Times: A Long View of Economic Crises
    Edited by Leon Fink, Joseph A. McCartin, and Joan Sangster
Redeeming Time: Protestantism and Chicago's Eight-Hour Movement,
    1866–1912   *William A. Mirola*
Struggle for the Soul of the Postwar South: White Evangelical Protestants
    and Operation Dixie   *Elizabeth Fones-Wolf and Ken Fones-Wolf*
Free Labor: The Civil War and the Making of an American Working Class
    Mark A. Lause
Death and Dying in the Working Class, 1865–1920   *Michael K. Rosenow*
Immigrants against the State: Yiddish and Italian Anarchism in America
    Kenyon Zimmer
Fighting for Total Person Unionism: Harold Gibbons, Ernest Calloway,
    and Working-Class Citizenship   *Robert Bussel*
Smokestacks in the Hills: Rural-Industrial Workers in West Virginia   *Lou Martin*

The University of Illinois Press
is a founding member of the
Association of American University Presses.

University of Illinois Press
1325 South Oak Street
Champaign, IL 61820-6903
www.press.uillinois.edu